Trifles Make Perfection

TRIFLES make Perfection

The Selected Essays of

JOSEPH WECHSBERG

EDITED AND

WITH AN INTRODUCTION BY

David Morowitz

DAVID R. GODINE · *Publisher*

Boston

First published in 1999 by
DAVID R. GODINE, PUBLISHER
Box 450
Jaffrey, New Hampshire 03452

Acknowledgment of previous publications appears on page 291.

LIBRARY OF CONGRESS CATALOGING-IN-PUBLICATION DATA
Wechsberg, Joseph, 1907–1983
Trifles make perfection : the selected essays of Joseph Wechsberg /
edited and with an introduction by David Morowitz.
p.   cm.
(hardcover : alk. paper)
1. Europe—History—Miscellaneous.   2. Europe—Intellectual life—
20th century.   3. Europe—Civilization—20th century.
4. Europe—Description and travel.   I. Morowitz, David A.   II. Title
D1051.W43   1998
940—DC21   98-29258
CIP

ISBN: 1-56792-092-6

FIRST EDITION

This book was printed on acid-free paper
in the United States of America

CONTENTS

INTRODUCTION

JOSEPH WECHSBERG'S OWN PHRASE, "a little fate is always involved," describes my first encounter with his writing. During an airplane flight on an autumn weekend in 1963, I chose *The New Yorker* from the stewardess's armful of offerings and began leafing thoughtlessly through it until snared by Wechsberg's profile of "Mado," both widow of and successor to Fernand Point, the legendary French chef. During that hour in the air, I read with unshakable intensity, almost wishing the essay wouldn't end. But, like the trip, it did, and after finishing, I knew that while dining with Mme. Point was likely to be a beautiful experience, an even richer treasure was to be found in the yet to be discovered writings of this kindred spirit whose essay I had just devoured. So I sought through libraries, bookstores, and book search services for Wechsberg's prior magazine articles and books, and found a treasury of music, European history, travel, food, and wine. Thus, my first pleasure in him became both a personal education and a dependency.

Thirteen years and countless pages later, our correspondence began, but only after his 1976 article on the Bois de Boulogne, which included his remark that he no longer operated a motor vehicle. Recognizing what one usually suppresses, that there must come a time when he and his writing would cease, I wrote him of my gratitude for the many pleasures he gave me but also to inquire of his health, particularly, whether there was anything that, as a physician, I might do on his behalf. My note was forwarded to him in Vienna, and this was his response:

Prinz Eugen Strasse 28
1040 Vienna, Austria
January 11, 1977

Dear Dr. Morowitz,

Your letter of November 26 arrived here yesterday. I no longer believe in accidents, a little fate is always involved. I am grateful for your letter and for your feelings. I am fairly well, maybe 95%, but I'll be seventy in

August, and time tells. While I don't know exactly what Gastroentero-logy means, I have a hunch; it is also my "specialty." Right now I cannot get rid of a kidney stone. No troubles, but it's just there and that is a bother. Too bad I can't come to Washington, though I'll be in New York in early February. I tell you all this because I enjoyed your letter and what you said about me. I still write, and I play the fiddle, and I cannot complain too much.

Thanks and my best to you.

More letters followed, and shortly thereafter, one of my patients began commuting between Washington and Vienna. After he was intro-duced to my precious teacher and friend, he acted as our courier, con-veying greetings and, occasionally, special bottles of wine between us. But over the next years, as expected, Wechsberg's publications became fewer, and eventually, from that patient, a letter arrived from Vienna telling me that this luminous man had died.

The loss was and still is felt by a select, devoted public, nourished by four decades of his unflagging humanism, personal grace, and intel-lectual breadth. His connoisseurship, that of the gentle, enlightened amateur seemed reflective more of the nineteenth than the twentieth century. A generous admirer of achievement in others, he had the addi-tional gift of a great teacher: demonstrating the enormous pleasure his subjects gave him and, in that enthusiasm, communicating a serious, intelligent love of life.

Perfectionism pervades the chapters of this anthology: the efforts and the ideals implied in deeds done flawlessly, with poise and elegance, as great gifts to deserving recipients. Whether describing the graceful pouring of a fine wine, musical artistry, the sheltering of war orphans, or setting a beautiful dinner table, each essay conveys a sense of life's preciousness, to be studied, appreciated, and rejoiced in.

To a writer preoccupied with music, history, and culture, the amass-ing of wealth could hardly seem less appealing. But like his philoso-phers, musicians, and chefs, the bankers he portrayed were men of extraordinary intelligence and classic education, whose wealth enhanced not only their own lives but also their world. All were linked, for the Warburgs of the world dined at the tables of a Soulé or a Point;

supported the operas; understood, bought, and donated the rare violins and paintings; and reposed in the great hotels and spas, where guests and staff alike were fellow connoisseurs.

Though Wechsberg's childhood in Moravia was torn by his father's death in World War I, the family hardships that followed, his mother's later disappearance into Auschwitz, and the destruction of his homeland, his readers must note the curious absence of any strident tone. While not unbiased, his historical writing only occasionally rises to sadness or irony, but never to rage. For while he could see both sides of life, it was only the good he chose to explore and preserve. Though Jewish, he chose to live his last years in Vienna, and when he wrote about that once great city, it was not Kristallnacht or Anschluss he described, but its art and its pastries, the times of Franz-Joseph, Schnitzler, and the Strausses.

Calling him a writer defines only the way he made his living; his essays reflect much more: an extraordinary mastery of European history, art, and civilization. And when he described these things, he did so much as a museum curator might offer up a shard of ancient glass whose preciousness and beauty is enhanced by its very fragility.

Accordingly, his death in 1983 was more than the simple passing of a productive, creative writer. For those who understand his real message, he remains a bright window to a lost, perhaps lovelier world, and he himself its celebrant and sometimes elegiac portraitist.

In preparing this book, many obligations were acquired and are noted here with my deepest gratitude: Miss Wendy Katz labored long and without complaint assembling all of Wechsberg's essays; Dr. and Mrs. Michael Rosenthal were my trusted "couriers" to and from Joseph Wechsberg in Vienna; Mrs. Constance Kelley has been more than secretary, sidekick, and model of selflessness, organizing my professional life, while patiently translating my editorial scribbles into logical computer language.

There are others. Mlle. Poppy Wechsberg graciously permitted the use of her father's literary bequest, seasoning it with personal reminiscences of this quiet man's worthy life. David R. Godine, unique publisher and another kindred spirit, equally familiar with Wechsberg's achievement, sustained this project from its inception. Simone Goodman, beloved friend and champion, was and is a muse to me and a beacon to my family and, indeed, to all who know her. Barbara Morowitz, doctor's wife and doctor's doctor for thirty-five years, owns and guards my heart and, as she well knows, can never be thanked adequately.

Nancy Morowitz and Joel Morowitz, daughter and son, embrace me ceaselessly with their generous friendship, intelligence, and humor. My life and this book are dedicated to them.

DAVID MOROWITZ

Conclusive Characters

HENRI SOULÉ
The Ambassador in the Sanctuary

OVER A PERIOD OF YEARS I HAVE, on my occasional visits to France, spent many a delightful hour in the company of one or another of that country's great chefs, a thoughtful, wise, and witty group of men who consider themselves the guardians of French civilization. In the land of Brillat-Savarin, where cooking is regarded as one of the major arts, these celebrated practitioners of *haute cuisine* easily eclipse cabinet ministers, novelists, and members of the Académie Française, and are almost as popular as the bicycling heroes of the Tour de France. The great chefs are interviewed by newspapers on problems of cuisine and life in general, asked for advice by young people and for comfort by old, invited to state functions, and decorated by the president of the Republic, and they are the friends of kings, former kings, statesmen, composers, philosophers, and poets. These chefs constitute a small, select circle; there have hardly ever been more than a score of them at any one time. Admission is gained only after years of strict devotion to the severe, exalted standards of the best French cooking. The great chefs have a low estimate of cooking, eating, drinking, or, for that matter, living anywhere but in France. They often wonder about so-called French restaurants in the dreary, unepicurean world beyond the borders of France and are disturbed by rumors drifting back from that void—rumors substantiating their suspicions that there is practically nothing French about such establishments except the names of some dishes on their menus and that even these are frequently misspelled. "French restaurants abound in New York," Raymond Baudouin, a member of the Académie du Vin de France and one of his country's most respected wine experts, wrote in the December 1949 edition of *La Revue du Vin de France*, "but their family connection with French cuisine is usually fairly remote, their gastronomy is Americanized, and the signs on their doors are there simply to attract customers."

One of the very few French restaurants outside France that French connoisseurs accept as worthy of the name is Le Pavillon, at 5 East Fifty-fifth Street, whose proprietor, Henri Soulé, is a member in good standing, *in absentia,* of the illustrious circle, despite the fact that he is a maître d'hôtel rather than a chef. A maître d'hôtel, so the great chefs say, is apt to think first of making money, whereas a chef, although he, too, must bear in mind the cost of things if the establishment he works for is to stay in business, thinks first of cooking. Soulé, who has spent a quarter of a century in the faithful service of *haute cuisine,* is undeniably far from absentminded about income and outgo, having built up the thriving Pavillon almost singlehandedly during the last twelve years. But his heart lies in the kitchen, and he has not let the success of his restaurant lull him into lowering his standards—standards that apply as much to good wine as to good food. He was given the supreme accolade three and a half years ago, when he was invited by Fernand Point, the owner of the Restaurant de la Pyramide, in Vienne, in the Département de l'Isère, and generally considered the greatest chef in all France, and Alexandre Dumaine, the chef and proprietor of the Hôtel de la Côte-d'Or, in Saulieu, Burgundy, and a worthy runner-up for the title, to share a Cuvée des Dames Hospitalières of the Hospices de Beaune, in Burgundy; he accepted, and the three of them became co-owners of the 1949 vintage of a distinguished vineyard. M. Baudouin, in striking contrast to his disparaging opinion of most French restaurateurs practicing here, refers to Soulé as *"Le Fernand Point des Amériques."* Simon Arbelot, of the Académie des Gastronomes (France is the only country that has academies devoted exclusively to the study of wine and food), has called Soulé *"l'ambassadeur de la cuisine française."* A transplanted Frenchman, C. C. Philippe, who is the successor to chef Oscar of the Waldorf-Astoria, has gone so far as to describe the Pavillon as "unquestionably the foremost French restaurant in New York."

Notwithstanding the enthusiasm of Soulé's fellow countrymen who have seen him in action, some of the great chefs of France remain skeptical. They are ready to grant that he has ability and the best intentions, but they still have their reservations about any French restaurant located three thousand miles away from its source of inspiration and the finicky demands of French customers. On my latest visit to France, M. Point himself expressed this view in his slow, musing way: "I'm convinced Soulé has done well by the French cuisine, but after all, how

French can *any* French restaurant be in America?" It seemed a reasonable question, and when I returned to this country shortly afterward, I decided to find out.

One's impression upon entering the Pavillon is that it is unmistakably French. The decor and the atmosphere of its three dining rooms are like those of a first-class restaurant in Paris. As is the custom in many French restaurants, the diners, instead of facing one another, sit side by side on banquettes that run along the walls. The dominant colors are soft red and light green, and there are many mirrors. On each table is a centerpiece of long-stemmed red roses; Soulé buys six hundred of them twice a week. The lighting is at once invitingly dim, yet bright enough to make no mystery of what one is eating. Confronting the guest as he enters is a *buffet froid* notable for its restraint; instead of the overwhelming profusion of dishes so often encountered on an hors d'oeuvre wagon, here are only a few carefully chosen delicacies—salmon from Nova Scotia, caviar from Russia (Soulé's monthly caviar bill comes [in 1953] to twenty-five hundred dollars), *foie gras aux truffes* from France and *terrine de canard, boeuf à la mode en gelée,* and *langue givrée* from the kitchen of the Pavillon. The official language of the restaurant is French. Soulé has eighty-five employees, practically all of whom either came from France or were born in this country of French parents; several have been working with him since 1939, when he got his start in America as head of the restaurant in the French Pavilion at the New York World's Fair. The waiters can also speak English, but some of them appear to do so with reluctance. The menus are, of course, printed in French. In fact, the only dissonant note—Soulé's concession to native custom—is a large bar at the far end of the *nouvelle salle,* as the dining room to the left of the entrance is called. Here martinis and daiquiris are mixed—much too close to the diners, in the opinion of those who prefer wine with their meals. Otherwise, everything about the place runs true to form, and more than one customer has been known to comment on how reminiscent the Pavillon is of the Café de Paris, that celebrated and gracefully old-fashioned Parisian restaurant on the Avenue de l'Opéra. This is no coincidence. The interior of the Pavillon was designed by Maurice Chalom, a French artist who also designed the Café de Paris. And Henri Soulé, the founder, sole owner, maître d'hôtel, and guiding spirit of the Pavillon, spent several years as maître d'hôtel of the Café de Paris.

It is almost impossible to dine at the Pavillon without encountering Soulé. He tries to greet each guest at the door and to say good-bye to them later. He pilots the customers to their tables or, if he can't take the time for that, instructs one of his captains to do so, and he also guides them gently past the unmapped shallows and reefs of the menu, suggesting *plats du jour* and recommending wines. During a lull, he is likely to serve a customer himself—carving a saddle of lamb, slicing a *châteaubriand,* or preparing a *carré de chevreuil flambé* at a table. The rest of the time, he is rushing to answer the telephone, whispering orders to his subordinates, initialing the checks of customers whose credit is good, or placing a centerpiece just so. Soulé is five feet five inches tall and, as befits a lover of good food and wine, inclines to stoutness, but his erect bearing and quick movements tend to camouflage this. His profile has been compared by one of his more admiring customers to that of the Duc de La Rochefoucauld and, by a less susceptible one, to that of a hardheaded French peasant from the Landes region, which, indeed, is where Soulé was born. His face is round, his forehead high, his nose prominent and curved, and his dark, shiny hair is always brushed back in a smooth pompadour. In moments of contempt or anger, he is capable of a glacial stare so devastating that one impressionable member of his staff claims to have seen a *sauce Béarnaise* curdle under it. Soulé is likely to respond with this stare if a customer makes what he considers an unwarranted request for a choice table; at such times, if the conversation has been in English, he switches to French. He speaks grammatically correct English and compensates for his French tendency to accent the last syllable of a word by hitting some words hard on the first syllable—"*Ken*tucky," for instance, and "*Conn*ecticut." His employees are loyal to him, although he isn't always easy to work for, being fastidious in his standards and uncompromising in his demands. During the busiest hours of the day, he is constantly tense, and his eyes, at least, rarely smile; he knows that something may go wrong at any instant and that a restaurant is only as good as the worst meal one has had there. He makes a point of being impeccable at all times in his attire, manners, and handling of business matters. His only hobby, he says, is paying bills promptly. His lieutenants, though hard-pressed themselves, sometimes wonder how he manages to bear up under the strain. "He would have had a nervous breakdown long ago if he didn't have the constitution of a healthy peasant," one of them said recently.

Since he opened the Pavillon twelve years ago, Soulé has not taken more than twelve days off, except for Sundays and legal holidays, when the place is closed, and a working vacation of a month or so each summer, when he shuts up shop and goes to France to reconnoiter the food and wine markets. The Pavillon is his life. He is fond of prizefights and, like most Frenchmen, was an ardent fan of the late Mardel Cerdan. When, on the evening of September 21, 1948, Cerdan fought for the last time in these parts, against Tony Zale in Jersey City, Soulé wanted desperately to attend, but he couldn't bring himself to leave the Pavillon until he had seen the last of his guests properly served. Finally, a few minutes before the fight was scheduled to begin, he was whisked off to Jersey City in the limousine of one of the promoters, a Pavillon client, and, thanks to a police escort thoughtfully provided by another Pavillon regular, arrived just in time. He was rewarded by seeing Cerdan knock Zale out in the twelfth round. Soulé feels that his aversion to leaving the restaurant during business hours has contributed to its success; he has witnessed the downfall of a number of similar establishments whose owners didn't feel it necessary to be constantly on the premises. "You don't have to be gone for a week or even a day," he says. "Turn your back on those *types* for only a few minutes, and right away they'll start to slow down."

Soulé had not been in this country long before he perceived that there are certain fundamental differences between the problems of running a French restaurant in France and those of running a French restaurant here. In France, most of the respected restaurants cater to people's palates and pay little attention to who those people are. Once, noticing that the paint on the ceiling of a fine old Parisian restaurant was peeling, I asked the proprietor why he didn't have it repainted, and he replied, "Monsieur, did you ever meet a Frenchman who looks at the ceiling while he's eating?" The greatness of French gastronomy is exemplified, besides Point's Pyramide and Dumaine's Côte-d'Or, by names such as Raymond Thuilier's Oustau de Baumanière in Les Baux, the Auberge du Père Bise in Talloires, Lapérouse and L'Escargot in Paris, La Réserve in Beaulieu, Dubern in Bordeaux, and the Hôtel de la Poste in Avallon.

These establishments are patronized by so-called "serious" eaters, to whom the location of their tables and the names of their neighbors mean nothing, while the *gratin de queues d'écrevisses* and the *râble de lièvre aux raisins,* accompanied by the right wines, are everything. Moreover, a Frenchman frequenting such a restaurant wouldn't think of devoting less than two and half hours to lunch nor, intent on the delicate taste of the sauces and the lingering aftertaste of the wines, would he concern himself with the number of calories he was consuming. To suggest that he smoke while eating would be an affront. Soulé acknowledges that things are not the same here. At the Pavillon, as at several comparable restaurants in the city, some of the steady customers have established a sort of social topography all their own. One of the Pavillon's principal landmarks is a small front room, sometimes perversely called the sanctuary, which opens directly onto the street and is cluttered with the constant traffic of customers making their way to and from other dining rooms. For all its hustle and bustle, many of Soulé's regulars regard the tables in the sanctuary as the most desirable by far. Second choice with them is the *nouvelle salle* to the left of the sanctuary, with its rattle and clank of cocktail shakers behind the bar, and in last place is what is known simply as the *salle,* a large room at the rear, where the tempo is slower, and one may dine quietly and at peace with the world. This is a state of affairs that Soulé has noncommittally, and profitably, come to accept, as he has the fact that a large number of his best customers prefer cocktails to wine, worry about their waistlines, smoke between courses, and are disposed to hurry through a meal in little more than an hour.

Having thus adjusted himself to his environment, Soulé diligently humors his customers, doing his best to seat them where they think they will be happiest and to serve them what they want as swiftly as they want it. His attitude toward his guests is courteous but cool. He never fraternizes with them and would rather be seen cooking with lard than slapping a guest on the back, pulling up a chair, and calling for drinks. In a city where the relationship between restaurateurs and their guests is often informal and on a first-name basis, Soulé remains unbending. Few call him by his first name, and fewer still are addressed by him in that way. Even outside the restaurant, Soulé treats his customers with a precise, calculated reserve. Last summer, a couple of Pavillon regulars crossing the Atlantic on a French Line ship discovered that Soulé was also a passenger and invited him a number of times to have a drink with them; he accepted only on the last day of the voyage, when he felt that any danger of *rapprochement* had passed. Because of his remoteness, some people consider him stuffy, but experience has taught him to be on his guard. People who consider themselves friends of a restaurant proprietor are likely to ask for favors that circumstances make it impossible to grant—a good table, for instance, when all the good tables are reserved—and upon being turned down might, no matter how apologetically, resolve to take their business elsewhere.

The Pavillon has sixty tables, with a seating capacity of a hundred-forty, and the demand for accommodations frequently exceeds the supply. Soulé is therefore obliged to require that diners make reservations for the most popular hours, which are from one to two-thirty in the afternoon and from seven to nine at night. Twice a day, an hour before the Pavillon opens—at twelve-thirty for lunch, and at six-thirty for dinner—Soulé consults his list of reservations and starts allocating his tables. This is a delicate task, for which he relies heavily on his knowledge of human nature in general and his familiarity with his customers' foibles in particular. As the guests arrive, Soulé, who carries the whole seating arrangement in his head, much as Toscanini carries a musical score, shows himself to be a true master of the arts of diplomacy—the half promise and the three-quarter assurance, the ability never to say no, saying yes when no is meant, and, when all else fails, appeasing with a smile.

Originally, the Pavillon consisted of only two rooms—the one that is now the sanctuary and was then the bar, and the big *salle* behind it. During the winter of 1943–44, Soulé rented the adjacent premises to the west—an office just vacated by Western Union—and broke through the walls, creating the *nouvelle salle*. Then his troubles began. Some of his regulars decided that the old *salle* was too stodgy and demanded tables in the *nouvelle salle*, where they could watch the comings and goings at the bar, which had not yet been moved to its present location. In May of the following year, Soulé became involved in a dispute with his waiters, who wanted, among other things, an arrangement whereby their stations would be rotated once a week, so that everybody could have a chance at the preferred tables, where, as a rule, the more liberal tippers were seated. The waiters went on strike and stayed out forty-two days, a situation that still makes Soulé wince. Soulé managed to keep the Pavillon going, after a fashion, by closing down the *salle* and serving meals only in the bar and the *nouvelle salle*, with the help of the non-striking members of his staff—two maîtres d'hôtel, twenty-two chefs and cooks, the cashier, the hat check girl, and a pantryman. As the days passed and the waiters showed no signs of giving in, Soulé threatened to close the *salle* permanently and to operate a condensed version of the Pavillon, tentatively named Le Petit Pavillon, in what was left of the place. To show the waiters and their union that he meant business, he called in workmen, had the bar moved to its present position in the *nouvelle salle*, and converted its former location into a dining room. At this point, the strike was settled by mediation; the waiters went back to work, and the Pavillon stayed in business, uncondensed.

As matters turned out, the strike was a good thing for Soulé. For some time before the walkout started, it had been his custom to set up a few small tables in the entrance room as emergency accommodations in the event of an overflow, but it was not until he moved the bar out that the room became the sanctuary and a social success—and the Pavillon a full-fledged commercial one. Soulé cannot explain this phenomenon, nor has he reason to complain about it. Today, space in the sanctuary is at such a premium that some people appear delighted to eat at tiny extra tables hastily set up in the middle of the aisle there during the rush hours, or so close to the revolving door that they are constantly fanned by it. "They would rather dine in the telephone booth than in the *salle*," Soulé says, with only a momentary lifting of his eyebrows.

Many leading chefs and maîtres d'hôtel have learned the elements of their trade in the establishments of their parents, but Soulé is a first-generation restaurant man. The son of a moderately successful building contractor, he was born on March 12, 1903, in Saubrigues, a tiny hamlet situated halfway between Dax and Bayonne, in the southwestern corner of France—a region known gastronomically for its cabbage soup, omelets with peppers, and foie gras. Soulé's mother was a housewife who was so gifted in the kitchen that her son still prefers the *brandade de morue* she used to cook—a purée of salt codfish—to such Pavillon specialties as *volaille étuvée* or *soufflé de homard.* "*Maman* would cut the cod into small pieces and poach them for about ten minutes," Soulé says. "Then, after removing the skin and bones, she'd mix in slices of potatoes she had boiled in their skins, and add vinegar, oil, garlic, and chopped parsley. She always served her *brandade de morue* neither hot nor cold, just tepid. What a dish, what a dish! Sometimes when I went home for a holiday, I'd eat it morning, noon, and night."

Soulé got into the restaurant business by accident. An uncle of his, a baker in Bayonne, supplied *brioches* and *petits pains* to the Hôtel Continental in nearby Biarritz. One day, he heard that the hotel had an opening for a busboy and recommended his nephew Henri, who had just finished high school and was looking for something to do. The boy was taken on, and soon, despite his lowly vantage point, became entranced by what he saw of how a restaurant is run. After two years of clearing tables at the Continental, he went to Paris and got a job as waiter in the late and lamented Hôtel Mirabeau on the Rue de la Paix, which then served an impressive lunch, with three wines, for twenty-five francs (about a dollar and half in those days). The dining room was under the supervision of Ange Valan, a great maître d'hôtel in the best French tradition, and it was from him that Soulé learned the basic precepts of his present occupation. He learned, for example, that a maître d'hôtel must be, above all, a subtle compromiser, capable of soothing not only the resentment of waiters toward overbearing guests but the far more deep-seated resentment of cooks towards waiters—a resentment based on the cooks' feeling that they do all the work and the waiters collect all the tips. Day after day, Soulé studied Valan's technique, which combined the talents of an actor, lawyer, doctor, and diplomat. Nobody was ever hurried into ordering at the Mirabeau; instead of standing impatiently with pencil poised, Valan appeared to take pleasure in watching a guest ponder the menu, scrawled in the traditional violet ink, with the *plats du jour* and *spécialités de la maison* in red and "special" specialties written upside down to attract proper attention. Sensing that a guest was unfamiliar with the Mirabeau's cuisine, Valan would tactfully steer him away from dishes that might call for an acquired taste, and recommend something of a deceptive simplicity that could not fail to please. If aware that a customer had a delicate stomach, he would prescribe a concoction both bland and succulent.

And always, of course, he stood ready to suggest, as the meal progressed, the proper concomitants from the Mirabeau's cellar.

Impressed by the intricacies of the calling, Soulé resolved that he
would become a maître d'hôtel. In 1919, to broaden his training, he
moved on, still as a waiter, to Claridge's Hotel, on the Champs-Elysées.
He was there only a short while, however—just long enough to become
acquainted with and marry a Parisienne named Olga Muller—before he
was called up for his two-year stretch in the French army. After ten
months of basic training, he was made a corporal and given the job of
running the officers' mess at Mülheim, in the Ruhr, and he spent the rest
of his stretch there. To hear Soulé tell it, he was an autocrat in a corporal's uniform, conducting the mess strictly according to his own ideas.
He decided what the colonels were going to eat, and there were no arguments. Upon getting out of the army, he went back to the Mirabeau, and
at twenty-three was made a captain of waiters—the youngest in Paris.
In 1930, he was offered the job of captain at Ciro's, which he quickly
accepted, for the Mirabeau was physically run-down and destined to
close, and Ciro's was, as it still is, one of Paris's most successful restaurants. It was managed by two of the greatest Frenchmen in the business—Maurice Chambenoit and Julien Rémoit. A few years ago, M.
Rémoit came to the United States to visit a granddaughter who married
an American soldier in France after the war, and Soulé proudly invited
his former employer to dinner at the Pavillon. "M. Rémoit perceived
everything that was going on—a perfect maître d'hôtel," Soulé recalls.
"He turned to me and said, '*Dites donc*, Henri, haven't I seen that *bombe*
before?' I said, 'But of course. We used to call it *la bombe de vanille
flambée* at Ciro's—chilled fresh fruit on a base of vanilla ice cream,
sprinkled with chopped nuts and topped with heated kirsch, lighted.' He
was so moved he kissed me on the cheek and started to cry."

In 1933, Chambenoit and Rémoit left Ciro's to manage La
Crémaillière, on the Rue de Faubourg Saint-Honoré, which they had
owned for some time. A short while later, Soulé also left Ciro's, to
become a captain at the Café de Paris, then run by the late Louis Barraya,
who was simultaneously managing three other distinguished restaurants—the Pavillon d'Armenonville, the Pré Catalan, and Fouquet's—
and who, in the course of his career, educated a whole generation of

French maîtres d'hôtel. Barraya was the brother-in-law of the late Jean Drouant, a member of a family long prominent in the operation of Parisian restaurants and himself the owner of three renowned establishments—Drouant Place Gaillon, Pavillon Royal, and Bois de Boulogne. During the next five years, Soulé rose to the position of manager and chief of staff under Barraya. Soulé and his wife were living comfortably in an attractive apartment near the Etoile, and had a car and a bank account. He was doing well. In the fall of 1938, Drouant sent for him and asked him how he would like to go to New York and help run a restaurant at the World's Fair.

"I was stunned," Soulé says. "I'd always wanted to visit America. As a boy in Saubrigues, I used to read all the books about America I could get hold of. But I'd never dreamed I'd really get there." It developed that Drouant had sponsored a plan to operate a semi-outdoor restaurant as part of the French Pavilion at the World's Fair, which was to open the following spring. Barraya and several other restaurant men in Paris had promised to chip in, but at the last minute all of them except Barraya got cold feet and quit. In this crisis, Drouant and Barraya decided to go ahead and, backed by the French Line and by the considerable resources of their own restaurants, started to recruit a competent staff. In March 1939, Drouant, together with Soulé and ninety-eight other Frenchmen (sixty kitchen workers and thirty-eight maîtres d'hôtel, waiters, carvers, and wine stewards), arrived in New York. Soulé was made general manager of Le Restaurant du Pavillon de France—or, as it soon became known, the French Restaurant.

It opened on May 9, 1939, and proved one of the outstanding attractions of the fair. By end of May, as many as 18,401 people had been served there; in June, another 26,510 were served. Word of the high quality of its food and wines got around, and by the time the restaurant closed for the winter, on October 31, it had served a total of 136,261 meals. Nowadays, its menu reads like a nostalgic memento of an earlier century: *Suprême de Barbue Mornay*, $1.50; *Homard Monte Carlo*, $1.75; *Coq au Vin de Bordeaux*, $1.60; *Gigot d'Agneau Boulangère*, $1.60; *Soufflé Palmyre*, ninety cents; *crêpes Suzette*, $1.25; and *tous les fromages*, fifty cents. The wine list featured Perrier-Jouet champagne, at $6 a bottle; Château Margaux '29, at $4.50; Château Cheval Blanc '29, at $5.50; Château Beychevelle '24, at $3; Cos d'Estournel '34, at $2.50; and Clos de

Vougeot '34, at $4. Soulé often worked eighteen hours a day; in addition to his regular duties as maître d'hôtel, he was tormented by problems of supply and bookkeeping. Business was excellent until the first of September, when war broke out. A few weeks later, Drouant called a meeting of all the employees. "There were a few short speeches but no oratory," Soulé recalls. "There was no doubt in anyone's mind about where our place was." At the end of October, when the restaurant closed, Soulé and the others went back to France. Only the fifty-eight-year-old Drouant stayed on in New York, to wind up its business affairs.

Soulé spent a few days with his wife in Paris, and then he left for Bordeaux, where he joined the 1st Machine Gun Company of the 168th Infantry Regiment, resuming the rank of corporal. During the so-called phony war, he spent most of his time doing close-order drill in front of a barracks in Bordeaux and proved sufficiently competent at it to be promoted to sergeant. In the winter of 1940, he was notified, through channels, that he was to be demobilized and sent to New York on a *commission civile,* by order of Prime Minister Edouard Daladier. The French government had decided to reopen the French Pavilion at the World's Fair and considered Soulé's services as manager of the restaurant there more valuable than as a sergeant in Bordeaux; the restaurant's staff, however, was to be reduced from a hundred men to twenty-eight, all of them over thirty-five. Soulé and the others arrived in New York late in April 1940 on the *Manhattan,* which had sailed from Genoa. Two weeks later, France was overrun by the Germans, and on June 14, Paris fell. Soulé and his men wept, as Frenchmen did everywhere, but then they pulled themselves together and carried on through the summer. The season was not a success. For one thing, the weather was bad—out of the 173 days the fair was open, sixty-five were rainy—and, for another, the fall of Paris discouraged many fairgoers from visiting the Pavilion. Between May 11, when the restaurant reopened, and October 31, when it closed again, it served only 83,365 meals—a good fifty thousand fewer than in the previous season. At the end of that time, Soulé and his men were out of work. Away from their ranges, pantries, wine shelves, and tables, they felt lost. It was, of course, an unhappy period for anyone French; three-fifths of France was occupied, and Pierre Laval was making a sorry spectacle of himself in Vichy. Soulé and his men talked things over, and ten decided not to go back to France. "We just couldn't face living under the Boches," Soulé says. "It wasn't an easy decision, for we had no idea what we could do in New York. Most of my men had saved no money and didn't know where their next meal was coming from. All of us had only temporary visitor's visas and were not allowed to accept steady employment. Ah, it was terrible, terrible! We sat around for weeks making vague plans, and every now and then one of the men would say to me, 'Why don't you start a French restaurant here in New York? We'll all be with you. And you made so many friends at the World's Fair.' Well, I began to think about it. It was true I had made friends. I had a book containing over three thousand cards inscribed with the names and addresses of people we had served at the French Pavilion—people who told me they had enjoyed themselves. Everybody I talked to encouraged me. Finally, I decided that I would take my men temporarily to Canada, so that we could reenter this country with the status of refugees, and I began to look around for a suitable location."

Soulé found that location—his present premises, on East Fifty-fifth Street—where an establishment called Palmer's 711 Restaurant was up for sale. Actually, it wasn't much; the kitchen was inadequate, and the location was supposed to be jinxed. A few years before the 711, a French restaurant called L'Apéritif had failed to survive there. But Soulé, who isn't superstitious, was convinced that it was ideal for a restaurant of the sort he had in mind, and he hastily took an option on it before doing anything about the requirements of the immigration authorities. Then, in June 1941, he shepherded his men to Niagara Falls, Canada, in order to be able to bring them into the U.S. again on the "French quota." The others were readmitted to the United States without a hitch, but Soulé, to his horror, was held up owing to some technicality connected with his papers. He spent three bleak weeks in Canada before the troubles were straightened out. On June 28, he was allowed to reenter, and without so much as a backward glance at the falls he hurried to New York. A little over five years later, on August 8, 1946, he became an American citizen.

Taking stock of his assets, Soulé found himself long on goodwill but rather short on cash. In the latter department, he had, in fact, only twenty-four thousand dollars—part of it as savings and a portion as loans from two silent partners (whom he has since repaid)—with which to equip and open his restaurant. He spent ten thousand dollars on furnishings and decorating, six thousand on rent, insurance, and the legal expenses of incorporating the restaurant as the French Pavilion Restaurant Corporation (for both commercial and sentimental reasons he had decided to keep the name of the World's Fair showplace), and another six to take over the lease to the premises. Two thousand dollars remained on which to operate. Happily, he was able to obtain most of his supplies on credit from wholesalers who had dealt with him while he was managing the French Restaurant and were familiar with his "hobby" of paying his bills on time.

The Pavillon opened on the evening of October 15, 1941. Of the forty members of Soulé's staff who worked that night, eleven are still with him: Cyrille Jean-Louis Christophe, the head chef; Martin Decré, Soulé's deputy; Pierre Franey, an assistant chef; Pierre Géraud, Gabriel Jofre, and Henri Rouget, captains; Gaston Large, a waiter; Charles Hubert, a steward; Mme. Marie Casanova, the cashier; John D. Trump, the accountant; and Mohammed Youbi, who is in charge of the pantry. A preamble to the Pavillon's wine card on that opening night read, "This distinguished offering of the great wines of France, most of which would be rarities at any time, has been made available through the joint efforts of Messrs. Bellows & Company and ourselves, to keep fresh the memories of happier events in that country, despite the tragedy of present conditions." The card (its tribute to Bellows represented a friendly gesture toward the president of the firm, a personal friend of Soulé's) listed twenty-two champagnes, twenty-six red Bordeaux, and twenty-seven red Burgundies. There had been no advance publicity—Soulé couldn't afford it—but the place was sold out. "I remember the opening night menu," Soulé says. "Caviar, *sole bonne femme, poulet braisé,* with champagne, cheese, and dessert. Everybody liked it. When it was over, I went up to my office and started to cry, because my parents were in Saubrigues, and my wife was in Paris, and there was no one to share my success with me."

Soulé's thoughts of success turned out to be premature. Fifty-four days later, the United States was in the war, and for a few months there were a good many empty tables at the Pavillon. Then, during 1943, as the nation's prospects became brighter, business gradually picked up, and it has gone on picking up ever since. When the Pavillon opened, it had a hundred and twelve seats and forty employees, or one employee for every two and four-fifths seats; today, with its hundred and forty seats, it has eighty-five employees, or one for every one and three-fifths seats. In 1941, a table d'hôte lunch, consisting of hors d'oeuvre, a *plat du jour*, dessert, and coffee, cost $1.75; today a *plat du jour* alone costs $3.50. The payroll the first year was $75,195; last year it was $277,573. Gross income the first year was $263,714; gross income last year was $831,732. In the past eleven years the restaurant has served over one million one hundred thousand people, paid out $2,017,022 in wages alone, and taken in a total of $6,582,854. Soulé likes to think of himself as an artist rather than a businessman, but there can be no doubt that, as such things go, he has succeeded. He now owns all 102 shares of the French Pavilion Restaurant Corporation.

In moments of introspection, Soulé sometimes dreams of the kind of restaurant he would like to own. It would be a comfortable, unpretentious place, with no glitter and only twelve tables, seating four people each, arranged in such a way that no one of them could be considered preferable to the others. People would feel at home there, easily spending three hours for lunch, while the chefs would think nothing of spending six hours or more on the preparation of *fumet de poisson* or *fumet de gibier*. Everything would be cooked to order, and customers would know to call a day in advance for such delicacies of *cuisine bourgeoise* as *tripes à la mode de Caen*, which must spend at least ten hours in the oven. Soulé realizes that a restaurant of this kind could exist only in Paradise, or perhaps in some remote French province where the costs of operating are still tolerable. With Manhattan wages, prices, rent, and taxes what they are, he has to serve three hundred people a day just to break even, and a good many more to make it worthwhile to stay in business. On a normal day, there are around 150 people for lunch and 230 for dinner. Quite a few are in a hurry and ask to be served quickly. Others express no less shocking desires ("Make my omelet on the raw side"), for which they might well be asked to leave a similar restaurant in France. Once, in Saulieu, I heard a customer tell M. Dumaine that he was in a hurry, to which that distinguished gentleman replied, "In that case, Monsieur, I think you had better go elsewhere and get yourself a sandwich." And the management of La Tour d'Argent, in Paris, gently tries to avoid such occurrences by printing this reminder on its menu: *"La grande cuisine demande beaucoup de temps."*

In becoming resigned to the tempo and customs of his adopted land, Soulé has acquired a pragmatic view of things that cushions the shock as he writes down some particularly barbaric order or assures a guest that he will hustle a meal along. "If I were to insist that my customers take their time, I would be out of business tomorrow," he says. "People here eat before the theater, not afterward, as they do on the Continent. They arrive at seven, want drinks and a full-course dinner, and expect to make an eight-thirty curtain. Well, it isn't easy, and good restaurants in France wouldn't do it, but with patience, practice, and teamwork, we've finally worked it out so that we can serve them a soup or hors d'oeuvre, an entrée, a soufflé, and coffee, all within an hour. We've timed our operations to the point where we can tell a guest that it will take, say, forty-five minutes to broil a saddle of lamb, or forty minutes to make a soufflé."

Each day, the menu at the Pavillon lists two *plats du jour* for lunch—dishes that are ready to be served instantly—and another two for dinner; typical of these are *selle d'agneau rôtie persillée, cuisseau de veau Pavillon, volaille Alexandra,* and *aiguillette de boeuf à la française.* And each day, though it's not on the menu, there is one *plat bourgeois,* which is the sort of thing Soulé likes to eat himself—*tête de veau vinaigrette,* perhaps, or a *choucroute* consisting of ham and Alsatian sausages with sauerkraut and new potatoes. No more than fifteen portions of the *plat bourgeois* are prepared, and Soulé offers them only to customers he knows will appreciate them. Two-thirds of the Pavillon's clientele order a *plat du jour;* the rest, except for the select few who have the *plat bourgeois,* order à la carte. Soulé's menus are merely suggestion lists; he will prepare anything for a customer, provided he is given enough time. One of his regulars, a sturdy female gourmet of biblical age, often sends him complicated orders prior to one of her appearances at the restaurant; not long ago, she asked to have a *châteaubriand* prepared in a marinade of vintage Châteauneuf-du-Pape—"just as I used to have it in France back in the good old days." Though Soulé was delighted to oblige, he was a little embarrassed when it came to adding up the bill. "We made the *château,* of course," he later told a friend. "But what with the price of steak and Châteauneuf-du-Pape, we had to charge eighteen dollars a portion. And then the wines and all the rest of it brought that lunch—

it was for two—to around sixty dollars." Less expansive customers of the Pavillon find that, not counting wine and other drinks, a lunch for two costs around eight dollars, and a dinner around fifteen.

Soulé, who is a great believer in the old saying that no dish can be better than the ingredients that go into it, buys only provisions he considers first-rate. This, of course, is in the best French tradition—one that sometimes sorely taxes Soulé's ingenuity to uphold in this country. Fernand Point, to whose restaurant Soulé makes a reverent pilgrimage each summer, once said, "In the *haute cuisine,* you can't think of money, or you're though before you start. The chef must be king." Soulé ocassionally quotes this dictum, and adds rather sadly, "How pleasant life must be in a land where one never has to consult one's accountant."

Every night at around ten-thirty, as the last of the Pavillon's guests are being served, Christophe, the head chef, takes an inventory of his supplies and compiles a list of his needs for the next day. Half an hour later, knowing this schedule, the merchants with whom Soulé deals—butchers and purveyors of poultry, fish, vegetables, butter and eggs, truffles, and caviar—start calling for orders. Soulé has faith in the men he buys from, and they in turn respect his high standards. (A few years ago, a butter dealer who had long held a standing order from Soulé for AA butter—the best grade—began slipping in a few pounds that were only A. He was warned once, but a couple of months later did it again and was dropped from the Pavillon's list forever.) No matter how diligently Soulé scours the markets, he finds a considerable gap between what he would like and what he can get. "If we had everything available to us that they have in Paris, we would be the *ne plus ultra,*" he says. "The youngest partridge, the freshest *fraises des bois,* the finest Brie and Pont l'Evêque when they are in season, the season's first truffles. The fact, alas, is that we never get any true 'firsts' here. Everything is fresh all year round, so, naturally, it is never *quite* fresh, if you see what I mean. While there are fresh vegetables throughout the year, we miss the *primeurs*—those tender garden vegetables that on the Continent they have only in spring." Soulé maintains a strict embargo on frozen foods and buys only fresh vegetables—or, at any rate, what Americans call fresh vegetables—with the exception of canned French *petits pois,* which he considers superior to any peas raised in this country, whether fresh, canned, or frozen.

*   *   *

Soulé rates American seafood as generally excellent but insists that he can find nothing here that approaches the delicacy of the Mediterranean *loup de mer,* or sea bass. He also pines for *rouget,* or red mullet—especially the Mediterranean rock mullet, known as sea woodcock—and for the *omble chevalier,* a member of the trout family that is found in the Annecy region and in the lakes of Switzerland. While he concedes that American beef, lamb, and pork are of unequaled quality, he thinks our veal is inferior. This view is shared by Arsène Tingaud, a French-American whose firm has delivered veal, lamb, pork, sweetbreads, and poultry to the Pavillon since the day it opened. "In France," Tingaud says, "the farmer puts a collar around the neck of a young calf, ties it up inside the barn, and feeds it milk three times a day—patiently, little by little, taking infinite pains, as with a child. The animal never sees the sunshine until it is taken to the slaughterhouse, at the age of four to six weeks. No wonder the meat is white and almost as tender as chicken! Here the young calves jump all over the place and are sometimes even fed on grass. Our poultry comes from some of the best farms in New Jersey and Delaware and is especially good from August to November, but even the best American chicken, no matter when, doesn't have the flavor and tenderness of chickens in the Bresse region, north of Lyon. There the chickens are kept cooped up all the time and maize is forced down their throats, much as geese are stuffed in Strasbourg and the Périgord region. A goose liver from around there sometimes weighs two pounds or more."

One of the Soulé's regrets is that New York State's fish and game laws are so stringent that they make it all but impossible to cook brook trout *au bleu* as it is prepared in France. There, every major restaurant has a small pool stocked with live trout, which are removed as they are ordered, killed by a blow on the head, cleaned, and thrown into a boiling court bouillon of water, salt, vinegar, minced carrots and onions, parsley, thyme, and bay leaves, after which they are served with melted brown butter and boiled new potatoes—as fine a dish, in the opinion of many epicures, as any in the world. Soulé could have a pool in his establishment if he chose, but the legalities of buying the fish to stock it and of removing them from the pool in the off-season makes the whole idea impractical.

When it comes to such things as forcibly fed poultry and captive trout, there isn't much Soulé can do about competing with his opposite numbers in France, but he feels that in the matter of the beef he has the edge on them, and he drives himself relentlessly to make the most of this advantage. Twice a week, on Tuesday and Friday afternoons, he visits the large meat packing house of Ottman & Co., at Ninth Avenue and Little West Twelfth Street, where he personally selects every piece of beef to be delivered to his restaurant. One Tuesday morning not long after my first visit to the Pavillon, he called and suggested I go along with him on his trip downtown that afternoon. "Why don't you stop by the restaurant at three-thirty?" he said. "We'll have lunch together before we start." When I arrived at the Pavillon, Soulé, looking tired but still immaculate, was bidding goodbye to a party of three loquacious ladies, the last of his lunchtime customers. While waiting for them to leave, I walked into the bar, where the barman, André Gros-Daillon, was polishing glasses. André, a veteran of the Paris Ritz and the old Ritz-Carlton in New York, joined the Pavillon a few weeks after its opening. *"Ah, c'est dur, le travail ici,"* he told me. "I get here at eleven-thirty in the morning, and often I am still here at twelve-thirty the next morning. I've got to serve twenty waiters who carry drinks to the tables, in addition to all the customers who line up at the bar. Everybody with their own tastes and everybody in a hurry. *Oui, c'est dur."*

The three ladies left at last, and I accompanied Soulé to the kitchen, which is in the basement and is reached by twenty-one steep steps that constitute a real challenge to the stamina of the waiters. At that time of day, a general air of letdown hangs over the kitchen. Two or three handymen were mopping up, and a couple of cooks in white toques were keeping an eye on some large vessels that contained veal stock and *fumet de poisson.* In one corner, a man was listlessly cleaning fish for dinner. In another, the head chef, Christophe, was conferring with three of his top lieutenants. He left them to come over and join us. A slender, modest man—surprisingly slender and modest for a member of a profession that abounds in well-fed prima donnas—Christophe is a native of Pouilly-Fuissé, the home of the famous white Burgundy wine of that name, and served his apprenticeship in Mâcon, another good wine region. Later, he worked in Lyon, Dieppe, and Evian-les-Bains, and then at the Hôtel de Paris in Monte Carlo, generally considered a tough postgraduate course for ambitious practitioners of his calling. He was a prominent member of the original French team at the World's Fair. "M. Christophe lives only for his work," Soulé said, with surprising warmth. "He is a bachelor and has no family life. This kitchen"—he made a sweeping gesture with his arm, just missing a stack of plates—"is his life. You should have been here a couple of hours ago. At one o'clock, no one was in the restaurant, and by one-twenty there were a hundred and forty people and all of them wanted their orders taken care of right away."

"And, as always, what orders!" Christophe said. "One man likes strong seasoning and another doesn't want any salt. One wants his *pommes en purée* liquid and another wants his omelet well done." He paused meditatively, and then went on, "I'm sorry to say that no matter how they want it, we can't make a real French omelet. The eggs don't have the color of those in France, and even the best American butter is factory-made. It lacks that mellow, hazelnut flavor of the butter from Isigny, Charente, and Savoie, where the farmers and their wives make their butter in small quantities by hand. People sometimes ask me whether we use a special skillet for our omelets and whether it's made of copper, aluminum, or iron, but they never ask me about the butter. It's the butter and eggs that make an omelet, Monsieur—not the metal. You know, I have come to the unhappy conclusion that certain things shouldn't be served in this country at all. Take calves' liver, for example. Even at a dollar-sixty a pound, the best American calves' liver can't be given the delicate light taste of a French *foie de veau*. We've tried everything, including preparing it *saisi* instead of *sauté*. Nothing doing. And filet of sole. Nothing here can compare with *limande* from the Channel. To be sure, the sole we serve is flown here from England, but that means packing it in ice, and so it is not perfect. Why, when I worked in Dieppe, we used sole right out of the Channel. It makes all the difference."

"It's a sad thing that even a rich man here can't buy the kind of lunch that every middle-class Frenchmen can afford from time to time," Soulé said. "Six *marennes*, a partridge—very, very young—and a piece of Brie."

"And *fraises des bois*," said Christophe.

"And *fraises des bois*," said Soulé.

After taking our leave of Christophe, Soulé and I went to the wine cellar, which adjoins the kitchen. Air-conditioning keeps it at a steady sixty degrees. Two sides are taken up by Bordeaux and champagnes, the rest by Burgundies, other French wines, German wines, and liqueurs. The *caviste,* Aimé Thélin, a cheerful, gray-haired, ruddy-faced Frenchman in a pharmacist's white jacket, was on hand to greet us. *"Voici le petit enfant de la cave,"* Thelin said, calling my attention to a Cuvée des Dames Hospitalières '49. "Only three years old—a real baby. All told, we have almost fifty thousand bottles of various wines, but we keep most of them in a warehouse. Ah, but M. Soulé is the true expert when it comes to choosing wines!"

I was already aware of Soulé's reputation as a connoisseur of wine, having heard in France of the discernment he shows on his buying forays each summer. Some time ago, one of the most celebrated châteaux in the Médoc marketed some 1929 wine that turned out to have been "heated": that is, fermentation of the young wine had been sped up artificially. Soulé, who had bought quite a quantity, discovered this flaw in the first bottle he opened back at the Pavillon, tried a half-dozen bottles to be sure that he was not making a fool of himself, and returned eleven hundred dollars' worth of the stuff. He buys wines as a speculator buys securities, always keeping a lookout for vintages that are inexpensive to purchase but may gain in value with the passage of time. This is risky business, but one for which he is equipped by thirty years of experience. As Thélin pointed out to me, it's easy to proclaim that the Château Cheval Blanc '37, now offered by the Pavillon at twelve dollars, is a splendid wine; it was less easy to spot this wine back in 1941, when Soulé laid in a big shipment of it at three dollars a bottle.

Soulé and I had lunch in the *nouvelle salle.* On a small side table were two bottles in baskets—a Vieux Château Certan '45 and a Musigny, Comté de Vogüé '34. Soulé filled our glasses with the Certan and served a *pot-au-feu* that a waiter had brought. In addition to the customary ingredients—beef boiled in a consommé with carrots, turnips, leeks, celery, blanched cabbage, potatoes, and a marrow bone—the Pavillon's *pot-au-feu* contains pork and breast of chicken. With it, we each had a cup of clear consommé. Soulé tasted the *pot-au-feu* and nodded approvingly. He loves to eat, but his tendency to put on weight restricts him to one large meal a day. "Yesterday for lunch I had six oysters, which I shouldn't have had, a small *bifteck,* and endive salad," he said. "Only a sandwich at night. If I ate Christophe's dishes twice a day, I'd gain ten pounds a week. Still, I think I'll have a little more of this *pot-au-feu*."

The waiters were setting the tables for dinner. As we ate, Soulé told me something about the mechanics of running the Pavillon. The restaurant's sixty tables are divided into ten groups of six tables each, and a team of two waiters is assigned to each group; one brings the food from the kitchen, and the other serves it. There are no sommeliers, because Soulé considers them superfluous; he himself suggests and takes the orders for wines, and captains serve them. Soulé has contracts with the Consolidated Dining Room Employees Union, Local 1, and with the Chefs, Cooks, Pastry Cooks and Assistants Union of New York, Local 89, both affiliated with the American Federation of Labor. In the contracts, the unions recognize that the "employer...operates a French-type restaurant of high-class clientele, and in the event that the union is unable or fails to furnish and supply the employer with workers of the type and qualifications formerly employed...the employer shall then have the right to employ any other person or persons that [he] may deem necessary...even though they are not members of a union at the time they are hired." Fifteen of Soulé's employees—the head chefs and stewards, and the like—are not members of any union. The weekly minimum union wage for the dining room help ranges from $29.50 for a busboy to $53.50 for a captain; kitchen salaries start at forty-six dollars for a dishwasher, and run up to a hundred and twenty-six dollars for a *chef saucier*. "That's one of the things that makes life so difficult in New York," Soulé told me. "A *saucier* in France gets less money than a dishwasher in America. Over there, the proprietor can afford to have a man in the kitchen who does nothing but strain the flesh of trout through sieves to make *mousse de truite*. If we did that here, we would have to charge a fortune for the dish. We charge four-fifty now for a *mousse de sole* and we're losing money on it. And there is another problem. Something seems to happen to my people as soon as they come to this country. Over there, they took pride in their work, had a sense of teamwork and a desire for perfection. Everybody tried to do his best. Here, everybody is just trying to get a bigger paycheck. The old sense of teamwork is gone. Terrible, terrible!"

We had cheese and a glass of the excellent Musigny, and then, after coffee, went up to Soulé's office on the second floor, at the end of a dark corridor. Soulé shares the office with his accountant and his secretary, and the little time he spends there is devoted mostly to signing checks, something he allows no one else at the Pavillon to do. To the right of the office is Soulé's dressing room which resembles an actor's, what with bright lights, multiple mirrors, and stacks of freshly laundered dress shirts. Soulé changed from the dark-blue suit to a pearl gray one, put on a pearl gray tie and a camel's hair coat, picked up a briefcase, and we went out and got into his car—a chauffeur-driven limousine. During the ride downtown, Soulé leaned back in his seat and closed his eyes. He looked worn. "Last night when I went home, my wife complained that I'm working too hard and that I have time for nothing but the restaurant," he said. "I suppose that's true, but the fact is I *like* to work hard. In my *métier,* you must never relax if you want to be successful, and only the successful man is respected."

It was clear that Soulé is respected at Ottman & Co., where Henry and Jack Ottman, the owners, greet him cordially. They were wearing the traditional butchers' white coats, and brought out two similar uniforms for us, which we slipped on over our overcoats. Soulé led the way to an elevator, carrying his briefcase. At the fourth floor, Jack Ottman opened a heavy double door and we stepped out into a cool, spacious chamber full of shelves, where sides of beef were lying like bottles in a wine cellar. Each piece was stamped PRIME and bore a sticker showing its weight. Soulé strode along past the shelves, inspecting the sides of beef and occasionally shaking his head and muttering. "Too much fat," he said as he slid his thumb over a filet, and again, "The grain must be smooth, as in fine silk. It must be marbled. Feel those fibres! In France, we call cattle like that *la cavalerie*—cattle that have gone in for gymnastics and overdeveloped their muscles."

At last, Soulé found a side of beef to his liking and nodded to Henry. "This one," he said. Henry pushed a wooden skewer through the layer of fat surrounding the carcass, to denote that the meat had been sold to Soulé, and Soulé opened his briefcase, took out a pair of pliers and several pieces of wire, to which were attached lead tabs marked "H.S." He stuck one of the wires through the fat and fastened the end to the tab with the pliers. This was to prevent any confusion about to whom the animal belonged. Then he continued his prowl past the shelves, poking, prying, inveighing against too much fat in one case and too much muscle in another. Presently, he selected another side of beef.

"Forty-seven pounds," he said, consulting the sticker. "By the way, what's the price today?"

"One-forty-two for short loins, and one-ninety for tenderloin," Jack said.

"This side is going to cost me over sixty dollars," Soulé told me. "There will be fourteen portions of meat on it. There is possibly a seven-pound fillet, but only the center part of it can be used for the kind of steaks we serve. That center part will cost me twelve dollars and will perhaps net three steaks. For each dollar's worth of steak I sell, forty-four cents comes right back here to the Ottmans, leaving me fifty-six cents for salaries, taxes, and all sorts of overhead. The customers think I'm getting rich because I charge them seven dollars and half for a steak. Why, back in 1941 we used to sell a *châteaubriand* that big for two"—he held up his hands to frame an imaginary *châteaubriand* the size of a desk blotter—"for eight dollars and a half. Today we've got to charge fifteen for the *château,* which is silly. I say people ought to eat less steak, and more lamb and poultry."

Soulé and his wife, who joined him here in 1946, have a four-room apartment on Park Avenue at Seventy-fifth Street, but he rarely goes there except to sleep, and he refers to it as his "place," never as his "home." Home to him is a house he and his wife bought four years ago at Montauk, on the tip of Long Island, and he persists in thinking of it that way even though he spends no more than seven hours a week there—on Sundays, when the Pavillon is closed. The trip to Montauk takes three hours in his limousine, and Soulé finds it restful; soon after crossing the Triborough Bridge, he usually falls asleep and doesn't wake until the car swings up in front of his house. Mme. Soulé typically accompanies her husband on these Sunday jaunts. Every now and then, she returns to France, to visit her family and scout wines for the Pavillon, but Soulé keeps on going out to Montauk every Sunday, just the same. One Saturday afteroon not long ago, shortly after he had seen his wife off on the *Liberté,* he called and asked if I would come along to keep him company on his journey out the next day. I replied I would be delighted to, and he said he would stop by and pick me up at nine at my hotel.

The next morning Soulé was wearing a sports coat and slacks, a checked topcoat, a woollen muffler, and a cap. All in all, he looked like one of those fashionable travelers seen in photographs taken during the early years of this century. He settled himself comfortably in the back of the car; I got in beside him, and the driver arranged a robe over our knees. As Soulé adjusted his muffler and put on a pair of calfskin gloves, there was a smile of cheerful anticipation such as I had never seen before. "Nine-twenty," he said, looking at his watch. "We'll be home at twelve-thirty. A pleasant lunch, time to repose, and then a ride to the very tip of the island. We'll leave at seven and be back in town shortly after ten. We'll have a fine day. By the way," he added with a chuckle, "I've got a little surprise for you out there."

It began to drizzle and then to rain, but Soulé seemed unconcerned. As we reached the open countryside, he became even more affable. "I left Saubrigues twenty-five years ago, but I'm really still there," he said. "I've never really become a city man. I always felt happy back home as long as my mother was there. My father and mother were wonderful, and they brought me up to show the proper respect for the amenities of living. At the table, it was always, *'Papa, permets-moi de prendre le sel.'* Father died in 1943. After the war, I went back to see *Maman* every year until she, too, died, in 1951. I've named the house in Montauk after her—Laetitia." He looked out the window for a while and then went on, "I'm glad I bought the house in Montauk. Until we began going there, I was always miserable on Sundays. I would sleep late, or my wife and I would go to Atlantic City for the day—since the Pavillon was closed, there was no other place to go—but we didn't like it."

As we approached our destination, Soulé told the driver to stop at the top of a hill, from which we could see both the ocean and the Sound. Soulé got out in the rain, stretched, and breathed deeply. The view reminded him of the coast of Bretagne, he said, with its sandy dunes and low underbrush. "I love the smell of the sea in the air," he remarked, and added, "This seems a long way from the sanctuary, doesn't it?"

Soulé's house stands on a slight hill overlooking Montauk Point. The gates to the grounds are flanked by a green and red light, like a harbor entrance, and these had been turned on. The wind was howling, but inside the house it was warm, and there was the smell of good food in the air. Soulé took me by the arm and opened the door to the kitchen. Behind the small range stood Christophe, tasting a sauce.

"Voilà!" Soulé said to me. "Our little surprise."

Christophe and Thélin, the *caviste,* had driven out the previous evening to prepare our lunch. Soulé often invites members of his staff who have been with him a long time to come out for the day, and Christophe and Thélin go there so much that they have their own rooms. Although the house stands empty during the week, it has a nice lived-in look about it. There are flowers and the Sunday newspapers and latest magazines in the living room. The plumbing and the kitchen are American style, but the furniture suggests an upper-middle-class house in Neuilly-sur-Seine; Soulé said the dining room table and chairs were ones he and his wife had used in their Paris apartment. A gallon bottle of cognac stood on the buffet. In the basement was a small but well-stocked wine cellar and a pantry with a refrigerator containing a bucket of crushed ice in which Thélin had buried a can of caviar.

"The finest of all, *mon vieux,*" he told Soulé.

"That's right," Soulé said, rubbing his hands in delight. "Nothing but the best for the *patron* and his friends." He slapped Thélin's back, and Thélin fondly pressed his arm.

Soulé, Christophe, and Thélin went into an earnest huddle on the subject of whether we should have an *apéritif* or champagne before lunch, and finally decided on a light Cramant *blanc de blancs,* which Soulé characterized as "stimulating and inspiring." By the time each of us had had two glasses, we indeed felt stimulated and inspired, and Soulé removed a pullover he'd worn under his coat. The table was set simply, with exquisite Limoges and glassware, but without the usual clutter of doilies, ashtrays, matches, vases, candlesticks, individual salt and pepper containers, and miscellaneous bric-a-brac. Thélin put the caviar on a small table next to Soulé, who served it with glasses of chilled vodka. For the next course, Christophe brought in a large, freshly caught striped sea bass he had bought down in the village only several hours earlier and had prepared according to a Pavillon recipe— braising it in buttered aromatics, white wine, and minced mushrooms, and making a beautiful yellow sauce to go with it. Thélin said, "Ah!" and inhaled the aroma, and then he, Soulé, and Christophe tucked the ends of their napkins into their collars, and we all ate in silence and devoted concentration.

"In New York, you'd never guess there was fish like this in America," said Soulé, sponging up every last bit on his plate with a piece of bread.

"Real freshness in a fish is all a matter of a few hours," Christophe said.

Next came *boeuf à la bourguignonne*—a beef stew marinated in brandy and red wine, braised with the marinade and a *sauce espagnole,* then cooked gently in the oven in a rich wine with mushrooms, bacon, and onions, and served with *pommes en purée.* Soulé sniffed the stew expectantly. "*Dis donc,*" he said to Christophe, "what wine did you put into it?"

Christophe laughed and said, "Make a guess."

So Soulé sniffed again and guessed that it was *le petit enfant de la cave,* and both Christophe and Thélin exclaimed wasn't it *formidable* how the *patron* always guessed right, and there was much slapping of shoulders and raising of glasses, which Thélin had now filled with a Château Cheval Blanc '28. In the midst of all this, Christophe brought in a cake with "HAPPY BIRTHDAY AIMÉ" spelled out on its top, and Thélin, whose birthday it was, started to cry. It was after four when we left the table—"a decent time to finish one's lunch," Soulé remarked with a significant sigh.

We had cognac and armagnac with our coffee, and later more champagne, and what little was left of the afternoon went fast. After a while, we drove down to the fishing piers to buy seafood, but the boats had come in early and the catch had already been sent to the city. Christophe stumbled and almost landed in a barrel of crushed ice, and it struck everybody as the funniest thing ever.

By the time we got back to the house, a local girl had washed the dishes. We prepared to leave, and Thélin switched off the harbor lights. Then the chauffeur brought the car around and the four of us got in. On the way into town, the talk was of France and food and wine, while the rain beat hard against the windshield and the wipers sang. Maybe it was the talk or maybe it was the weather, but two hours later we were all hungry again, and Soulé had the driver stop at a roadside stand. "Let's get out and have a couple of hot dogs," Soulé said. "They're delicious here."

WARBURG
The Nonconformist

"Progress in thinking is progress towards simplicity."
—S. G. Warburg

SIEGMUND GEORGE WARBURG is the most discussed and least advertised among the great merchant bankers of London. The City's gossip-filled bazaars reverberate with the faint echoes of glorification and suspicion. No banker is more glorified and more suspected. His friends admire him; his enemies distrust him; no one remains indifferent at the mention of his name. The London *Sunday Times* has called him "the postwar wonder of merchant banking." Anthony Sampson, in *Anatomy of Britain*, names Warburg "the most spectacular newcomer in the City." And the *Statist* declared in 1961, "It would be hard to find in New York a close parallel to the Warburg...success story."

An immigrant of relatively recent vintage who set up his merchant bank as late as 1946, S. G. Warburg is considered something of an upstart in the City's ultra-conservative partners' rooms where some may not remember that their ancestors were upstarts once. Being very successful makes Warburg only more suspect to the City's Old Guard who like to forget how suspect *their* forefathers were to British society in the early nineteenth century.

Whatever people may say about Warburg, and they say a lot, they agree that he has done very much very fast. He arrived in London one day in 1934 with less than five thousand pounds to his name—admittedly a great old name, respected in the citadels of international *haute finance*, a name carrying tradition and prestige which is an asset in itself. In 1964, the profits of Mercury Securities Limited, S. G. Warburg's holding company, were about 2,300,000 pounds sterling before taxes. Mercury owns the whole equity of S. G. Warburg & Co., his banking subsidiary, and a diversified empire of enterprises ranging from insurance and metals to advertising and market research.

The Warburg legend has created the image of a dynamic, aggressive financial genius and go-getter who streamlined and modernized merchant banking, is said to never have lost a takeover battle, plunges with gusto into City fights, handles big international deals, commutes between London, the Continent, and New York, is listened to respectfully in Whitehall and Washington, launches new companies, is always surrounded by secretaries and satellites, dictates while he is being driven out to the airport or on his way to the next appointment, casually makes telephone calls involving millions of dollars. And so on.

There is some truth in the legend but not the whole truth. The real Warburg emerges as a somewhat different man—diffident, doubting, soft-spoken, slightly stooped, with dark hair, a sensitive forehead, melancholy brown eyes, a melodious voice. He looks like, and might well be, a poet or philosopher. He reads Greek and Latin and often quotes in the classical languages. Speaking of a brilliant friend driven by impatience, Warburg was recently heard to say, "He is a man who doesn't know the difference between *kairos* and *chronos*." Such sentences puzzled his acquaintances, most of whom didn't know the difference themselves. *Kairos* is the right time; *chronos* is time in the abstract sense. Even Warburg's banking associates are often puzzled when he admits being prouder of his thorough knowledge of the classics, and of English and German literature, than of his widely admired skill in banking. Warburg is probably the only man in the City of London who has read Thomas Mann's *Dr. Faustus* three times—truly a feat of emotional discipline and intellectual endurance.

If this should give some people the idea that Warburg is a dreamer who lives in the clouds, he will quickly set them straight. His associates say that he is just being practical: he considers a working knowledge of Greek and Latin a better preparation for merchant banking than a study of modern finance, management technique, and economics.

"Classical education is a wonderful thing," Warburg has said. "It helps one to develop logical thinking and to perceive quickly and accurately what is read." He emphatically opposes the widespread belief that to think deeply means to think in a complicated way. "Deep" authors are often respectfully read and rarely understood. Obscurity is taken for profundity, ambiguity for wisdom. Warburg feels that symbolism is greatly overestimated these days and he quotes Kafka's definition, "A symbol is something that can be expressed only through a symbol and nothing else." Simplicity combined with thoroughness has helped Warburg more than anything else in life. "To think deeply means to think lucidly," he says. His motto is reflected by his words inscribed on his library book-plate, "Progress in thinking is progress towards simplicity."

Warburg has strong opinions about what to read and what to ignore. He reads books on history and philosophy; he loves good fiction and good poetry. He avoids business publications and ignores most newspapers. He used to read many before the war but came to the conclusion that "newspaper reading leads to a gradual loss of memory, since most people read the paper with the subconscious wish of trying to forget as fast as possible what they read"—an interesting theory that may yet be scientifically proven some day. The very sight, and the weight, of America's Sunday papers are apt to frighten visitors to these shores who are not used to America's wealth (and waste). Warburg solves his newspaper problem by glancing quickly over the index and discarding the rest. He allots himself ten minutes a day of index-glancing for the perusal of the leading journals from England, the Continent, and America. Warburg's friends claim that this alone proves his wisdom. He spends many pleasant weekends reading and rereading the books he loves. He keeps his favorite authors on special shelves in his London apartment. When he goes to his secluded villa near Grosseto, Italy, his car is always filled with books.

People often ask Warburg how a modern, successful merchant banker can get along without a thorough, daily study of contemporary politics, economics, and finance. He may shrug in his quiet way and answer, "I keep my ears open. People tell me everything that's important."

Such unorthodox views are characteristic of Warburg, who is an enthusiastic nonconformist. Warburg wants to be right and he doesn't mind being different. In his scheme of things, theory and practice must always mesh. The life of the nonconformist is not always easy in modern society. Warburg doesn't mind paying the high price of unconventionality. He is quite certain that some potential clients who might otherwise have come to S. G. Warburg & Co. did not do so because they know Warburg's "resistance to conformity."

Warburg often startles young men who come down from Oxford or Cambridge for a job interview by asking, "Would you dare speak up against everybody if you didn't agree with them, or would you remain silent? Would you go it alone, be an outspoken nonconformist?" Quite a few of the candidates, mindful of the trends toward faceless uniformity and uncritical adjustment in modern business life, give the wrong answer so far as Warburg is concerned.

The atmosphere at S. G. Warburg & Co. is distinctly nonsycophantic. Warburg does not like to be surrounded by yes-men. He has the quiet authority of the natural leader, the determination of the born executive, and he is boss in his bank, the master of his ship—a well-built ship with crisis-tight compartments and the latest safety devices to make it financially as unsinkable as possible. The crew is well trained, enthusiastic, hardworking and, by the competitors' almost unanimous consensus, brilliant.

There is a saying in publishing circles that "everybody has at least one book in him." Warburg has two books in him, and he hopes to write them some day. One, which he calls "The Businessman's Book of Quotations," will be the outgrowth of his interest in epigrams. He collects and writes them all the time. Samples are: "Influence is more important than power. This applies both to nations and individuals." Or, "Life and imagination are in continuous conflict with each other. Imagination tears the material elements of life to pieces and creates a world beyond us which is in opposition to the world around us."

Warburg's second nascent book, tentatively called "Education of the Adult," will deal with his favorite thesis that self-education relatively late in life is far more important than earlier academic learning. He is concerned about higher education in the Western world where many of the more advanced institutions have become educational factories with pedagogic assembly lines, turning out the latest models—students less concerned with acquiring knowledge than with getting their degree. Warburg's interest in education, both in the sciences and the arts, has led to his generous support of the Weizmann Institute of Sciences in Rehovoth, Israel.

Warburg is a man of many paradoxes. He loves tender poetry and tough banking deals. He has not much hope in the ultimate future of capitalism but leads his forces in dramatic City battles with infectious confidence. He surveys the state of the world with Schopenhauer-like gloom but feels the West must fight on with firm determination. He is sensitive about criticism in public but not in his own shop. He is amused by occasional parodies which a staff member writes about intramural goings-on at the bank.

Men of talent are often complex and hard to understand. Warburg's complexity is heightened by much internal conflict. Although he appears very sure of himself, he cares very much about what others think of him. He is said to be dominating, but his closest associates know that this perception is provoked by the wish of doing the best for others. He knows the importance of publicity but gives orders to avoid personal publicity. Mercury Securities owns, among other companies, an interest in a successful advertising agency in London, but Warburg makes a sharp distinction between his business and his private life. He was one of the first in Britain to anticipate the future of commercial television and acted as adviser to Associated Television, Britain's second largest network, known for its "half-American feel," as Sampson calls it, and for its close relations with American programs. But Warburg rarely looks at TV himself.

He does not like to be interviewed. In fact, he agreed to this one only after we had established a rapport and he was assured that his story was going to be one in a series about the world's great merchant bankers, that his was not the first that had been written, and when he was convinced that there was no reasonable suspicion of his seeking personal publicity. That very day the London papers had headlines on their front pages about a City financial battle in which Warburg figured prominently.

YOUTH AND THE TEAM SPIRIT

Warburg's command post and the headquarters of S. G. Warburg & Co. are at 30 Gresham Street, London EC2, just a short walk from the Bank of England. Merchant bankers never like to stray far away from the Old Lady of Threadneedle Street. Warburg's organization reflects his innermost belief in youth and the team spirit. "Youth" to Warburg means just that—men in their late twenties. He collects able young people with the same enthusiasm that other rich men show for old paintings. Of the firm's ten executive directors, four are in their early thirties. The average age of the top people is well below forty—which makes S. G. Warburg & Co. in one respect the world's youngest merchant bank.

Warburg calls youth "the greatest strength of our firm." (He rarely talks of himself, always of the firm, avoids the word "I" in favor of "we.") His son works as an accountant—but not at S. G. Warburg & Co. His father tolerates no nepotism.

Warburg's other business credo is team spirit. Ever since he entered the Warburg family bank in Hamburg as a trainee in the twenties, he has had definite ideas about the organization he was going to build. The ideas have matured without any basic changes. In his statement of March 31, 1964, as retiring chairman of Mercury Securities, Warburg said:

> My belief is that the priority task for private enterprise is to build up competent management teams. If we want to development management teams with strong vitality and dynamism, it is not sufficient to engage a group of individuals of good character and ability, nor is it sufficient in itself to mould them into a well-knit unit and to inspire them with courage and team-spirit. It is, above all, continuously necessary to change and develop the composition of such a team and especially to rejuvenate it. It is part of this process that the older members of the team must gradually move from the foreground to positions backstage and to advisory functions, making room for the younger members of the team to take over the lead in policy and management.

Warburg has dismissed people—unhappily and politely, pointing out that "in our mutual interest" it may be better to part—because they didn't get along with the team. He always reminds his older associates that it is their primary duty to act as a sounding board for ideas of the younger men. Elderly executives who are not willing to give their juniors the benefit of their accumulated experience may find themselves in trouble with the master of the ship. Another Warburg epigram says, "In order to build a good team of men, the head of the team must, in critical moments, not only support the members of the team but must protect them." Teamwork is a two-way street at Warburg's. The members of the team can give their best, knowing they are not only supported but even protected. They can also take a hint from yet another Warburg epigram, "The highest degrees of human potency are reached in enthusiasm, on the one hand, and in suffering, on the other." Senior members at 30 Gresham Street admit their familiarity with this epigram.

Obviously Warburg is a born teacher and never stops tutoring. He introduced what some people in the City call "the nursery principle" at his bank. One of the younger men must always be present at all important meetings. Afterwards he is asked to write a lengthy memorandum of the meeting. Often Warburg himself corrects the wording, as carefully as a professor when scrutinizing his students' homework.

Warburg expects everybody to try to be as punctual, meticulous, and well organized as he is. He freely delegates authority in big matters and shows himself as a man of vision and scope; but at the same time he can be pedantic about detail, a weakness that may be inherited from his German-Jewish ancestors. "Siegmund," says a famous merchant banker, "is the mixture of Jewish dynamism and German thoroughness—an unbeatable combination in modern merchant banking." Warburg fondly remembers one of his uncles, back in Germany, who used to say, *"Der liebe Gott wohnt im Detail"*—the dear Lord lives in the details.

At S. G. Warburg & Co. every verbal promise, telephone conversation, and oral statement must be confirmed later in writing. This is not due to any lack of trust on Warburg's part. On the contrary: his associates complain that he trusts people far too much. Only lately, at the repeated urging of his wife, has he become accustomed, on his frequent travels and in hotel rooms, to keep his attaché case locked.

Usually mild-mannered, Warburg cannot stand incompetence of any kind and has no patience with people who don't know their job: he can get very irritated by an airline ticket clerk fumbling with vouchers, as his serenity may be shattered by a sloppy waiter. His secretaries earn their salaries: any letter containing a minor mistake or an unclear sentence must be retyped. A fast reader who notices the slightest fault, Warburg is very strict about clarity of style and lucidity of expression. Some people call this an example of German *Grundlichkeit* (thoroughness). But written German is rarely lucid, often merely vague when trying to appear deep; clarity of style is not a premium.

Warburg was pleased when a director of the Bank of England once told him he wrote better letters than many born-and-bred Englishmen. Leaving nothing to chance, he is terrified at the mere thought of the gifted dilettantism and "ingenious sloppiness" that are widespread in the City. He never loses a big battle for lack of preparedness. That doesn't mean that he doesn't have those failures resulting from too much wishful or superficial thinking about human character and its reliability.

Warburg's organization works almost with the precision of a fine Swiss watch. There is no touch of amateurism. This new attitude of tough and thorough professionalism is beginning to affect some of the older houses. Bankers now rely more on memoranda than memory, work longer hours, even talk shop during the once-sacred lunch ritual.

"A PESSIMIST SURROUNDED BY RISKS"

Warburg is superstitious, always afraid of provoking the wrath of the gods—possibly the psychological aftereffect of his classical education. He walks through life like a character in a Greek tragedy, forever expecting the worst to happen, the last man in the dead center of a hurricane, continually amazed that he is still alive. The frightful sound of the Erinyes is always in his internal ear—especially when all goes well. *That,* he feels, is the moment when one must watch out for the danger signals. As a banker, he is "a pessimist surrounded by risks." But there are degrees of pessimism. In the financial world, Warburg is described as a "white" or cheerful pessimist, not a "black" or even a "gray" one. His premonitions of disaster are often balanced by faith in his God and his fellow men.

He rarely enjoys the fruits of success or victory. After twenty-four hours, while his associates are still celebrating, Warburg is worrying again. At the beginning of a big transaction he always asks, "But what are we going to do if it doesn't work out?" He tells his associates that they must learn to listen to "hints of fate" and to react accordingly. He himself has learned "by painful experience," in the early 1930s in Germany, that people in the banking world often foresee a crisis but do nothing about it.

When Warburg is away from his London headquarters, which happens frequently nowadays, he receives a large daily envelope with two files. Number 1, the most important, contains the "Management Mail and Memoranda List," which mentions every conversation and important telephone call inside the bank, every incoming and outgoing letter, cable, and other related communication, with initials indicating the names of the executives assigned to the case and those reading copies of the mail. The file also contains the day's press clippings; a summary of all bonds and stocks bought or sold; minutes of the daily 9:15 A.M. or weekly investment meeting; Secret Memoranda; travel schedules of all directors and top executives from London; all luncheons given at the bank, with names of guests; New Accounts; and the Daily Statement.

File Number 2 contains "Companies to be Kept Under Review"; "Current Propositions" (brief résumés of all pending matters); "Personnel Problems"; names of "Volunteer Trainees at the Bank" (particularly close to Warburg's heart strongly beating for youth); and, finally, all "Money Dealings."

Thus, no matter where he is, Warburg knows exactly what happened in London yesterday (or the day before). This knowledge gives him a comforting sense of security and a pleasant feeling of good organization. He reads his lists as a conductor reads his scores; they are the blueprint of his creative thinking, inspiring him to new, imaginative feats in the artistry of finance. (He compares such feats to surgical operations or theatrical productions.) To him, his lists are tangible proof, daily renewed, of the smoothly functioning mechanism of a team that he built and perfected through years of tutoring and training.

The team itself is a group of about twenty who work as closely together as members of a chamber music ensemble. Each knows at any given moment what the others are doing, just as a good chamber player knows not only his part but also those of all his fellow players. They are held together by "enthusiasm and suffering," by loyalty, "the steel girders of the organization," and by a shared devotion to the master of the ship. Warburg cannot cut the inevitable high-tension wires between able, ambitious people, but he tolerates no short circuits and remains the final arbiter when fuses threaten to blow.

The team and several specialists—about thirty in all—meet every morning at 9:15, usually for less than a half hour. Important current transactions are reviewed, and all the bank's inside activities coordinated. Nowadays, Warburg rarely attends those meetings—"after years of training, they can get along without me"—but he reads the minutes carefully just the same.

New ideas, which Warburg calls "the bloodstream of a merchant bank," are discussed informally among the top executives and tested at the daily meeting. There is no spacious "partners' room" at 30 Gresham Street, as in many of the City's older merchant banks. The senior directors have their own (small) offices. But the *esprit de corps* makes up for the somewhat cramped conference rooms.

In each important transaction, the organization is dominated by "the rule of four," a Warburg invention. Four people must represent S. G. Warburg & Co.—one director and one chief executive, each with his deputy. In less important deals, at least two people must be present. Warburg himself is not excluded from the rule: when he travels alone, another member of the team will join him at his meetings.

THE CONTINENTAL INFLUENCE

Siegmund Warburg's emotional and intellectual makeup is dominated by three factors. First, he is a European, probably the reason that, as an émigré, he chose London rather than New York as the base for his new life, though he had strong family connections on Wall Street. Second, he feels himself the product of the ethical and intellectual heritage of his Jewish ancestors. Third, though at home in London and in love with the City's bizarre tribal customs, he never forgets that he was brought up in southern Germany. He became naturalized in 1939—his application was sponsored by several prominent merchant bankers—but he never attempts to pose as a "genuine" Englishman in the manner of many who came a little late. He speaks correct English with an unmistakable German accent and doesn't try to hide it. He has close friends among the leaders of the City and is fond of the English—yet, as a man from Central Europe, he remains puzzled by their inscrutable ways.

There is, for instance, the predilection of the English for "playing dumb." Warburg affectionately remembers a merchant-banking elder statesman, now long dead, who would listen to one of Warburg's proposals and then ask him, with a perfectly straight face but with that certain twinkle in his eyes, "Now, do you *really* believe we should do it, Siegmund?" Actually, the old fox, as Warburg knew well, had already made up his mind to do it.

Siegmund delights in asking his English friends embarrassing questions and watching their reaction. There is often a long, slightly uncomfortable pause, and then the friend will say, "Well, Siegmund—let's cross that bridge when we come to it." At S. G. Warburg & Co., such answerers are called "bridge-crossers." Or he will tease his friends with the sort of question they think only a foreigner would ask and is told, "Well... very interesting...there we are." End of conversation.

Warburg does not believe in the virtue of English understatement. His London associates often feel that he tends toward the other extreme— Continental overstatement. They are often disturbed by his tendency to step on highly sensitive English toes and implore him not to tell people the awful truth.

"No matter how tactfully you talk to them, you are bound to offend them," they say to Warburg.

He pays no attention to such admonitions. In Warburg's world there are two groups of people. The one to which he belongs wants to do everything right, even at the risk of conflict. "Many Americans and Scots belong to this group. The other group, which includes many prominent City figures, is so anxious to avoid unpleasantness that they may do the wrong thing solely to circumvent conflict."

Warburg believes in strong praise and strong criticism—things "not done" in the City. He lavishly commends people when successful and mercilessly reprimands them for failure. Where an Englishman will say, at most, "I'm afraid, old boy, I don't quite agree with you," Warburg disagrees dramatically with the "old boy." He is perturbed by the low standards of secrecy in the City, which, like any big marketplace, is always filled with rumors. He holds a theory, based on his study of various psychologists, that gossip is a compensation for sexual incompetence. A serious study on the relationship between Bank Rate and libido may be overdue. There is less secrecy and more secret sharing in today's merchant banks than ever before. In the old days the Barings, Rothschilds, Schroders, Morgan Grenfells, Hambros, and Lazards kept their secrets to themselves and used them to their advantage. Warburg remembers his maternal grandfather saying that there are three degrees of secrecy: in the first, a man promises to keep something to himself, but tells his wife; in the second, he doesn't tell the secret even to his wife; in the third, when he is reminded of the matter three years later, he claims he no longer remembers that he ever heard it before.

Among Warburg's favorite epigrams is the advice of an old friend, "Don't ever think of what you want to put into a letter—think only about the answer you might get to it." Another friend once told him, "Your strength in business is that you don't change your coat when you leave your home; you are always the same man." And he never forgets what was said at the grave of the murdered German statesman Walther

Rathenau: "Each man has the shortcomings of his merits but few have the merits of their shortcomings."

There is no doubt that the Continential influence is strong at S. G. Warburg & Co. Young Englishmen, known to arrive there in traditional style, wearing bowlers and carrying umbrellas, soon divest themselves of such City paraphernalia. Some are quite surprised when the chairman of the board expresses a lively interest in their private affairs. Warburg feels that a man's personal life affects his efficiency in business. They also note that he believes in giving second chances (he has had some very good results with this theory) and harbors no grudges. They may not know that Warburg forgives, but never forgets, a mistake; that he won't mention an unpleasant experience, but cannot erase it from his memory.

A fellow merchant banker, Lionel Fraser, the former chairman of Helbert Wagg (now merged with Schroder and known as J. Henry Schroder Wagg & Co.) wrote in his autobiography, *All to the Good*, "I admire Siegmund Warburg not only for his courage in starting a new life in this country and making an unqualified success of it, but for an almost monastic indifference to passing pleasures which seems to endow him with an unusual appreciation of the intangible, yet very real, things in life. I rate him high in the international banking fraternity."

Warburg discourages any attempt at show. He has never owned a Rolls Royce or a Bentley and once talked one of his directors out of buying one. Too conspicuous. He owns neither a yacht nor a town house. He breeds no racehorses, raises no orchids, shoots no grouse. In London, Warburg and his wife entertain ("more than we really like") in their apartment in Belgravia's Eaton Square. The apartment is furnished in quiet taste and filled with books. They are everywhere—in the hall, in the drawing room, in Warburg's ascetic bedroom—a modern version of a Trappist monk's cell. The books are arranged first according to languages and second by Warburg's reading preferences. Warburg likes to be with stimulating people and loves the forgotten art of conversation. His standards for both are high.

Mrs. Warburg, the former Eva Maria Philipson, a slim elegant woman of quiet charm, comes from an old Jewish banking family in Stockholm. (The Warburgs, like the Rothschilds, are known as a Jewish house in the City, but on the board of S. G. Warburg & Co., Gentiles outnumber Jews.) Mrs. Warburg passed the all-important test during their early years of exile when she told her husband, more than once, that if worse came to worst, they would live in a two-room apartment with their two children, then six and three years old. While worse never came to worst, Warburg still discusses all important matters with her and frequently quotes her advice when he makes a decision.

Like many people who spent their early childhood years in comfortable circumstances and later lost their possessions, Warburg is relaxed about the attributes of wealth. He doesn't care much about food and drink, "stays with a dish" for days; on a recent trip to Frankfurt he ordered boiled beef five days in succession. He doesn't experiment in food, only in banking. He says, "If orange juice were as expensive as champagne, people would serve it at elaborate parties." Orange juice is probably healthier than champagne, and Warburg strongly believes in the healthy life. Every second year, he spends ten days or so in a sanatorium in England, where he pays a lot of money for a massage and a few glasses of orange juice a day. To ban the pangs of hunger, he plays bridge with his wife, who diets with him (though she doesn't need it). He loses ten pounds and unspecified amounts of "toxin," happy and rejuvenated for a return to the rigors of modern banking life, more boiled beef and an occasional glass of wine.

Money *per se* has no attraction for him. He remembers his grandfather, the late Siegmund Warburg, who said, "It was the Warburgs' good fortune that whenever we were about to get very rich, something would happen, and we became poor and had to start all over again."

A TALE OF SEVERAL CITIES

A great many things have happened since 1798, when the brothers Moses Marcus and Gerson Warburg founded M. M. Warburg & Co. in Hamburg. Actually, the family's banking tradition is much older, dating from one Simon von Cassel, a sixteenth-century ancestor who was a pawnbroker and money dealer. (The prefix "von" has merely a geographic, not aristocratic, meaning; it denotes that Simon came *von*, or from, Cassel.) In 1559 Simon obtained permission to settle in the Westphalian town of Warburg from which the family later took its name. (Warburg, population 9500, is known for a twelfth-century "double church" with a Romanesque foundation, and a thirteenth-century church, St.-Maria-in-vinea.) This gives the Warburgs a clear historical lead over such early merchant-banking upstarts as the Barings who began their activities in Exeter, as late as 1717, and the Rothschilds who became court factors to His Serene Highness Prince William, Landgrave of Hesse Cassel, doing business only after 1785.

Some Warburgs were known to have lived in the sixteenth century near Hamburg in Altona, then under Danish rule. There, the Jews—who gained full rights as citizens in Hamburg only in 1849—were allowed to be active as merchants and shipowners. One of the Altona Warburgs, Marcus Gumprich Warburg, moved in 1773 to Hamburg where the situation had become a little easier for Jewish merchants and bankers. He was the father of the two brothers who founded M. M. Warburg & Co.

Like London, Hamburg owes its commercial prominence to its port which then connected northern Europe with the Atlantic and the Mediterranean, making it a fine base for merchant adventurers and bold entrepreneurs. Hamburg's status as a neutral, free city was another big asset. In time of war, its merchants traded with all belligerent parties.

The new bank was less than one year old when, in 1799, the boom suddenly collapsed from competition in Portugal, England, and Scandinavia, causing sharp price breaks. In Hamburg alone over a hundred and fifty firms went bankrupt.

The Warburgs had been cautious and rode out the storm. But in 1806, French troops occupied Hamburg and seized some of its more substantial citizens as hostages. Among them was Gerson Warburg who was interned in Rothenburg. According to a cherished family story, Moses, who had often quarreled with Gerson, was reluctant to pay the high sum demanded for his brother's release. He had to be severely admonished by the Jewish community before agreeing to redeem his brother. Even then, he appears to have made a deal with the French, paying much less for Gerson than they had demanded originally.

In 1814, the French left, and immediately the Hamburg Giro Bank began to replenish its silver stocks. M. M. Warburg & Co. helped provide the silver supplies on which the new Mark Banco currency was based. The Warburgs were already dealing with N. M. Rothschild & Sons in London. In a letter of August 4, 1814, the Warburgs offer gold or *louis d'or* "for early delivery," assuring the Rothschilds that they are capable handling business of this kind "as effectively as anybody in Hamburg."

After the death of the founding brothers, the bank was taken over by

Moses Marcus's son-in-law, Abraham Samuel Warburg, who remained in charge until *his* death in 1856. Money changing and trade bill activities were the foundation of the firm. Among the old merchant bankers, the Warburgs were the exception: they were not merchants before they became bankers.

In 1863 the designation of the firm was changed from *Geldwechsler* (money changers) to the more elegant title *Bankiers* (bankers). Five years later, the *Bankiers* moved to their present address at Ferdinand-strasse 75. These were disturbing times. Prussian powers began to threaten the small territory of their Free Hanseatic Town, and some people worried that Hamburg might lose its independence, as had Frankfurt in 1866.

The firm had acquired great prestige in trading with commercial bills and foreign exchange—typical merchant-banking operations that demanded sound judgment and thorough knowledge. The Warburgs had good intelligence sources and a network of agents. They weathered the crisis of 1842 and the more severe one of 1857, which in America had started with the failure of the Ohio Life and Trust Company. Its shock waves reached all the way to Hamburg, where many merchants and bankers had accepted trade bills not based on genuine transactions. While the Warburgs had endorsed many bills that came back to them under protest, there is no evidence that they had to impawn securities or commodities, like many other local firms. But it was not easy to meet all their obligations. They were among the contributors to the "Garantie-Diskonto-Verein von 1857,"a fund set up by the Senate of Hamburg to bail out troubled firms.

By that time the firm was managed by Abraham's wife, Sara, a remarkable woman who piloted the bank through troubled waters until joined by her two sons, Siegmund and Moritz. When Hamburg needed a silver loan of ten million Marks Banco, the Senate approached Prussia. The Prussians refused and sent Hamburg an insulting answer. Then the Warburgs suggested Austria. A sister of Siegmund and Moritz was married to Paul Schiff, director of the Creditanstalt in Vienna. Schiff submitted Hamburg's request to Baron Bruck, the Austrian minister of finance. Baron Bruck went to see Emperor Franz Josef I, and, at once, got permission to send a special train with silver ingots to the Hamburg Giro Bank. The silver was never needed and was returned—with interest—six months later to Vienna, the ingots still unpacked. Its mere presence spread calm and confidence in Hamburg; the crisis quickly ended.

Hamburg remained grateful to the Habsburgs but particularly to the Warburgs who had engineered the transaction. The Warburgs' prestige increased, as they now became known as a serious, reliable house. Both Habsburgs and Warburgs enlarged their respective empires through well-planned intermarriages. The Warburgs became related to the Rosenbergs of Kiev, the Gunzburgs of St. Petersburg, and the Oppenheims and Goldschmidts of Germany. The five sons of Moritz Warburg later became known as the "five Hamburgers." Though less famous than the "five Frankfurters" (the Rothschilds), the Warburgs were doing all right. The oldest, Aby, studied humanities, becoming the founder of the Kulturwissenschaftliche Bibliothek Warburg, now the Warburg Institute, attached to the University of London.

Under Siegmund and Moritz Warburg the bank expanded, floated loans, and helped to set up the big commercial banks that developed in the major cities of Germany at the turn of the nineteenth century. Siegmund had close connections with Baron Lionel von Rothschild in London. In a letter dated May 31, 1871, the Warburgs requested and were granted a share in the French loan to be issued by the Rothschilds. The Warburgs had arrived at the inner city of international high finance. They were involved in the second French postwar loan of three billion francs. Floated by the Rothschilds in 1872, it was twelve times oversubscribed.

Moritz Warburg, whose maxim was *labor et constantia*, was a conservative banker. Like the great merchant bankers of London, he preferred dealing with big firms and important banking correspondents having no wish for many private clients. In 1878, the firm had only sixteen employees. The German offices were small and unpretentious, as in England: one didn't show one's wealth, despite friendly connections with Baron Alphonse Rothschild in Paris, Baron Leopold in London, Baron Albert in Vienna. Moritz's wife, Charlotte, wrote her memoirs, as many Warburgs did. She describes with great charm a journey to the Paris Exposition of 1878 and a visit to the Rothschild château at Ferriéres, still the family's showplace.

In a historical essay on M. M. Warburg & Co., a Hamburg sociologist, Eduard Rosenbaum, quotes the advice given to him in 1921 by Max M.

Warburg when they discussed the project of a history of the firm:

> It should be shown [Warburg wrote], and I attach great value to this, how much the development of such a firm is governed by chance, and how the economic development anyhow is much more dependent on chance events and inherent tendencies than on the so-called consciously aimed activities of the individual. The description should be pervaded by a certain feeling of humility towards these forces. For most people suffer from exaggerated self-esteem, and specially bank managers, when they write their annual reports three or six months later, are inclined to adorn their actions with a degree of foresight which in reality never existed.

Among the members of a family whose achievements in art, science and literature are as notable as in banking and commerce, Aby M. Warburg, the "Professor," as he was called, was one of the most gifted. As a young man he half-jokingly had renounced his right to enter the firm and asked his brothers only to support him in his scientific work—to pay for his books, as he put it. This turned out to be quite an expense, as visitors to the Warburg Institute in London will easily realize. Yet the "Professor" was no unworldly dreamer. He had a sort of sixth sense for an approaching financial crisis, the lingering premonition of disaster that never seems to leave his younger relative, S. G. Warburg.

Of the other "five Hamburgers," Max was an entrepreneur whose motto was *en avant*. Paul chose *in serviendo consumor* as his maxim. Paul and Felix were connected through marriage with the New York firm of Kuhn, Loeb and Co., then second only to the Morgans as an issuing house in America. This additional connection enhanced Warburg's special position in the international banking world.

Kuhn, Loeb & Co. had been founded in 1867 by two retired Cincinnati clothing merchants, Abraham Kuhn and Solomon Loeb, with a reputed capital of $500,000. It was a good time to start in business. The Civil War was over; the United States had just purchased Alaska from Russia, and the Dominion of Canada had been established. Steel mills were built; telegraph lines went up across the continent; out west, railroad crews laid down hundreds of miles of tracks.

Kuhn, Loeb & Co.'s guiding spirit was Jacob H. Schiff, a Jewish immigrant from Germany. He became a partner in 1875 and spent forty-six years with the firm. He had faith in the country's economic future and realized that a banker's function is, above all, to be ready to help in times of adversity. When the Union Pacific got in serious trouble after the panic of 1893 and its reorganization was said to be impossible, Kuhn, Loeb & Co. achieved the impossible. That reorganization was approved by President McKinley in 1897 and the new management entrusted to Edward H. Harriman. The new Union Pacific became so strong that it later acquired control of the Southern Pacific and ultimately bought over forty percent of the shares of the Northern Pacific.

Felix Warburg married Schiff's daughter and joined the firm, while Paul Warburg married the daughter of founder Loeb and moved to New York in 1902. By that time, the flow of credit was going in both directions. America was beginning to provide financing for Europe and the Far East. Kuhn, Loeb & Co. floated several loans to Japan during the Russo-Japanese War. The firm's position was established by Schiff, who called the Russian (Imperial) government an "enemy of mankind" because of its treatment of its Jewish population. When Lord Reading came to New York during the First World War to seek a loan for the British and French governments, Schiff demanded assurances that none of the benefits would pass to Russia. The Western Allies were unable to give such a guarantee, and Kuhn, Loeb & Co. withdrew from the sponsorship of the loan, although individual partners, among them Schiff's son, became personal subscribers. Bold individualism was still possible in the conduct of international financial affairs.

They were civic-minded people. Mortimer L. Schiff was president of the Boy Scouts of America. Otto H. Kahn was a power behind the Metropolitan Opera Company. In Felix Warburg's room the walls were lined with filing cabinets relating to his charitable activities. Paul M. Warburg accepted an appointment by President Wilson to the Federal Reserve Board in 1914.

LA BELLE ÉPOQUE

In Hamburg the years prior to the First World War were *la belle époque* of private *Bankiers*. The balance sheet totals of M. M. Warburg & Co. had been 18,229,494 marks in 1891; 45,832,324 marks in 1900; and 127,325,616 marks in 1914. Warburg's was the leading German banker in the market of commercial bills that sometimes reached fifty million marks. And they were strong in foreign-exchange. In 1900 Max and Paul Warburg placed a loan of eighty million marks in *Reichsschatzscheine* (treasury bonds) in America. Later, the firm joined the select Reichsanleihe-Konsortium, the inner sanctum of German financiers.

The Hamburg Warburgs were invited by Kuhn, Loeb & Co. to participate in the floating of the Japanese loans, which Max Warburg discussed in London with Korekiyo Takahashi, the Japanese delegate. Takahashi later became prime minister and a liberal elder statesman, only to be assassinated in 1936. Warburg called him "the best arithmetician among all the finance ministers I ever met."

The Warburgs became active all over the world. They took part in loan negotiations for the Chinese State Railways, increased their business with Scandinavia and America, and set up a special department trading in copper, tin, and lead. The firm survived the First World War and the astronomical inflation that followed in Germany, helped to set up the Hamburger Bank of 1923, which issued its own notes based on gold—and received the gold through the help of the Warburgs. The Hamburger Bank was the first German institute granted a dollar credit from the International Acceptance Bank in New York. Its chairman happened to be Paul M. Warburg. Sixty-six years earlier, a crisis in Hamburg was ended by the arrival of Austrian silver; this time American dollars did the trick. In both cases, the Warburgs had been the intermediaries.

Paul M. Warburg carried through the reorganization of the American banking system with Senator Nelson W. Aldrich. In 1928, the International Acceptance Bank was combined with the Manhattan Bank. Paul M. Warburg remained its chairman.

FULL CIRCLE

The Wall Street crisis of 1929 was felt in Hamburg the following year, when depositors were beginning to withdraw large amounts of foreign money. Max Warburg went to New York and talked things over with his brothers Paul and Felix. The New York Warburgs took "a new financial interest" in the Hamburg house. The immediate danger passed. But the crisis deepened when the Austrian Creditanstalt collapsed in 1931. Earlier, from December 21 until December 31, 1930, Warburg's had to repay eighty percent of its foreign and fifty percent of its German deposits. It is doubtful whether it would have come through without the help of the brothers in New York.

By that time, two members of the younger generation had joined the Hamburg firm. Eric M. Warburg, the only son of Max, became a partner in 1929. And Siegmund G. Warburg was a partner from 1930 to 1936 (even after he had emigrated to London).

But the end was near, and the Warburgs knew it. Hitler had come to power. There was no *Lebensraum* in Germany for Jewish bankers. During the 1930s Max Warburg's number of directorships had fallen from over one hundred to eighteen. He tried to reason with Papen and Schacht, and he took dangerous risks to his personal safety. One day in 1938 Hjalmar Schacht informed Max Warburg that the firm was no longer a member of the august Reichsanleihe-Konsortium. The Warburgs had helped Hamburg in that city's critical days. Now no one helped the Warburgs in their big crisis. They were through. The firm was handed over to a group of banks and other firms. At the express request of the Nazis, the name remained M. M. Warburg & Co., Kommandit-Gesellschaft (limited partnership). In 1942, the name was changed to Brinckman, Wirtz & Co. Brinckman had been an employee of Warburg's, Wirtz a client.

After the end of the Second World War, the firm became again a leading private bank in Germany. Members of the Warburg family were again financially interested; Eric M. Warburg became a general partner in 1956.

And in July 1964, S. G. Warburg of London acquired an interest in the private bank of Hans W. Petersen in Frankfurt am Main, and it was renamed S. G. Warburg. Once more the Warburgs are private *Bankiers* in Germany, just as in 1797. They had come full circle in the country where they started.

EPITAPH

Siegmund George Warburg is a banker by inheritance rather than environment. He was born on September 30, 1902, the only child of the late Georges Siegmund and Lucie K. Warburg. (The Warburgs, like the Rothschilds, almost always use the family's traditional first names.) Georges Siegmund, a "nonbanking" Warburg, a cousin of the "five Hamburgers," was a trained agriculturist who owned a large estate near Urach, an old town in the Swabian Alps not far from Stuttgart. It is lovely country, with green hills and clear streams. Siegmund Warburg is fond of the region, sometimes goes back to visit, and still feels somehow "at home" there. This shocks some of his less forgiving Jewish friends. How can a man passionately devoted to the future of Israel and active in Jewish philanthropies feel even remotely "at home" in the country of Goebbels and Hitler?

Warburg tries to explain (he doesn't always succeed) that the Germany he thinks of when he goes there is more the country of Goethe and Heine. Heine once wrote, *"Denk ich an Deutschland in der Nacht / so bin ich um den Schlaf gebracht."* ("When I think of Germany at night / I cannot sleep.") Warburg himself feels that way about Germany. But he dislikes easy labels and facile generalizations, no matter whether Jews or Germans, Americans or British are concerned. On his merchant banker's map of the world, four countries—England, the United States, Israel, and Germany—are "Warburg countries."

The Swabians are similar to the Scots, with their mixture of realism and romanticism, their love of lyric poetry and sober prose. Theodor Heuss, Germany's cultured, highly respected former federal president, was a Swabian, a neighbor and friend of the Warburg family. So was Baron von Neurath who rose to international prominence as Hitler's foreign minister and Reichsprotektor of Bohemia-Moravia. Heuss, representing one Germany, remained Warburg's friend to his death. Von Neurath, who stood for another Germany, later played a brief, decisive, but different part in Warburg's life.

Siegmund was devoted to his mother, a kindhearted, selfless woman who taught her son the importance of self-discipline, and lived the way she preached. "If you see an ugly girl standing alone you should go and ask her to dance," she told her son as he went to his first dancing lesson. She came from Stuttgart (her maiden name was Lucie Kaulla) and was brought up under the strict, almost puritanical principles of her Jewish ancestors. Warburg often quotes her without being aware of it—when he lectures on the dangers of smoking (though he would like to smoke) or when he refuses chocolates (which he loves). After his mother's death, in 1955, he wrote a moving epitaph, "mostly for my children," about the way she helped shape his principles and his whole philosophy of life:

"My mother told me that her father often used to say, 'My child, if you have to choose which way to go, always ask yourself first which is harder and choose it. It will be the right one.' She had a deep sense of duty which she managed to combine with cheerful serenity. Goethe and Beethoven formed her conception of life. Her home was strict, almost Spartan, but at the same time, happy. What had to be done was done with absolute thoroughness; what had to be thought out was thought through toward the last consequence; what had been recognized as the important aim, was pursued with utter tenacity....

"My mother loved music and wrote some compositions. They express her feelings succinctly. In them, one hears her happy dreams beyond all earthy conflicts and worldly problems. After her marriage, she had to take care of a vast estate—a task for which she had not been trained and which sometimes severely taxed her frail constitution. In those years she developed an enormous willpower.... When my father became ill after they'd been married over twenty years, my mother kept him away from all work and worry. Despite my father's prolonged illness and his deep depressions, there was great harmony in our home. This sense of harmony was the most important thing she gave me in my formative years.

"She would always assist me with my homework, and she was very strict about it. If I made a small mistake, I had to rewrite the whole page, and sometimes there were tears. She would repeat her criticism of something I'd done, again and again, until she was certain I would not forget it. Today I am deeply grateful to my mother for being so strict with me.... She made me pray every night, but she was never dogmatic about religious matters, and always tolerant of those who did not agree with her. Until I became thirteen, she would always join me at my night's prayers; often she would come from downstairs to my room for a few minutes, even when my parents had guests.

"Later, when I was told to say my prayers alone, she would tell me, 'Before you pray, my child, ask yourself what you did wrong today and could have done better. All of us make mistakes every day. One must be critical about one's mistakes.'

"During my father's sickness she had given up her music, but a few years after his death she began to play the piano again, her beloved Beethoven sonatas and Bach fugues, taking lessons and writing more compositions. She got along very well with her grandchildren who adored her. She would say, 'The old people can learn more from the young people than the young from the old ones.' When she had to leave her beloved Swabian homeland for England, she settled down quickly to learn about her new country and its people. She admired their gentleness and fairness, their self-discipline and strong faith. She remained in London during the war and never worried about the danger of the air raids. She was convinced that Hitler would be defeated, because to her this was the battle of the good forces of mankind against the evil ones. But she was not sure that she would live to see the day of victory. She was seventy-three when she emigrated.

"Mother believed in the importance of real values, things that mattered. She had no patience with snobs and social life. She never stayed in her children's homes. 'An old mother is there to love and help, not to interfere and be a burden,' she would tell us.

"Once we discussed the difficulty of telling the truth to close friends—the reason why people often lie to each other because they don't want to hurt one another's feelings. My Mother would say that a lie always corrupts, even a well-intentioned one, that one must tell one's friends the truth, as tactfully as possible. And she would always tell us that one must never stop doing the best for other people. She liked to quote Hofmannsthal, 'It makes much difference whether people live their lives merely as spectators, or are actively involved, suffering, enjoying, feeling guilty or happy with others; only such people really live.' Another favorite quotation of Mother's was:

> Dein Glück, oh Menschenskind,
> Glaub es mitnichten,
> Dass es erfüllte Wünsche sind
> Es sind erfüllte Pflichten."

The stanza means "Happiness is not the fulfillment of desires but the fulfillment of duties," and it accurately expresses Siegmund Warburg's philosophy of life. He is always conscious of his responsibilities—toward his family, his business associates, his clients, his friends, even his bridge partners. He plays the game with great concentration; he does not want to let his partner down.

Warburg remembers the day—he was hardly eight years old—when he came home with a chocolate bar that he'd bought himself out of his pocket money. His mother reproved him severely. He might spend his money on something worthwhile, perhaps a book, but not on chocolates! Warburg never forgot. Even now he often buys things for his family and friends but rarely for himself.

He went to the humanistic *Gymnasium* in nearby Reutlingen and after the *Abitur* (the final examination), he entered the Evangelical Seminary—a former canon chapter house in Urach, founded in 1479— where he distinguished himself in the classical languages with consistently good marks. He was the first Jewish student in the history of that institution, where teaching had a strong philosophic emphasis.

As it does for all young Warburgs, the time came "to go into the bank," when a summons arrived from Max Warburg, one of his uncles, then the senior partner at the Hamburg house, offering Siegmund a job as trainee.

Siegmund hesitated. He would have preferred to continue his studies and later to teach. The Warburgs have always been scholars as well as bankers, students of both art and commerce. The family has produced some remarkable scholars—his American cousin James P. Warburg in New York is the latest—and Siegmund is convinced that if he hadn't become a banker, he would today be a university don, or perhaps a scientist, philosopher, or writer.

Max Warburg thoughtfully looked at the young man and said, yes, he understood, but how about coming into the bank for a couple of years, just to try it? If Siegmund didn't like banking, he could still become a scholar.

Siegmund agreed to try it. The rest is merchant-banking history.

THE FOREIGN MINISTER WAS AFRAID

Warburg's father had been rich before the First World War (his fortune estimated at about six million marks, *gold* marks), but like many other patriotic Germans, he invested nearly everything in *Kriegsanleihe* (war loans). But after the lost war, they became valueless. But a Warburg has much even if he has nothing. Related through marriage to other German banking dynasties, Warburg grew up among Rothschilds and Oppenheims. There were still lavish parties and musical soirées at the house of the music-minded Mendelssohns in Berlin. Many German merchant bankers remained prominent in politics, literature, society, and the arts.

Siegmund Warburg probably inherited his predilection for politics and literature from generations of politically interested and literary-minded Warburgs. Since 1905, when the firm had been involved in the Japanese loan, the Warburgs had kept in close touch with the German Foreign Office and were strongly interested in German's colonial enterprises. During the Morocco crisis in 1911, a member of the Warburg staff, Dr. Wilhelm Regendanz, was on board the cruiser *Panther* which the German Naval Command sent to Agadir at the request of the German Foreign Office. This was merchant banking in the twilight zone between politics and economics. Max Warburg had several talks with Lord Milner about the Anglo-German Bank in Morocco and with Sir Edward Grey about a Warburg-headed syndicate trying to acquire the majority of the Nyasa Consolidated in the Portuguese colony of Nyasaland. In June 1914, shortly before "the lights went out all over Europe," the Warburgs concluded agreements between Germany and England for a delineation of financial interest spheres in Turkey and Africa.

During the First World War, the Warburgs (together with most German Jews) loyally supported their country's precarious war economy. Dr. Fritz Warburg was named honorary commercial attaché at the German embassy in Stockholm. Once, he was authorized by his foreign office to talk with a member of the Russian Duma, a man called Protopopov, about the possibility of a separate peace treaty with Russia. The talk remained without result. (Years later the Nazi demagogues revived the matter and called the Warburgs "pro-Russian.") Two members of the firm, Max Warburg and Dr. Carl Melchior, were delegates to the Peace Conference of Versailles. Both were against signing the peace treaty and resigned in protest before the German National Assembly voted for acceptance. (The same Nazis ignored this when they reviewed the Warburgs' past.)

In 1925, S. G. Warburg went to N. M. Rothschild & Sons in London as a trainee. The Warburgs and the Rothschilds had a long-standing agreement concerning the exchange of their young men as trainees. Anthony Rothschild at one time worked in Hamburg. Later, Siegmund continued his training in Boston with the accountants Lybrand, Ross Bros. &

Montgomery, then in New York, first with the International Acceptance Bank, and finally with Kuhn, Loeb & Co. In 1930 he was taken as partner into the Hamburg firm; the following year he started a branch office of M. M. Warburg & Co. in Berlin.

By then the Nazi handwriting was on the wall, which Warburg, the pessimist, chose not to ignore. Unlike so many others, he was haunted by the premonition of approaching disaster. One lives harder that way, but perhaps one also lives longer. In March 1934, after some of his Jewish and Catholic friends were arrested in Berlin (officially taken into *Schutzhaft*, protective custody) Warburg did an impetuous thing and called on Baron Neurath.

In pre-Nazi days the Warburgs had paid an occasional visit to the Neuraths in the Swabian Alps. After a suitable interval *Rittergutsbesitzer* ("manor's owner") Neurath would return the visit. When Siegmund returned from abroad, he would see Neurath, then a *Ministerialdirigent*, at the foreign office. Warburg would report his impressions, and the able bureaucrat seemed to value the young man's remarks, for he always told him to come back.

Since then Neurath had become Germany's foreign minister, first in the caretaker government of Von Papen, and later under Hitler. Neurath received Warburg jovially. Well, well—had Siegmund come to report from another trip abroad? Where had he been?

Siegmund shook his head.

"On the contrary, *Herr Minister*. I've come to report on some happenings right here in Berlin which worry me a great deal.... Do you know that people are arrested in the middle of the night and sent to prison without any judicial procedure?"

Neurath, no longer his jovial self, admitted he'd heard that such things happened "occasionally." *Sehr unerfreulich*, really most unpleasant. And he mumbled about "the inevitable aftermath of the revolution."

"It's brutal injustice," said Warburg, with the directness of a young idealist of thirty-one. "*Ein Willkürherrschaft*." That means "rule by arbitrariness," and was, under the circumstances, not exactly diplomatic language.

Neurath seemed very uncomfortable. He claimed that no one regretted these happenings more than he did. "But after all," he said, "what can I do?"

Warburg knew his Weimar Constitution. He boldly suggested that the *Herr Minister* should see President Hindenburg. According to Paragraph 19, the *Reichspräsident* was authorized to dismiss the chancellor (Hitler) who had committed an obvious offense against the Constitution. If Hitler were dismissed, the Reichswehr would stand firmly behind *Generalfeldmarschall* von Hindenburg.

"And it is well known, *Herr Minister,* that you have the ear of the president," concluded *homo politicus* Warburg.

Neurath admitted that this was true. And then he said, in his broad Swabian dialect, "I have to tell you, my friend, that I myself am considered *national unzuverlässig* (politically unreliable) and must be very careful. Sorry, but there is nothing I can do. Good luck, and good-bye."

After leaving the foreign office, Warburg did not go back to the bank. Instead he went straight home, and told his wife to start packing their bags. They were going to leave Berlin. Yes, at once.

"If the foreign minister himself has a bad conscience and is afraid, I have no doubt what will happen here to all of us sooner or later."

At the bank Warburg was called a defeatist. But looking back now, he is convinced that his talk with Neurath was "a hint from heaven," like a powerful motivation in ancient Greek drama. If he hadn't gone to see the foreign minister, he might have stayed in Berlin, until it had got late. Perhaps too late.

In early April 1934, Siegmund Warburg, his wife, and their two small children moved their home to London. He was convinced that war was unavoidable. He expected it to break out in 1936, when Hitler occupied the Rhineland, and again the following year. There seemed no point in starting a new banking business in London. It was like "building on sand." During the early phase of the war, when the Allies seemed paralyzed, Warburg was not sure they could win. But after Hitler invaded Russia, Warburg became convinced that this madness would ultimately lead to German disaster and defeat.

Only at the end of the Second World War did Warburg truly begin to build his new life. Before then, he worked day and night. In 1939 he had founded a small firm, the New Trading Company, with four employees; later there were six, then eight. By 1946, the name of the company was changed to S. G. Warburg & Co. (Like his "merchant banker" predecessors, Warburg was never a merchant but began at once as banker.) In

1957, after joining an old merchant bank, Seligman Brothers, S. G. Warburg & Co. became a member of London's Accepting Houses Committee—the City's elite, the *true* merchant bankers; there are only sixteen of them.

Looking back now at these early years, "the postwar wonder of merchant banking" is supposed to have recalled a long, hard uphill struggle. The firm grew with the international expansion of trade. But even in the late 1950s Warburg's was not yet considered preeminent. Just another important house in the City. The outcome of the "Aluminium War of 1958–59" changed all that.

It was the most sensational takeover battle in the history of London finance. In the Aluminium War, Siegmund Warburg was the Biblical David who defeated Goliath—the powerful phalanx of great, old merchant bankers and august "institutions." With one stroke Warburg moved right up to the top of the Big League. Prior to 1959 he was not loved, often ignored. He is still widely unloved, but no longer is he ignored.

The conflict started in late 1958, when two American aluminum giants—the Reynolds Metals Company of Virginia and Alcoa (the Aluminum Company of America)—were trying to get control of the British Aluminium Company, the largest British producer and a highly strategic prize. British Aluminium had just completed a new reduction plant in Quebec that would fit well with Reynolds's expansion plans. Britons are understandably sensitive about American takeover bids, which often create outbursts of a kind of national inferiority complex, with laments about the sad fate of "the poor relations." In the words of London's *Financial Times,* the Aluminium War was "a fight between two vast empires [Reynolds and Alcoa] for a distant province—almost like Russia and Austro-Hungary fighting in the Balkans in the old days." (A good thing that Kipling was no longer around to see the *Financial Times,* once a pillar of the empire, comparing the City to the Balkans.) The paper warned that the fight was "building up grudges which should not exist between leading institutions of the City."

Among the "leading institutions," two great merchant banks, Lazards and Hambros, acted as joint advisers for British Aluminium. They represented the "old" forces, guardians of the merchant bankers' glorious past. The press called them "Gentlemen." Reynolds was advised by S. G.

Warburg & Co., which joined forces with Schroder's and with Helbert Wagg, whose chairman, W. Lionel Fraser, was a "self-made" banker, thus also something of an upstart by conservative City standards. The press called them "Players."

Reynolds was told by Warburg to cooperate with a British firm to make the takeover bid less painful for the British public. Reynolds went into partnership with Tube Investments, one of the leading British industrial groups, owners of an aluminum rolling mill. Reynolds and Tube Investments, at the advice of Warburg, began to buy shares of British Aluminium, carefully and, in accordance with London Stock Exchange customs, "through nominees," which means anonymously. Thus they had a good head start when "the war" erupted into the skirmishing stage. By October 1958, they held ten percent of the shares of British Aluminium.

"It was the best-kept secret in recent history," a merchant banker in the losing camp later said.

British Aluminium knew something was up, and people had a feeling there was danger. Somebody was after their shares, but who? Such mysteries make life in the City of London forever exciting. British Aluminium's chairman was Viscount Portal of Hungerford, Britain's air chief of staff during the last war. Its managing director, Geoffrey Cunliffe, was the son of a former governor of the Bank of England—a pair of "Gentlemen" if there ever was one. The cast of characters in this great financial drama couldn't have been more colorful.

Lord Portal and Cunliffe knew that their firm was a natural target for a takeover bid. Its shares had been around eighty shillings two years ago and now were as low as thirty-seven. Their current earnings were small, but their potential profits were considerable. They needed money to expand. Their own choice was Alcoa, with whom they had a "special relationship." While the buying of their shares by unknown, "sinister" forces went on, the board of British Aluminium counteracted the pressure by increasing the authorized capital from nine million pounds to thirteen and a half million, entitling them to issue four and a half million pounds' worth of new shares without consulting their own shareholders.

The war moved quickly toward a climax. On November 3, Sir Ivan Stedeford, the chairman of Tube Investments, met with Lord Portal and told him he would like "to have an association for future development."

(The City has certain formulae for takeover bids, like marriage vows. The traditional phrases are uttered politely, even while the antagonists are mentally rolling up their sleeves for the free-for-all.)

Portal and Cunliffe turned down the proposal— "stiffly," the papers reported—since they were already negotiating "with another group." Undaunted, Stedeford two days later made a definite, attractive offer for British Aluminium shares. Portal listened and later replied that he had reached an agreement with Alcoa and would sell them British Aluminium's four and a half million pounds' worth of shares, *unissued* shares. He refused to pass on Stedefor's attractive offer to British Aluminium's shareholders.

Stedeford summoned a press conference and spilled the beans. He would bid the equivalent of seventy-eight shillings per share (half cash, half in shares) for all British Aluminium's shares. The shares would be vested in a United Kingdom company with a fifty-one percent British ownership interest. The fine merchant-banking hand of Warburg became almost visible later on, when it turned out that the hapless British Aluminium board had asked only sixty shillings per share as the price of issue to Alcoa.

Headlines exploded all over the front pages. Lord Portal and his advisers, Lazard's and Hambros, were angrily criticized. Why hadn't the board of British Aluminium consulted its own shareholders before making such an important decision? Some commentators spoke of "an authoritarian attack against the shareholders' democracy." Lord Portal didn't exactly improve matters by declaring, "Those familiar with negotiations between great companies will realize that such a course would have been impracticable."

Further criticism was provoked when the British Aluminium board decided to jack up the 1958 dividend from 12½ to 17½ pence per annum. Many people in the City regarded this clearly as "an opportunist move." By that time, there was such excitement all over the City that no one took seriously the Lazard's-Hambros claim that the Alcoa deal was "American collaboration" (one third of British stock to the Americans) while the Reynolds deal was "American domination" (forty-nine percent of British stock to the Americans). Experts quickly and sardonically pointed out that even one-third of a company's shares is enough to give absolute control, as long as the rest of the shares are widely spread.

Reminiscing now about the Aluminium War, Warburg is reminded of Churchill's description of the Second World War as "the unnecessary war." Warburg didn't anticipate a big battle when he agreed to advise Reynolds and Tube Investments. But as the fronts began to stiffen and the distant thunder of heavy guns was heard, he became very worried. In fact, he went to see his opposite numbers at Lazard's and Hambros, pleading for compromise. He tried his best to convey the impression that he didn't suggest this compromise from a position of weakness. He did not succeed: Lazard's and Hambros decided to call what they thought was Warburg's bluff and determined to fight. There are many parallels in world politics.

And so, on New Year's Eve of 1958, the Aluminium War spread from the boardrooms of the merchant bankers to all over the City. In a letter to British Aluminium's shareholders signed by Olaf Hambro, chairman of Hambros, and Lord Kindersley, chairman of Lazard's, it was declared that the Reynolds-Tube Investments offer must be resisted "in the national interest." The two old merchant bankers represented a formidable consortium that held two million shares of British Aluminium, and now offered eighty-two shillings in cash—four more than the other side—for any additional shares. Many great merchant bankers had joined the consortium, among them Morgan Grenfell, M. Samuel, Samuel Montagu, Brown Shipley, Guinness, and Mahon. One banker was quoted as saying, "We must save British Aluminium for civilization."

A noble task, no doubt, but the consortium failed to perform it, though this was by no means certain at that time. For Warburg, these were nerve-racking weeks. In a takeover battle, even great financial wizards don't know the outcome until the very last moment. Big blocks of British Aluminium shares were held by the "institutions"—insurance companies, pension funds, the Church of England commissioners—where the truly big money is now. The institutions' managers didn't tell the merchant bankers which way they were going to jump. Warburg admits that much of the power once wielded by the banks has gone to the managers of these institutions, whose holdings in the industrial giants are enormous and growing every day.

Gradually the fog began to lift, and the battlefield became visible. The institutions were beginning to sell large blocks of shares—not directly to the consortium, but at the Stock Exchange. There, brokers for Tube Investments-Reynolds, alerted and organized by the Warburg forces, were buying up every share offered. Happy days were here again for British Aluminium shareholders. In a single week, 1,300,000 shares were traded—ultimately at over four pounds per share! Happy for Warburg too. Nine days after the battle begun, Tube Investments-Reynolds held an eighty percent interest. The consortium had suffered a crushing defeat. The managers of several institutions later said they had been disgusted by the consortium's attitude and decided to sell their British Aluminium shares.

The war was over, but for some the grudges remained. Lord Kindersley of Lazard's was heard to mutter at the mention of S. G. Warburg, "I will not talk to that fellow," and several merchant bankers were seen crossing the street to avoid meeting other adversarial members of the fraternity.

All this is now forgotten, and today Lazard's and Warburg's have close relations. "Big people will forgive others, though they may never quite forgive themselves" is a favorite epigram that fits the occasion. Some of his erstwhile opponents have now become Warburg's friends. There are still a few "big people" in the City of London.

SHOCK WAVE IN THE CITY

S. G. Warburg's personal concept of merchant banking—"the fluctuating nature of activities by a group such as ours"—has sent shock waves through the City. Warburg considers the traditional money-lender function of the merchant banker outdated. In a statement made as retiring chairman of Mercury Securities, "advisory services to industrial clients in England and abroad" was first among the firm's activities, followed by "management of investment accounts" and "issues of foreign bonds and domestic issues." Only in fourth and last place did he mention "credit and money business."

Warburg sees the modern merchant banker as the trusted adviser to financial and industrial enterprises. He compares the merchant banker to the family doctor, who calls in specialists when needed—accountants, lawyers, engineers, efficiency experts. He doesn't see a paradox if the merchant banker often knows more about the client's industrial organism than does the client himself. It is just as a good family doctor knows more about his patient's body than the patient does. And talking to a firm with financial problems is like X-raying a man's body. Warburg gets great personal satisfaction out of giving constructive advice. Occasionally, he is consulted by statesmen and political leaders. He is gratified when his advice is accepted.

"Basically, merchant bankers do what lawyers in America do, only more so," a Warburg teammate explains. "Lawyers in the United States act mostly under instructions. We act more like friends who help the client formulate instructions. We try to reconcile differences between companies. It's not strictly a scientific business, but full of intangibles. Often it means doing the right thing at the right momemt. Suppose two partners in a firm are not on speaking terms but each has a friend. The friends sit down and try to straighten out the partners' differences. We are the friends. Yes, a thorough financial knowledge is necessary but not sufficient. One can read many things out of a balance sheet—but the intangibles have to be considered and can only be guessed. Management is made up of people, and people are unfathomable. You would be surprised how many big corporations are badly managed. When faced with serious financial problems, their boards may prove utterly helpless and often prone to make wrong decisions. We offer a thinking service, acting as a group of advisers. Often we move in as a team, sit down with the management, diagnose the problems, try to find solutions."

When Warburg's advised Chrysler on the projected merger with Rootes (which retained Lazard's) the advisers got together and tried to reconcile the inevitable differences. A member of the British government who had watched the negotiations with some misgivings—it was another "symptomatic" case of an American firm taking over a British firm—said, "If Siegmund has his fingers in that pie, it will come out all right," and it did. There was a basis of mutual trust. Much water had run down the Thames since Warburg's and Lazard's had fought against each other on the battlefields of the Aluminium War.

"First one tries to bridge the basic differences. Then there is some give-and-take involved until one reaches a meeting ground in between. It is very important to make one's own client listen; that often takes a long time. Yes, only then can we make decisions for the client. At that point, the accurate science of finance enters the field, though no one can really explain precisely how it is done. The technicians take over. The deal is made."

KNOWLEDGE THROUGH PAINFUL EXPERIENCE

S. G. Warburg acquired his merchant-banking knowledge through "painful experience," a recurrent expression in his private vocabulary. He will never forget the lesson of the crisis of 1929–30. In Vienna, the Bodenkreditanstalt, Austria's largest agricultural institution, had got in terrible trouble. At the federal chancellor's personal request, Baron Louis von Rothschild agreed that the (Rothschild-controlled) Credit-anstalt, Austria's largest bank, should take over the Bodenkreditanstalt's liabilities. As a result, the Creditanstalt itself had to suspend payments the following year. This time, even the Rothschilds couldn't prevent the *Krach*.

"It was fantastic," Warburg remembers. "People everywhere had said it couldn't happen. Well, it did happen. The fall of the Creditanstalt started a terrible chain reaction all over Europe. Many other institutions collapsed. People withdrew their deposits, causing the liquidity of many banks to become endangered. That's the sort of experience one never forgets. Sometimes I try to explain this to my young people at the bank, but I don't really succeed. They listen politely—and forget. No theoretical teaching equals the value of painful experience. There were brilliant people all over Europe who did foresee the great crisis—but did not act accordingly."

Could something like 1929 happen again? Warburg doesn't think so. The teachings of John Maynard Keynes have taught people a great many things, given them confidence that capitalism can be made to work, that a violent depression can be averted by skillful manipulation. Warburg now worries about different problems—the population explosion in Asia and Africa and the rapid expansion of Red China.

Warburg, the tutor, always tells the young men at his bank that a good merchant banker, like a good doctor, must rely on a blend of idealism and knowledge, common sense and applied psychology. The most important single component is idealism. "A banker and a surgeon must not think of money when they start to operate." This also answers the question about the merchant banker's function in the future. There will be larger hospitals as the world's population increases, but there will always be a need for good doctors and surgeons. Warburg tells his associates, "The satisfaction of rendering a good service is more important than the size of the anticipated bill." The great merchant bankers whom he met as a trainee after the First World War never thought of money as the primary purpose of banking. "For most of my colleagues in the City merchant banking is a constructive achievement, an intellectual sport."

There is hardly a technical problem in merchant banking that cannot be solved, but there there will always be the nearly insoluble psychological problems. Just as well: Warburg is fascinated by the challenge. When he advises a client about a projected merger, he always tries to find out what the other side is thinking. This is the tactical part of the problem. Then comes the strategic question: do the people really mean what they say? This is where "the occult powers of the successful merchant banker" come in.

"Every good doctor will admit that a cardiogram tells you a lot—but not everything. The rest is a matter of instinct, *Fingerspitzengefuhl*, extreme sensitivity that comes with knowledge and experience. Even sound instinct, however, won't prevent the merchant banker from making mistakes."

When Warburg is asked by a young man how to train for the profession of merchant banker, he points out that he can suggest only the technical part of the training. In England it's accountancy; in America, a few years' practice in a good law office. Some good American bankers started out as lawyers. Warburg is not impressed by many economists who spend their time and energy redefining definitions and renaming terminologies.

Mergers and amalgamations have become an important activity in merchant banking. In this era of mass production, industrial units are getting bigger, and the trend toward bigness continues. Warburg is against bigness for its own sake, but he realized at the end of the last war that Europe would have to follow the American trend of amalgamation and rationalization or risk being eased out. In these bigger units, the merchant banker must act like a living cell, creating new ideas. To the outsider, such mergers are often mysterious riddles of high finance, camouflaged by enigmatic figures. To Warburg the operations are necessary, simple, and lucid. At Warburg's, they didn't invent the art of the merger and the technique of the takeover. It is true that the firm has never yet actually lost a takeover battle. But defeat in battle can often be avoided only by slow or quick retreat, "prior to irrevocable involvement in an acute struggle." This certainly applies to takeovers no less than to military battles. Warburg's has on several occasions retreated when it came to the conclusion that the price to be paid was too high.

In the past years, Warburg's has acquired so much experience in takeover operations that it almost has made a science out of it, a very profitable science. Fees usually range from one-half to two percent of the amount at stake, and these amounts are often very large. Fees are not mentioned in the City until the operation is completed. A great surgeon saves a millionaire's life first, then sends him his bill. The merchant banker often saves a millionaire's financial life. At S. G. Warburg & Co. advisory fees now account for a growing slice of profits. Merchant banking remains a profitable business, though for different reasons.

DRAMA IN FLEET STREET

Warburg, the student of history, has always closely followed the changing trends in merchant banking. As a trainee after the First World War, he was taught that the merchant banker's primary obligations were to give credit, issue domestic and foreign bonds, or arrange large loans. As the shadow of Nazism darkened the Continent, credit became restricted and finally stopped flowing out of Europe altogether, as it began to come from the other side of the Atlantic.

At the end of the war, as Warburg started to build up his new business in London, the established merchant bankers of the City were picking up the pieces, trying to reestablish old connections. Warburg was way behind, and he had the added handicap of being an upstart. But he perceived, perhaps a little earlier than his colleagues in the venerable old houses, that the role of the merchant banker was changing fast in a changing world. In the "era of the migration of capital" (a Warburg expression) the issue of bonds, the credit business, even the management of accounts became mere sidelines. Merchant banking became a service business, and the merchant banker a combination of doctor-consultant-financial-engineer-friend-adviser.

In those early years, Warburg's primary concern was to get customers. He felt like a doctor who is not permitted to advertise, but must wait until the patients come in. As they indeed began coming in and more experts were needed, he started to build up his team of specialists, headed by Henry Grunfeld, a coolheaded banker from Berlin who shrewdly assessed people, figures, and risks. Business kept expanding but Warburg's was ready. The team spirit was a reality at the bank. There were complicated financial constructions, great amalgamations, highly involved transactions. They didn't mind: the more complicated, the better. The modern merchant banker must always be one step ahead of the big commercial banks if he wants to survive.

In the late 1950s, the Warburgs—the team—were known among knowing insiders as brilliant advisers. "It is always pleasing to a man's vanity for his services to be sought by opposing interests at the same time," wrote Lionel Fraser. Warburg's has had several such pleasant experiences. As adviser to Roy Thomson, the Fleet Street tycoon, Warburg's engineered the smooth, painless transfer of Kemsley Newspapers— including England's great *Sunday Times*—from Lord Kemsley into the hands of Roy Thomson for four and a half million pounds.

A big deal and a symbolic change. Instead of the old gentlemen who had a ticker tape in the hall of his country house, where important news items were brought in on a silver tray by an impeccable butler, Thomson, the son of a poor barber from Toronto walked into Kemsley—sorry, Thomson House, in Gray's Inn Road—shook hands with everybody, and went on to collect more newspapers as philatelists collect stamps.

The transfer was a complex operation. Aside from the shares held by the Kemsley family, there were one and a half million shares in Kemsley Newspapers held by the public. All shareholders, it was agreed, must have the opportunity of selling their shares for cash at the same price as the price received by the Kemsleys. Eventually all shareholders had a chance to sell at that price, ten pounds and ten shillings.

At a later stage, Warburg's became "temporarily and reluctantly" the opponents of Roy Thomson. Odhams Press, one of the largest British publishers of magazines, trade journals, and also owners of *The People* and the *Daily Herald,* saw the danger signs of being taken over by Cecil Harmsworth King, another Fleet Street entrepreneur. It hastily contacted Thomson about a possible merger.

When King heard of the "secret" negotiations, he hit the ceiling. The situation became extremely delicate for Warburg's. It had advised King for years before it had become adviser to Thomson. Cecil King, a cultured man with a great ambition for power, had been one of S. G. Warburg's first important clients. They had met in the early 1950s, several years after King had taken over the *Daily Mirror,* now with a circulation of over five million, "the largest on earth." It is probably the most successful venture in tabloid publishing.

King had been in need of financial advice. He approached a great old merchant bank earlier and was turned down; the "Princes of the City" wanted to have nothing to do with the unconventional Mr. King. Warburg's, which likes nonconformists, became King's adviser.

After Odhams Press started to negotiate "secretly" with Roy Thomson, Cecil King quickly issued a counterbid that was much more attractive to Odhams's shareholders than was Thomson's. When it became clear at 30 Gresham Street that there might be conflicting interests between King and Thomson, Warburg's informed Thomson, regretfully, that on the principle of seniority of client relationship, it was acting for King in this matter. Thomson understood and called in a well-established merger expert, Kenneth Keith of Philip Hill, Higginston, Erlangers.

The fight for Odhams Press developed into a big drama. Lionel Fraser, who, jointly with Warburg's Henry Grunfeld, looked after King's interests, later wrote that "financial blood, newspaper blood, and labour blood" was spilled in the process. The battle ended with a clear victory for King who, after a tense week found himself in control of the biggest newspaper empire in British history, "to the astonishment of Parliament, the Prime Minister and most of Odhams," as Anthony Sampson reported. Happiest of all were Odhams's stockholders whose shares went up from forty shillings when talks began, to sixty-four shillings when they ended. Cecil King now controls about thirty-eight percent of Britain's daily newspaper circulation, and forty percent on Sunday, and has reached his ambition of being the biggest newspaper publisher in the world.

For Warburg's it was another spectacular success. But what pleased them most was that Roy Thomson, the loser, came back to them after the battle was over. Today Lord Thomson of Fleet, another very big and powerful publisher, remains an important client of S. G. Warburg & Co.

RISKS ARE CAUSED BY PEOPLE

People who meet Warburg for the first time sometimes wonder how this quiet man with his dreamy eyes and soft voice is able to argue with tough tycoons and brilliant bankers and come out on top.

"Siegmund's greatest asset is his inner authority," says a friend who often watched him during intricate negotiations. "There are other men with exceptional minds in the merchant banking fraternity. Siegmund has the brilliant mind and also the conclusive force that comes out of a man's innermost conviction. I've seen him enter a room where some of the world's great industrialists were assembled, men of authority, accustomed to issuing orders, to be listened to respectfully. Siegmund would sit down and they became silent. They paid attention to him, because they'd learned that Siegmund will not utter a single superfluous word. Big people gladly pay a premium for lucidity of thought and economy of expression. Warburg clarifies, never merely simplifies, complicated matters."

What the friend calls Warburg's inner authority comes out of Warburg's sense of duty, his Spartan self-discipline. He is never playful, neither with ideas nor with words. He approaches every matter with complete intensity. When he wastes an hour, he has pangs of conscience, brought up as he was in the belief that to waste even a minute of one's life is a sin. He applies the same rigorous standards to everybody else. He has no use for people who tell him lightheartedly that something can't be done. "If you want to do it, you can do it," Warburg may answer. He believes that energy and perseverance can move mountains, even in business. He talks to an apprentice in his bank with the same intensity that he displays to persuade a member of government that devaluation is no cure for England's economic ills. And why not? The apprentice may become a member of government himself and will remember the talk with S. G. Warburg as a milestone in his life.

Great bankers are said to have the minds of calculating machines. Warburg is also a keen observer with a highly trained memory. No detail, no matter how insignificant, escapes him. He notices the different hairdo of a stenographer whom he hasn't seen for months, or the worn heels of a man's shoes. Because nothing is unimportant to him, he is better suited to discover quickly people's hidden strengths and little weaknesses—an indispensable talent of a merchant banker whose job is to assess risks. "Risks," Warburg says, "are caused by people."

His associates, clients, and friends depend on his reliability. "When Siegmund says that he's going to call you on the seventeenth of December, at four P.M., you know he's going to," a prominent client says. "There may be a war, a blizzard, an earthquake, the lines may be down, a general strike—but Siegmund will get through. In this careless world of ours, his attitude is a source of great comfort. You know there is at least *somebody* left on whom you can rely absolutely. He *never* forgets a promise. It took the people in the City a long time to realize that Warburg never utters these conventional phrases, as we English so often do, without really thinking. Warburg means literally what he says, which is a phenomenon in this loosely talking age. Some accuse him of being too intelligent—'clever,' you know—which is always somewhat suspect here. Those who know him well realize that his attention to detail, in thought and word, comes out of his sense of inner duty."

Warburg never makes a promise if he isn't certain he can fulfill it. He also can be very tough when he feels that somebody was treated unfairly. He once flew to the Continent and spent several days there aiding somebody he hardly knew who had been wronged. He can also be very tough with people who are unfair to him. He doesn't mind being disliked, envied, or justly criticized. But he gets angry when people accuse him of something he hasn't done.

In action Warburg is precise, effective, polite, and generous, and always skillfully conveys the impression that the other fellow thought of the great idea first. Masters of the hard sell are often captivated by the melancholy charm of this master of the soft sell. He is one of the world's best-organized men. On his trips, he has everything arranged for weeks beforehand, down to the meals, appointments, things to do. "Siegmund knows whom he's going to have dinner with three weeks from now," says a friend. "He knows he must call up a widowed aunt at five-fifteen in the afternoon." Outside Warburg's simple private office at the London bank, a red light is installed to keep people away when he is occupied with other matters. But he rarely uses the red light; people wander in and out all the time. Warburg interrupts his dictation, talks to the visitor, makes a couple of telephone calls, turns back to his secretary, and resumes his letter midsentence, exactly where he had stopped. He applies his meticulous sense of organization where it matters most—to himself. Before an important meeting, he prepares for every contingency, every possible objection, and thus is ready to counter every argument. As a congenital pessimist, he always expects the worst to happen, and so is perfectly prepared for it. He is not as flexible as many merchant bankers, who make a fetish out of flexibility. Once Warburg has taken a line of conduct, he follows it strictly, and concentrates completely on whatever he is doing. Everything else becomes unimportant for the time being.

He is not jealous of his competitors. The merchant-banking fraternity has its own prima donnas who react like prima donna sopranos, prima donna baseball players, or prima donna field marshals. Warburg admires people who know something better than he does. He hates incompetent bankers, of whom there are quite a lot. His sense of justice sometimes gets him in trouble. Once he got into a terrible argument with a London Underground ticket collector who accused him of having traveled one station too far with his ticket. Warburg said he had asked for the right ticket and hadn't noticed that he was sold one that cost three pennies less. He was upset for days, wanted to go to court to prove his innocence, and only after long, painful discussions was persuaded by his terrified associates that arguing publicly with the London Underground (and making headlines in the tabloids) would hardly help the image of one of the world's leading merchant bankers.

"What can you do with a man who likes to pay his taxes before they are due and won't let you bring a small bottle of perfume from France without declaring it in customs?" asks a friend. "Siegmund will declare *any*thing."

But he is also a practical man who does much for people he likes and nothing for those he doesn't like. He may spend days at the bedside of a sick relative, but he doesn't waste any time with funerals. He feels, perhaps not unreasonably, that he is more useful to the living than the dead.

A STUDENT OF GRAPHOLOGY

Warburg's intellectual curiosity embraces a wide range of subjects— literature and philosophy, politics and psychology, the arts and music; and modern currency problems has long been a favorite hobby. He is convinced that money is becoming less valuable all the time. He speaks wistfully about the wise law of Solon in Athens, that all debts not repaid within seventy years must be cancelled. People who contract debts pay the interest. But with the progressive development of production, people inevitably want to pay back their debts—knowing the money they pay back is always worth less than that which they borrowed. Only during the second half of the nineteenth century and the early years of the twentieth were the world's leading currencies tied to gold. Since then the values of all currencies have gone down slowly and inexorably.

The gradual devaluation began much earlier, though. The great fortunes of the eighteenth and nineteenth centuries were not made by people lending money, but by those who owned and developed land, traded with raw materials, built railroads and utilities, and financed industry. They considered obligations only for a short-term investment. Warburg's "painful experience" after the First World War, when bondholders lost nearly everything, while shareholders who didn't sell eventually came out all right, has formed his basic investment philosophy.

Next to currency problems, his main extracurricular interest is the science of graphology, "which some people unfortunately still consider something akin to astrology." Several years ago, when he worried about an associate with some emotional difficulties, he sent a page of the man's handwriting to a noted graphologist in Zurich. He received a lengthy character analysis which convinced Warburg that the graphologist knew more about the man (whom he had never seen) than Warburg did after talking to him every day for years.

Warburg endowed the European Foundation of Graphological Science and Application, now attached to the University of Zurich. The Swiss, a sober-minded, analytical people with an inborn sense of precision, seemed especially qualified. At the opening of the foundation in April 1963, Warburg, though he considered himself merely a dilettante, explained why he endeavored to further the development of graphology.

"My experience convinced me that graphological analysis enables us to gain insight into the psychological structure of other people, to find out more about them than years of personal acquaintance or spontaneous, intuitive impression will tell us...."

"I learned that the handwriting of a person contains signs of tension that tell more to the expert graphologist than that person's facial, muscular or verbal expressions reveal to the amateur. If we don't take people for granted, but always try to strengthen the forces of good, we must find the direct way that leads from psychological knowledge to psychotherapy. Graphology helps us to understand certain psychological connections and to undertake the solution of complicated psychological problems. If I were indiscreet, I could tell you of many experiences when, at the advice of expert graphologists, I changed my attitude about difficult psychological situations, and adopted a different course of action so that seemingly insoluble problems could be straightened out in a new, happier way.

"I realize that many people still consider graphologists to be cranks and eccentrics. Actually, graphologists have pioneered new segments of psychological knowledge. Many sciences started as myths. The knowledge of the stars began as astrology and only gradually became the accurate science of astronomy. Today no one would call an astronomer a crank. Eventually, I am convinced, graphology will become *hoffahig*—presentable at the court of profound knowledge, comparable to the established sciences of astronomy, chemistry and physics...."

"A LIVING FORCE OF ITS OWN"

Of all the great merchant bankers of London, only Baring Brothers & Co., founded in 1763, and S. G. Warburg & Co., founded in 1946, have their names in the telephone directory without any description, such as "bankers," "merchant bankers," "merchants and bankers." Both firms consider themselves well enough known in the City to dispense with any title. The atmosphere at S. G. Warburg & Co. contrasts strongly with the Dickensian mood at Barings, where Sir Edward Reid, the chairman, is a personal and business friend of S. G. Warburg's.

There is nothing Dickensian about 30 Gresham Street, a rather functional structure with simple, modern lines that could stand unobtrusively in Wall Street or in Frankfurt am Main. They do have a grandfather clock and many old prints there, but these old-fashioned appurtenances are canceled out by electronically steered elevators and automatic machines, and by the conspicuous absence of ancestral portraits and coal fires in grates.

This is obviously Modern Business. Big Business. Long, white corridors are divided by rooms on both sides. Few of the 250 employees are visible. Everybody walks with a brisk pace. The doors of the individual rooms are closed, and there is a sense of secrecy. The rules of the game are enforced severely at S. G. Warburg & Co. No merchant banker would use advance knowledge of an intended merger for personal gain. That's elementary. One doesn't even talk about it. Except at Warburg's, where they do everything differently. There, they do talk about it. But at both institutions, anybody suspected of the slightest infringement of the unwritten rules will be summarily dismissed.

From the start, the firm has acted as a catalyst in international business. In 1947, Warburg's and the Banque Nationale Pour le Commerce et l'Industrie formed the British & French Bank, a very important transaction that, for the first time in years, brought British and French monetary business together again. Afterwards, Warburg's made a specialty of repatriating companies uprooted during the war. It brought back to England, from the United States, a twenty-five percent interest in Associated Electrical Industries that had been acquired by General Electric. A number of London office buildings that had been purchased by an American group were returned through Warburg's to British ownership. The Brazilian Warrant Company, a coffee plantation and trading firm, was transferred from Britain back to Brazilian hands, and the International Telephone & Telegraph Company's twenty percent interest in the L. M. Ericsson Telephone Company was sold back to European investors. Warburg's also advised the Timken Roller Bearing Company when it bought up all the shares of its British subsidiary, and the bank introduced a number of foreign securities on the London Stock Exchange, including Chrysler from the United States, Farbenfabriken, Bayer and Hoeschst from Germany, Finsider from Italy, and the Discount Bank of Israel. Warburg's also floated the stock issues of a number of private companies that became public.

In the past years Warburg's has built up a network of manifold interests. It advises British firms expanding on the Continent and American firms entering Britain and Western Europe. It financed industrial modernization in Austria and floated a fifteen million dollar loan to help develop Italy's *autostrade* (superhighways). It has had its fingers in many British pies, from hire-purchase (as the British call finance companies) to television. In Switzerland it placed bond issues of the International Telephone and Telegraph Corporation, British Aluminium, and Reed Paper Group. In Canada it has had an investment trust and a finance company since 1953. And in the summer of 1965, S. G. Warburg & Co. opened a branch in New York City.

In his last statement as chairman of Mercury Securities, Warburg said that while the circle of clients expanded slowly during the early years, the expansion recently proceeded "at such a pace that we are having continuously to increase the size of the departments concerned." He admitted that the higher business volume might lead to a deterioration in the quality of service, and exhorted everybody to make "special efforts to maintain the personal style and character which we consider essential for a merchant-banking house."

Last year S. G. Warburg decided to step aside "before the doctor told me I had to stop." He would no longer continue as chairman but would remain a member of the board "to render whatever contribution I can to our Group's further progress." A favorite Warburg epigram says, "Good organization means to make oneself dispensable."

In his final statement, Warburg said:

> Leaders in industry and finance are often inclined not to step down before the decline of their capacity becomes manifest, holding on too long to their positions and thus preventing the formation of a strong chain of potential successors. It has all along been our principal aim in the Warburg-Mercury Group to achieve a management structure in depth, self-recharging, free from nepotism, and based on integrity and humility, on imagination, courage and efficiency.

A characteristic Warburg statement, placing old-fashioned virtues ("integrity and humility") ahead of the "courage and efficiency" constantly preached today. It was forthright and unorthodox, provoking angry mutterings in paneled boardrooms and vintage banking parlors where "leaders in industry and finance" still "hold on too long to their positions" although "the decline of their capacities" has long become manifest to everybody but themselves.

Yet it expressed nonconformist Warburg's conviction that a well-made organization must go on, irrespective of its members. The team is more important than the totality of the individuals who form it. Of the twenty-five names on the letterhead of S. G. Warburg & Co., ten are "executive directors" and fifteen are "directors." Among the latter is S. G. Warburg.

"This division of the board is very important to me," Warburg says. "It does not mean that some of the 'directors' do not work just as hard as those called 'executive directors.'" "Director" S. G. Warburg certainly works as hard as anybody else in the organization. On a recent business trip to Frankfurt am Main, he had his first appointment at 9 A.M., spent most of the day in seven different meetings, and talked about business matters until shortly before midnight. Certain merchant bankers never retire—they just work a few hours more every day.

The division on the firm's board between "executive directors" and "directors" means that when some of the executive directors reach a certain degree of seniority, they should move from the executive side to the advisory side. "They should become, to use the Japanese expression, wise elder statesmen," says Warburg.

He hopes that in due time the "wise elder statesmen"

> will want to make room for other colleagues well trained to follow them. Thus, I am convinced that my stepping down as Chairman will not weaken, but on the contrary strengthen our Group. Over the years our team has developed into an organism which is now a living force of its own. This organism is today stronger than the sum of the individuals who compose it.

Which echoes the wise words of Walter Bagehot, the great Victorian banker, economist, and critic, "The business of a great bank requires a great deal of ability and an even rarer degree of trained and sober judgement."

ALBERT SCHWEITZER
Toccata and Fugue

ONE DISMAL NOVEMBER EVENING IN 1932, I was walking aimlessly through the streets of Aarau, a dull factory town in northern Switzerland. I was between trains—on my way to Paris—and I was not due to leave until midnight. A slow rain was falling, and I felt lonely and rather lost, as one is apt to feel on a dreary night in a strange provincial town. As I passed Aarau's late-Gothic *Stadtkirche,* I heard the organ being played inside. The music was Bach's Great Fugue in G Minor, and I could tell at once that the organist was a master. The main entrance to the church was closed, but a small side door stood open, and I went in. Except for a dim light from the organ loft, the church was dark, and, as far as I could make out, it was empty. I sat down in a pew near the door and closed my eyes. The organist was performing with understanding and authority, his phrasing was intimate, and his legato beautifully lucid. He managed to convey all of Bach's sweep and grandeur without sacrificing, as so many organists do, his fascinating detail. The drab, damp streets of Aarau began to seem a long way off. After the fugue, the organist played the moving chorale prelude, "Nun danket alle Gott," and then one of the Leipzig Preludes, during which the church seemed to be ringing with a multitude of exquisite voices.

When the music came to an end, I continued to sit quietly in the pew, with the sound of the fine organ still in my ears. After a moment or two, I heard steps, and a man came down from the loft and walked swiftly toward the door. As he passed through a patch of light, I could see that he was perhaps sixty years old yet carried himself with remarkable vigor. His face was deeply lined; he had an aquiline nose, and a bushy mustache drooped around the corners of his mouth. I stood up as he approached, and he raised a hand in greeting. "I played the chorale too fast, didn't I?" he asked, and nodded vigorously, as though in answer to his own question. He spoke German with an Alsatian accent. I apologized for having come in without permission, but he didn't seem to be listening.

"Do you like this music?" he asked, with the directness of a teacher quizzing a pupil.

I told him that I certainly did, but that, as a student of the violin, I had never felt as close to Bach as an organist would.

He shook his head. "You mustn't say that," he told me firmly. "Bach was an accomplished violinist. He knew a lot about the the technique of violin playing. If he didn't, how could he have written all that great polyphonic music in his violin sonatas and partitas? Many of his works for the organ demand a violinist's phrasing and modulation. Have you ever played the Chaconne that concludes the Second Partita?"

I said I had tried to.

"An astonishing work," the organist said. "One doesn't know what to admire most—the wealth of the variations, the development, or the polyphony." And then he smiled, raised his hand again, and left.

I stared after him, wishing that I'd been bold enough to suggest walking him home. In a moment, another elderly man came in and told me gruffly that the church was now closed. I asked him who the organist was. He gave me an odd look. "You mean to say you don't know Albert Schweitzer?" he said.

As a matter of fact, at that time I knew next to nothing about Albert Schweitzer. He wasn't, of course, as celebrated then as he is now. I was vaguely aware that he was a doctor somewhere in the African bush and that he had written a number of books, but otherwise his name meant little to me—so little that a few years before, when Schweitzer visited Prague, where I was then living, to receive an honorary degree and deliver some lectures, I hadn't bothered to attend any of them.

When I got to Paris, I bought Schweitzer's autobiography, *Out of My Life and Thought,* which had come out a year or so before. I was impressed by his modesty and clarity of style ("I was born on January 14th, 1875, at Kayserberg, in Upper Alsace, the second child of Louis Schweitzer, who just then was shepherding the little flock of evangelical believers in that Catholic place…"), and when I finished it, I began to read everything else I could lay my hands on by or about Schweitzer— Schweitzer the organ builder, the organist, the interpreter of Bach and Goethe, the architect, the philosopher, the minister, the theologian, the apostle of the universal spirit, the lumberman, and the doctor, or, as his African patients call him, "the fetishman." The more I read, the more eager I became to see Schweitzer again face to face, and once, years later I even thought of visiting him at his hospital in Lambaréné, French Equatorial Africa, but a friend who had been there dissuaded me. He told me that I had no business going, for Schweitzer was all too frequently pestered by casual visitors who went to Lambaréné out of curiosity and, once there, took up a lot of his time and kept him away from his patients. "Schweitzer can never say no to a caller," my friend said. "If you want to see him, wait until he comes back to Europe. In Africa, he belongs to the sick."

In his *On the Edge of the Primeval Forest,* written in 1920, Schweitzer explains, with customary directness, why he cut short a brilliant career to Europe to establish a hospital in the jungle: "I gave up my position as professor in the University of Strasbourg, my literary work, and my organ playing, in order to go as a doctor to Equatorial Africa. How did that come about? I had read about the physical miseries of the natives in the virgin forests; I also heard about them from missionaries, and the more I thought about it, the stranger it seemed that we Europeans trouble ourselves so little about the great humanitarian task which offers itself to us in far-off lands. Moved by these thoughts, I resolved when already thirty years old, to study medicine and to put my ideas to the test out there. At the beginning of 1913, I graduated as an M.D. That same spring I started with my wife, who had qualified as a nurse, for the River Ogowe in Equatorial Africa, there to begin my active work. I chose this locality because some Alsatian missionaries in the service of the Paris Evangelical Mission had told me that a doctor was badly needed there on account of the constantly spreading sleeping sickness." Schweitzer left for Lambaréné on Good Friday, 1913, and it has been his headquarters for more than forty years.

Every once in a while he returns to Europe to study, catch up on medical progress, play the organ, raise funds, or simply take a rest, but in recent years these visits have become shorter and more widely spaced. He has always run the hospital as a private venture, never seeking aid from either the French government or the Paris mission, because he wants to preserve his independence. When he set out, however, he promised the mission, which had misgivings about his religious orthodoxy, to be "as silent as a carp" in theological matters. He has long since been released from that promise.

Not long ago, I read in the papers that Schweitzer had arrived in Bordeaux on his way to spend a few months in the small Alsatian village of Gunsbach, where he makes his home when on the Continent. Later, I heard on the radio that he had given an organ recital in Strasbourg and, as the winner of the Nobel Peace Prize in 1952, had attended a meeting of Nobel laureates in Lindau, on Lake Constance. I figured that now was my chance and wrote to him in Gunsbach, asking if I might see him there, but I received a prompt reply from Mme Emmy Martin, his private secretary, expressing her regrets. "Dr. Schweitzer is going through a fatigue crisis," she wrote in French. "He must concentrate on a special manuscript, which must be completed by a certain date. He has called off all his lectures. Please try to understand...." There was a post-script in German, written in a small, vertical hand: "Please forgive a man who is so tired and swamped with work that he cannot fulfill your request. For the first time in my life, I must try to live as quietly as possible." This was signed by Schweitzer.

So that was that, I thought. But recently I was taking a leisurely drive through Alsace with two friends, on the way from Strasbourg to Zurich. At lunchtime, we arrived in Colmar, a lovely old town with a fine restaurant, the Maison des Têtes, and I suggested that we stop there for some Alsatian *choucroute*. While we were waiting for our lunch, I glanced at a map of the region. Eleven miles from Colmar, on Route N-417 to Munster, was Gunsbach. A couple of months had gone by since I had written my letter, and I found myself speculating whether Dr. Schweitzer might be less tired now and more in the mood for talking. I went to the phone and put in a call to Schweitzer, and after a nip-and-tuck struggle with the whimsicalities of the local long-distance telephone service, I heard a voice saying, "This is Mme Martin, in Dr. Schweitzer's house." I introduced myself, mentioned my letter, said I happened to be passing by, and asked if Dr. Schweitzer was at home. "I knew you would call someday," Mme Martin said, with a sigh. "If I ask you to come at three o'clock, will you promise not to stay too long?" I promised. Returning to the table, I finished my *choucroute* almost without noticing how good it was. My friends had decided they wanted to visit a museum in Colmar, and this fit in perfectly with my plans. After arranging to meet them at the Maison des Têtes for dinner, I set out to find Route N-417.

The day had been gray and cloudy, but as I left the picturesque, brightly painted houses of Colmar behind me, the sun broke through, and the countryside, washed clean by recent rains, looked sparkling. The air had a brisk edge to it. I drove through the valley of Munster, between vineyards and potato fields, with the Vosges looming ahead and on either side. Everything was so peaceful that it was hard to believe this was one of the most fought over regions in the world. As I drove along, I passed many road signs, but Gunsbach didn't appear on any of them. As I approached that town, I saw a separate village nestling in the foothills, with a pointed church spire at its center and well-kept vineyards around it. A road branched off toward it from the highway, but it was not marked. Obviously, the community preferred to remain anonymous. A man, wearing the light blue overalls and apron that are the uniform of winegrowers on both sides of the Rhine, told me in a very thick Alsatian accent that the village was indeed Gunsbach. Reaching it was only a matter of a minute or two. It was an attractive hamlet—a few old but sprucely kept-up houses with small gardens behind them, a town hall, a schoolhouse, an *épicerie*, a bakery, a butcher shop, and, on the side of a steep hill, a church.

Three women were standing on a corner, chatting, and I asked them the way to Dr. Schweitzer's house. One of them told me to take the next turn to the left. "You'll know the house when you see it," she said. I was dubious, but she proved right. The third house I came to was a three-story structure, a good bit larger than its neighbors. It had gray shutters and freshly painted window frames, and its sides were covered with ivy. Schweitzer, I knew, had built this house in 1930, with money from the Goethe Prize, given to him by the city of Frankfurt am Main "for his general services to humanity."

I parked my car, walked up to the door, and pulled an old-fashioned bell cord, which produced a tiny sound inside. In a moment, the door was opened by a young woman wearing a nurse's dress of unbleached linen. She gave me a questioning and, I thought, dismayed glance, and I quickly explained that I had an appointment with Dr. Schweitzer and gave her my name.

"Oh, yes. Mme Martin mentioned that you would be here," the young woman said, looking relieved. "Come in, please. I was afraid you were another passerby. We had a quite a few this morning. Everyone who passes through the village wants to see Herr Schweitzer. Come upstairs to his office, won't you?"

As she led me toward the stairway, we passed a closed door with a printed sign, in French: "If possible, don't stay more than five minutes. Dr. Schweitzer must work." The walls of the house were white—hospital white, I thought—and along the stairway hung photographs of church organs in Holland, Denmark, Switzerland, France, and Germany, with the name of the church written on each in Schweitzer's small, vertical script. On the second floor, the nurse opened a door with the same forbidding sign on it and asked me in. It was a big, not very tidy room, with two large windows commanding a view of vine-covered slopes. The nurse told me that Herr Schweitzer had gone to Munster that morning but was due back any minute, and that meanwhile she'd wait with with me here. After we sat down, she introduced herself as Ali Silver, a native of Holland, and said that she had been working for Herr Schweitzer in Lambaréné for the last nine years and would return there with him and his wife in December. Mrs. Schweitzer, she said, was visiting her daughter Rhena, near Zurich. Rhena, the Schweitzers' only child, is the wife of an Alsatian organ builder and the mother of four children. As I looked about the room, Miss Silver explained that it was here that Herr Schweitzer (she apparently made it a point not to refer to him as "Doctor") worked with Mme Martin, who acts not only as his secretary when he is in Gunsbach but as his European representative when he is in Africa, ordering supplies for Lambaréné and carrying on a worldwide correspondence with pharmaceutical firms, medical authorities, publishers, philanthropic institutions, autograph collectors, prime ministers, volunteers who want to work with him in Africa, and various committees that have been formed to help him—such as the Friends of Lambaréné and the Albert Schweitzer Fellowship—in Great Britain, Switzerland, Germany, Holland, Scandinavia, France, and the United States. On the walls were paintings of Schweitzer and photographs of him in Africa with his wife, hospital staff, and patients, and in Europe with friends and family. At one side of the room stood a large round white-tiled stove. There were books everywhere, including a complete set of Goethe, as well as a collection of curios that Miss Silver told me grateful patients had given Schweitzer—small elephants crudely carved out of ivory and ebony, a tiny stuffed doe, and a model of the Ogowe riverboat *Alembe,* which looked something like an old Mississippi stern-wheeler. Miss Silver said that a new boat now makes the hundred-and-eighty-mile trip once a week from the coastal town of Port-Gentil, in Gabon, to Lambaréné, in twenty-four hours, instead of the forty-eight the *Alembe* required. I gathered that it is nevertheless quite a journey. The Ogowe, infested with crocodiles, changes abruptly from a narrow channel to a broad lake and back again, and threads the tropical forests, full of pythons and gorillas. Lambaréné is no place for people who cannot stand solitude and a hard life, Miss Silver told me. The equator is only fifty miles to the north, and the coolest the temperature gets—and only during the rainy season—is about eighty-five. After a couple of years, people accustomed to a temperate climate begin to suffer fatigue and anemia. There is a constant struggle to keep the jungle from reclaiming the land. White ants eat into the foundations of the buildings, and the plantations that provide the hospital with food—mostly bananas, tapioca, and rice—are often ravaged by wild elephants. Other supplies must be brought in by boat, for there is no railroad or road—only footpaths.

Miss Silver went on to tell me that at the moment the hospital staff consists of three doctors, in addition to Schweitzer, and nine nurses—all volunteers and all European. They keep extremely busy. Two of the worst ailments they have to contend with are diphtheria and leprosy. "We've had good success in recent years, though," Miss Silver said. "There's a good diphtheria toxoid from England, and there are two good drugs for leprosy—one from Madagascar, called *Hydrocotylus asiatica* and one from America, called promine. Sleeping sickness, elephantiasis, malaria, osteomyelitis, and amoebic dystentery are common, too, and there are a good many cases of mental derangement, brought on by poisoning. (Some natives still do poison their enemies.) But there is no cancer, appendicitis, or empty beds. We have more than two hundred and fifty patients at the hospital proper, and two hundred and forty in our leprosy village. Some travel hundreds of miles from the interior by canoe, and often the entire family comes along. Relatives insist on staying near the patients, and that creates a number of problems. When we tell Herr Schweitzer that there is absolutely no more space, he smiles and says, 'Arrangez-vous, mes enfants.' And we do. No one is sent away. Herr Schweitzer holds a service every Sunday morning. He plays the harmonium and gives a simple sermon in French, and then two native interpreters translate it into the Galoa and Pahouin dialects. At night, he makes the rounds of the wards, and then goes to his house, where he plays the next best thing to an organ. A real one wouldn't last long in the climate down there, so the Bach Society in Paris gave him a special instrument—a zinc-lined piano fitted with organ pedals. When he starts to play, the rest of us turn out the lights and listen."

The door opened and Mme Martin, a gray-haired woman in her sixties, came in. She is a widow and has her own apartment in the house. Her husband was a classmate and close friend of Schweitzer, and she has worked with him for forty years. Miss Silver introduced us, and then remarked that something must have held up Herr Schweitzer.

"He should have been here half an hour ago," Mme Martin said to me. "He went to a funeral. I suppose he got to talking to people in the street. Meanwhile, his work piles up."

"But he loves to talk to people," Miss Silver said. "And they need him."

"Yes, Ali, but think of all the things he's got to do here," Mme Martin said. "This morning there were so many interruptions. The bell didn't stop ringing once, and everybody promises to leave in five minutes, and then everybody stays for an hour." She sighed, and looked signifi-cantly at me. "Of course, the Doctor sends no one away. And then he stays up half the night working."

In Gunsbach, Mme Martin told me, Schweitzer gets up at seven and, after a simple breakfast, retires to a room on the ground floor to work on a book about ethics—the "special manuscript" she had mentioned in her letter to me that he started many years ago and is determined to finish before he returns to Africa. The room is as bare as a monk's cell. It is just above street level and passersby can see his head as he bends over his small desk. Sometimes, to Mme Martin's despair, Schweitzer strikes up a friendly conversation through the window with his neighbors about the health of their grapes or their children. At around eleven, Schweitzer retires to a small house nearby, where he and Edouard Nies-Berger, an Alsatian-born organist who studied the instrument under Schweitzer in Strasbourg and is now an American citizen, work together at assembling a complete edition of Bach's Choral Preludes in their original form. Then Schweitzer comes home for lunch, in the dining room on the second floor. It can comfortably seat a dozen people, but there are often more than a dozen at meals, for Schweitzer, who is unconcerned about the mechanics of housekeeping, invites whoever happens to be around and brings in strangers he has met on the street. "*Arrangez-vous, mes enfants*," he again will murmur to the staff. In the afternoon, he writes or sees people, and then takes a walk through the fields or to the Gunsbach church shared by the Catholics and the Lutherans in the village, to play the organ—an ancient instrument that he had had rebuilt, according to his own specifications, in 1928. (He also plays for the Sunday morning service.) After dinner, he works with Mme Martin on his correspondence.

"If only we could get some of these letters out of the way," Mme Martin said, gloomily surveying a pile of papers on a table near one of the windows. "That's just today's mail."

The doorbell rang, and Mme Martin and Miss Silver looked at each other apprehensively. A servant girl stuck her head in and said that the two ladies from Strasbourg had arrived. Mme Martin closed her eyes. "Oh, yes," she said after a moment. "They should have come yesterday. Ali, ask them to wait downstairs, and when the Doctor comes in, see that he doesn't stay with them more than five minutes. Tell him we're waiting up here.

As Miss Silver started downstairs, the doorbell rang again, and a minute later, a little girl came upstairs to the office, followed by two little boys. The girl wore thick glasses, through which she stared at us timidly, and had braces on her teeth. Under one arm she carried a bulky packag wrapped in newspaper, which she gave to Mme Martin, asking if the Doctor would autograph a book for her. Mme Martin said he would and told her to leave the package.

The girl was silent a moment, evidently trying to muster up courage. Then she said, in a frightened whisper, "Madame, it isn't only one book."

"How many, then?" asked Madame.

"Five," the girl replied, almost inaudibly.

"Five books?" Mme Martin said severely. "Child, the Doctor hasn't got that much time."

"One is for Marcel, here—my brother," the girl said desperately. "He wants to have a book by the Doctor when he grows up. One is for my cousin Philippe, in Paris, and one is for—"

The door opened, and Schweitzer came in.

At seventy-nine, Dr. Schweitzer had the sparkle of a young man. His hair was white now, the lines in his face had deepened, his mustache still drooped, and he made me think of a figure in an Alsatian woodcut, the sort that my friends in Colmar were probably admiring at that very minute. He was wearing the clothes of a country doctor or a pastor—black trousers, a black coat, a black waistcoat, and a high wing collar with a black bow tie. Mme Martin introduced us, and he shook my hand. In my letter, I hadn't mentioned our brief meeting in the darkened church in Aarau, for fear I would seem to be stretching a casual acquaintanceship too far and didn't mention it now.

"Marie-Louise asked if you would autograph a book, and then she produces five," Mme Martin said. The little girl stared at the doctor through her glasses, unable to speak.

"Five!" Schweitzer exclaimed, in mock horror. "Did you buy five of my books, Marie-Louise?" His eyes twinkled.

Marie-Louise smiled; she was at ease now. She quickly unwrapped the package and handed him five copies of the French edition of his *Memoirs of Childhood and Youth.*

"One is for my brother Marcel, who is here," the girl began breathlessly. "And one is for my cousin—"

"Of course, I'll sign them," Schweitzer said and touched her hair lightly. "Just leave them here and come back tomorrow. Give Madame all the names. We might as well do this right." He smiled radiantly. When the children had gone, Mme Martin asked him if he would like a cup of tea. "Not now," he said. "I think I'll go over to the church. Where's the key?"

The key was not in its usual place—a nail by one of the windows—and there was some consternation. Mme Martin called to Miss Silver and asked her to look for it. While we were waiting, Schweitzer explained to me that he'd run into a few old friends after the funeral and had been delayed and then he had had to see the two ladies from Strasbourg downstairs. The phone rang, and Mme Martin answered it. It was from Paris—an invitation to Schweitzer to deliver a lecture. She politely declined. After she had hung up, he said to me, "I've got to practice some Bach chorales that I'm going to record next week. Would you like to come along and listen?"

"Dr. Schweitzer needs no practice," Mme Martin said. "He knows three-quarters of Bach by heart."

"These chorales belong to the fourth quarter," Schweitzer said, and laughed—a fresh, youthful, ringing laugh.

Miss Silver returned with the news that Domkantor Emilius Bangert, a friend of Schweitzer's from Copenhagen, had borrowed the key and was at the church, playing the organ. "He comes here every year to play the Gunsbach organ, because he loves it so much," Schweitzer told me. "Wait for me downstairs. I'll be right down."

Several people had gathered in front of the house, for word had gone about that Schweitzer would be playing that afternoon, and everybody wanted to go up to the church with him. Standing apart was a frail, thoughtful-looking man with fine features who, I found out later, was Professor Robert Minder of the Sorbonne, and another of Schweitzer's old friends. He was spending a week in Gunsbach. After a while, Schweitzer came out, wearing a somewhat battered black felt hat, and carrying a linen bag in one hand and a folder of sheet music in the other. Mme Martin appeared right behind him, looked about her with an air of resignation, and managed to detach Schweitzer from two newly arrived admirers. Schweitzer took my arm, and we moved off up the road toward the church, the whole party falling in behind us. En route, we met several villagers—men in blue aprons and women with children. They said, *"Guten Abend, Herr Doktor"* or *"Bonsoir, Docteur,"* and each time Schweitzer smiled, shook hands, and inquired about the children. I was reminded of the familiar description of him as "a combination of Goethe and Saint Francis of Assisi."

"They're good people," Schweitzer told me. "There are little over four hundred in the village. They work in the cotton factory in Munster, and on their evenings and weekends take care of their vineyards. Strictly speaking, this isn't my native village—I was born on the other side of the mountains—but I was brought here when I was only a few weeks old; my father had become pastor of Gunsbach."

Schweitzer stopped walking, looked me straight in the eye, and asked, "Do you still play the violin?"

I was taken aback.

"That night in Aarau, we talked about Bach the violinist, didn't we?" he continued as we walked on.

I said it was astounding that he should remember.

"I've trained myself to remember," he said. "Now, are you still playing the violin?"

"Sometimes for pleasure," I replied. "Mostly chamber music."

"Chamber music is the finest, purest music of all, better even than organ music," Schweitzer said. "Bach played viola in small groups. He liked to sit in the middle, so that he could hear what was going on on both sides. Playing music for the joy of it is truly wonderful. Unfortunately, I have usually had to play for money. With my music, I made the money needed for my medicine. Without the organ, there could have been no Lambaréné. Music became my refuge when I began to study medicine. Theology and music came naturally to me—my father and maternal grandfather were both musical pastors—but medicine was a strange new world. Sometimes, while I was at medical school in Strasbourg I felt I had to escape from my classes, and I would run over to a church and find peace of mind in an hour with Bach. I've often wondered how the violin was played in Bach's time. I once published an essay on the use of the round bow, and I had a lot to say about the round bow and his partitas. I believe the violinists in those days used a bow with a slightly curved stick. The hairs of the bow were fastened to the wood without screws and could be adjusted by pressure of the right thumb. For double-stops, the player would relax the bow so that it curved over the strings. When the bow is relaxed, the violin has a soft, organlike tone—almost ethereal. Of course, modern audiences would object to its weakness. The louder the better, they say. But I believe it would be altogether proper for chamber music. Bach's solo works should be moved out of the concert hall into the salon. That's where they really belong."

The three women who had given me directions were still chatting in the corner, and Schweitzer waved to them gaily. Then he stopped again, turned toward me, and said, with finality, "You will stay for dinner."

I mumbled something about a previous appointment.

"Can you stay or can't you?" he asked. "Quickly! No foolish excuses!"

I explained that I had to rejoin friends in Colmar for dinner, and that Mme Martin had emphasized that under no circumstances must I linger.

Schweitzer laughed. "Always listen to a woman, but never too much," he said. "That's how I get along with them. It's too bad you can't stay."

We had reached the foot of a rather steep path leading up to the church. Some workmen were building a stairway up the side of the hill, and the path was blocked by large slabs of stone. There was also a winding dirt road that made its way up the hill at a more leisurely grade, but Schweitzer would have none of it. Instead, he set off up the path, leaping from stone to stone. I managed to keep up with him, but I was soon out of breath. And all the while he went on talking about music. He said he'd recently been to a symphony concert in Strasbourg conducted by Charles Münch, whose uncle, Eugene Münch, had once been Schweitzer's organ teacher. Had I heard anything good lately? Yes, I panted—a magnificent *Tristan*, in Vienna.

"Ah, *Tristan!*" he exclaimed. "I still get as excited about it as I did when I heard it for the first time."

I said I'd often thought how singular it was that he, a Bachian, should admire Wagner.

"But why not?" he said. "Wagner himself greatly admired Bach. I've been an ardent Wagnerian since I was a youngster in Mulhouse, where I heard my first *Tannhäuser*." I was sixteen then. I was so excited I couldn't sleep for two nights. *Tristan* affects me that way, too, and it always has. So they like *Tristan* in Vienna now, do they?"

"Yes, very much," I assured him.

"They didn't always," he said, still bounding along. "The powerful anti-Wagner camarilla kept *Tristan* out of the Court Opera for a long time. If I'm not mistaken, the prelude to Act One was first performed there at a garden concert conducted by none other than Johann Strauss. Wagner reciprocated by conducting one of Strauss's waltzes at the first Bayreuth Festival."

To my relief, Schweitzer became winded himself after this speech, and he had to slow down. "No more talking," he said abruptly, and we climbed the rest of the way in silence.

As we approached the church, we could hear organ music. Schweitzer stopped at the door, took a deep breath, and cocked an ear. "My Danish friend, playing Buxtehude," he said. "How soft and lovely the organ sounds! I must admit it, even though I had it rebuilt myself. The number of fine old organs is decreasing rapidly these days, and I don't think much of the new organs they're building. The pedals are coarse. People have become obsessed with strong tone, and forget beauty and softness.

Someday, our lovely old Silbermann organs will all be gone, and then people will have no way of knowing how Bach's music was played in our time. I'm afraid I can't speak very highly of American organs. Harsh and tuberculous—that about sums them up."

Not all modern organs are inferior, Schweitzer admitted. He admires César Franck's organ, in the church of Sainte-Clotilde, and Charles Marie Widor's organ, in Saint-Sulpice, both in Paris. These two, as well as the magnificent organ in Notre Dame, were constructed by the great French organ builder Aristide-Cavaille-Coll. "But best of all I like my Gunsbach organ," he said. It was on this organ that Schweitzer recorded a number of Bach works for Columbia in 1952.

While we were talking at the entrance to the church, the rest of the company caught up with us. The crowd had grown along the way, as people discovered that Schweitzer was going to play, and there were several children, including Marie-Louise and her two small escorts. Schweitzer went inside and walked quickly up the creaking, steep wooden stairs to the organ loft. Most of the people sat in the pews, but a few of us—including the members of Schweitzer's staff, Professor Minder, and Marie-Louise—climbed up to the loft and sat on the choir benches flanking the organ.

The Danish organist, who was still playing Buxtehude as we came up the stairs, made as if to stop when he saw Schweitzer, but Schweitzer motioned to him to keep on. While he played, I looked out over the church. It was small and austere, but the afternoon sun pouring in through the colored windows made it seem warm and friendly, rather like a large living room. Schweitzer removed his shoes, opened the white linen bag, and took out a pair of organist's slippers, with soft rubber soles. More people entered the church in groups of two or three. Schweitzer sat with his hands crossed on his lap and his head lowered in meditation. In a few minutes, his friend had stopped playing, and he walked over to the organ. He sat down, put on a pair of spectacles, arranged his music, and then beckoned to me. "Careful!" he said softly as I tiptoed over. "Don't touch the pedals with your feet! Turn the pages for me. I'll tell you exactly when." He lowered his head again, as if in silent prayer, and sat motionless for a couple of minutes. There was a great stillness in the church. Then he raised his head, set the manuals, and began to play.

He started with "An Wasserflüssen Babylon," one of the eighteen chorales Bach wrote in Weimar and revised toward the end of his life. The organ had a sweet, soft, almost tender sound. When the time to turn a page drew near, Schweitzer whispered, "Wait," and then, "Now." Throughout the chorale he didn't once change the manuals, and only once or twice did he glance down for an instant to ascertain the position of his feet on the pedals; otherwise his eyes remained on the score. After he finished, he sat staring hard at the music. "I'm afraid I played too fast," he said, shaking his head. His friend from Copenhagen said he thought the tempo was just right, but Schweitzer disagreed. "I always feel I play the chorales too fast," he said. "So much detail of Bach's magnificent architecture comes to light only when you play the music slowly."

Schweitzer played another chorale, "Allein Gott in der Höh' sei Ehr," and then "Schmücke dich, O liebe Seele"—one of those Bach compositions in which the structure is hidden behind a lovely haze of melody. Schumann once wrote that Mendelssohn had told him that "if all hope and faith were taken out of your life, this chorale alone would be enough to restore them to you." Schweitzer played it with deep feeling. His expressive hands were in complete command of the keyboards. He repeated the second part of the chorale, and then complained once more that he had played too fast. As he took down the score, he said, "Now I don't need my glasses." He laid them aside, and, after a few seconds, during which he seemed to withdraw completely into himself, plunged into the magnificent chords of the great D-Minor Toccata and Fugue. For me, this has always been one of the most dramatic of Bach's works, and now I was overwhelmed by it. I closed my eyes, and when I opened them, as the music ended with a majestic *fortissimo*, the sun had fallen below the level of the windows. No one in the loft stirred, not even the children. It was Schweitzer who broke the spell. He put down the organ lid resolutely, locked it, and turned off the light.

One by one, people rose, but nobody spoke. After Schweitzer had changed back to his street shoes, we all filed down the narrow stairway. Some women were still in the pews; one of them was wiping her eyes. There were a number of people out front, standing near the little church cemetery. They smiled at Schweitzer in a grateful, affectionate way. One man, nervously twisting a blue beret in his hand, told him that he and his wife had walked to Gunsbach from a village three hours away in the hope of hearing him play, and that they had arrived just in time; the man's father had been a missionary at Lambaréné during Schweitzer's first years there. Schweitzer asked the father's name and then, upon hearing it, exclaimed happily, "Of course I remember the missionary!" The man's wife joined them, and for a few minutes the three talked together in high excitement; Schweitzer was plainly delighted to see someone who, as he said, "belonged to Lambaréné." He told the couple that he missed his hospital. "I'm needed there," he said.

"You ought to stay with us now, doctor," the woman said. "You're needed here, too."

Schweitzer shook his head. "No, no," he said. "I've got to go back."

Mme Martin came up and announced that it was time to go home. Schweitzer shook hands with the couple, and then he walked down the dirt road. The sun had set and the sky was a mass of color. Schweitzer stood for a moment looking west and said the sky reminded him of Africa, where darkness comes quickly. "At this hour, I would make my last rounds of the wards."

We were only a few steps from Schweitzer's house when a large bus came by, filled with tourists. Schweitzer quickened his pace, but it was no use. The tourists had seen him. The driver stopped the bus, and the passengers rushed out, armed with cameras and asking for his autograph. Mme Martin tried to hurry him into the house, but he shook his head and said, "No, no, leave them alone. It doesn't matter." A second bus came up and stopped, and more people sprang out. The tourists pleaded with Schweitzer—please sign here, please smile, please look this way—and he stood helpless and amiable, unable to say no. Only when a guide with a megaphone stepped out of the second bus shouted *"Mesdames et Messieurs, le grand Docteur Albert Schweitzer!"* did he show any irritation; he shook his head and said, "No, no, not that!" He asked me if the car parked in front of his house was mine. I nodded. "Let's get into it," he said. "Get me away from here."

I slid behind the wheel, Schweitzer slipped agilely in on the other side, and we drove off. He laughed at the way he'd outwitted the guide, and then he turned around and waved to the tourists. "I should have stayed," he said regretfully. "But too much is too much."

Down the road we saw the man with the blue beret and his wife trudging along, and Schweitzer asked me to pull up beside them. They were on their way home. Schweitzer turned to me. Their village was not far from Colmar, he said; it would mean only a short detour. Would I drive them home? I said, "Of course." Schweitzer smiled, got out of the car, and helped the woman in. "Now I must really go," he said. "No long good-byes." And he was off.

Preferred Places

THE BOIS DE BOULOGNE

ON A RECENT SATURDAY AFTERNOON, as I walked in the Bois de Boulogne, it seemed that Paris hadn't changed at all since I first came here almost fifty years ago. To be sure, the elegant carriages of yesteryear had disappeared, as had the Hispano-Suizas and Panhard & Levassors. Now there are other automobiles, hundreds of them, and not always elegant ones. That day everybody with a car had come to spend the shining afternoon in the Bois. But the ambiance was as Parisian as ever: families having a picnic with wine on the meadows; children playing; fragile old ladies walking under the trees, sometimes escorted by elderly gentlemen proudly wearing their Légion d'Honneur; and couples in rowboats on the lakes. At the Jardin d'Acclimatation, happy youngsters with their happier fathers rode the narrow-gage railroad. Nearby, people watched the men playing *boules* (lawn bowling). The Bois is very large, well over two thousand acres, and the wise Parisians have left it what it always was, a natural forest that now happens to be in the middle of a very large metropolis. The city is crowded, noisy, and polluted, but the forest is still unspoiled and often very beautiful.

The best route to take to enter the Bois is via the Etoile and down the Avenue Foch, once known as the Avenue de l'Impératrice, and, after a period as the Avenue du Bois-de-Boulogne, renamed in honor of Maréchal Foch upon his death in 1929. A masterpiece of Baron Georges Haussmann, it remains one of the most beautiful avenues in Paris, a hundred and twenty meters wide and bordered on each side by a strip of lawn with beautiful flowers and trees. Running parallel to the avenue is a *contre-allée*. Under the Etoile end is the largest subterranean parking lot in Paris. The grand private residences and embassies, the fine apartment houses and well-kept gardens still make the Avenue Foch a good address in the capital. The Porte Dauphine, at its far end, is dominated by a modern, A-shaped building that was to have been the headquarters of the North Atlantic Treaty Organization. After De Gaulle threw NATO out of Paris, the Université de Paris installed some of its far-flung facilities here.

Across the road, at the entrance to the Bois itself, is a large sign further proving that some things do change after all, even in the Bois. It says, "The Bois de Boulogne is a place of promenade placed under the *sauve-garde* (protection) of the public," and goes on:

> The Bois is reserved essentially for children and *promeneurs;* for pedestrians, cyclists and horseback riders. Motorists—it is specially forbidden to park on the lawns, in the undergrowth, and on narrow and winding roads, even on the shoulders. Drive slowly; Speed limit: 45 and 60 kilometers an hour, depending on the road.

Actually people leave their cars everywhere, even on narrow and winding roads, and sometimes they drive very fast. Pedestrians are advised to be careful when crossing. An afternoon in the Bois de Boulogne can tell you more about the French than a seminar at the Sorbonne.

Parisians take the Bois for granted, like the Eiffel Tower and the Métro, the *grands boulevards,* and the Place de la Concorde. Many citizens know something about the history of the Louvre and the Tuileries, but few know that as early as the sixth century, during the Merovingian era, the Forest of Rouvre (named after the *chêne-rouvre,* a species of oak one sees everywhere in the Bois) was part of a vast wooded area that included the modern forests of Meudon, Montmorency, and Saint-Germain-en-Laye. It was four times as large as the present Bois and was the preserve of hunters seeking bears, wolves, and wild boar.

The name of Bois de Boulogne has a curious history. In 1308 Philippe le Bel made a pilgrimage to Notre-Dame de Boulogne-sur-Mer on the Channel that must have been quite an excursion. After his safe return he built a replica of the Channel church at Les Menus, a tiny village in the forest, and called it Notre-Dame de Boulogne-le-Petit. Later the names of Les Menus and Rouvre were forgotten, and the forest became the "Bois de Boulogne." It belonged to the kings of France and was a favorite hiding place of brigands.

In 1556 Henri II had the Bois surrounded by a wall with several gates, among them the Porte Maillot and Port de la Muette. They are still there, though the walls have disappeared. In the seventeenth century, Colbert built rectilinear roads through the Crown's hunting preserve. They meet at certain crossroads, or *croix,* such as the Catelan. Today the forests of Meudon and Saint-Germain have similar roads. Gradually the Bois became the favorite promenade of Parisians, and Louis XIV opened it to the public. Not everybody went there for a promenade, however, and it was said, *"Les mariages du bois de Boulogne ne se font pas devant Monsieur le Curé"* (the marriages of the Bois are not contracted before a priest). During the Regency the Bois became the favorite rendezvous of the Four Hundred and beautiful mansions were built in it, among them the châteaux de Madrid and de la Muette, the Bagatelle, and the Folie Saint-James.

Come the French Revolution, the Bois harbored the now hunted Four Hundred, assorted "enemies of the people," and many untitled poachers. When British and Russian soldiers camped in the Bois in 1815, they did such damage that parts of the forests had to be razed. Those areas were later replanted with chestnut trees, acacias, and sycamores, which have brighter foliage than the old oak trees. The beautiful mixture of leaves now gives the Bois its unique character and dappled light.

The "modern" Bois was created by Emperor Napoleon III. Having learned a few lessons from history, he ceded the Bois to the City of Paris in 1852, on the condition that the city spend two million gold francs in the following four years to embellish the park. Baron Haussmann, the great city planner of the Second Empire, and his staff, did exactly that. The walls around the park were removed, and the forest was transformed into a large English-style park. That was no accident; Napoleon had much admired Hyde Park during his exile in London.

The many straight roads were replaced with more inviting, curved walkways. Ninety-five kilometers of new promenades, two artifical lakes, and several ponds were created. To fill them, water was brought from an artesian well in Passy that had been dug under the supervision of the Engineer Adolphe Alphand of the Corps des Pontes et Chaussées. Restaurants and chalets were built, and the racetrack at Longchamp was constructed. It remains one of the best-known courses on earth.

After the Avenue de l'Impératrice was inaugurated in 1854, the Bois became the favorite rendezvous of *le Tout-Paris,* as one would say today. Rich people rode there in their fancy equipages, and poor ones stood along the avenue, gazing in admiration and envy. Some went to the Jardin d'Acclimatation and Pré Catelan, popular amusement parks. In 1870, just before the siege of Paris, the steeplechase racecourse at Auteuil was opened at the southeastern corner of the Bois. More recently, when the Boulevard Périphérique was built as a new belt highway around Paris, part of it ran within the eastern boundary of the Bois, which caused much anguish among park enthusiasts. So did the construction of the new stadium at Parc des Princes and the creation of the Jardin Fleuriste, the municipal nursery, which contains the largest collection of plants and flowers in the capital. Budding plants are grown there and taken later to the various municipal parks; flowers for receptions are also bred there. Among the Jardin Fleuriste's special attractions are a *jardin à la française,* a fine assortment of tropical and exotic flowers, and special expositions of azaleas in April and chrysanthemums in late October.

The local authorities know, however, that the Bois is sacred territory to many. The new superhighway A-13 from the Saint-Cloud tunnel to the Porte d'Auteuil will draw much motorized traffic away from Périphérique; the Bois can remain a refuge.

During the week, especially in the morning, the Bois is often tranquil, frequented mainly by residents of the nearby sixteenth *arrondissement* or the western outskirts of Neuilly and Boulogne. Many stroll or drive in the park. The main roads and alleys are paved, but the byways are still soft, covered with needles, leaves, or moss. Parents take their children there to discover the superb pleasure of quietly walking under the trees. There are Parisians who know the Bois as intimately as many Viennese know, the hills, valleys, meadows and marked paths of their Vienna Woods, or as some New Yorkers know Central Park.

Experts agree with the green *Guide Michelin* that it would take "several days" to walk through the large park. Most strollers especially like the "wild" parts that appear as they must have centuries ago, some of the great attractions of the Bois. Others keep close to the lakes and flower gardens, the cafes and amusement areas. Tourists in Paris rarely spend much time in the Bois because there is so much to do and see elsewhere. But on a sunny day it's nice to spend a few hours there, walking at random and finally visiting certain spots, according to one's special interests. The Bois really offers something memorable for just about everyone.

Though I was often in Paris, it had never occurred to me to investigate the great park. I might ride through it in a taxi on my way to the suburbs to visit friends, but I never stopped. In the 1920s, when I lived in Paris as a student and musician, I sometimes went to the Stade Roland-Garros, the mecca of French tennis players, near the Porte d'Auteuil. There, in 1927, I watched the "four musketeers"—Cochet, Lacoste, Borotra, and Brugnon—win the Davis Cup against the Americans, Tilden, Williams, Johnston, and Hunter. I couldn't afford a ticket and climbed over the fence to find myself face-to-face with a *gardien*. I said I hoped the French would win and gave him five francs; he smiled and said, "Yes, that's the light that shines day and night." He put the money in his pocket, and we shook hands. How right he was! The light is still shining. Everywhere.

Thus it was with a genuine sense of anticipation that I entered the Bois recently via the Porte Dauphine. As I no longer drive, I had hired a car driven by Mac, whom Alfred, the chief concierge at the Hôtel Lancaster, called "the man who knows the Bois." As always, Alfred was right. Mac, a Frenchman, looks like a cross between Rex Harrison and Fernandel (which is better than it sounds). His comments often are subtly ironic and always to the point. He knows astonishing bits of random information and once quoted the sarcastic epitaph that Cardinal Richelieu had written for his own tomb, more or less what Mayor La Guardia expressed with the words, "When I make a mistake, it's a beaut."

Like many Frenchmen, Mac rarely does anything strictly illegal, like going through a red light, but often something he calls "half-illegal," like parking "on narrow and winding roads." He said that *pour faire le Bois*, one needs a sense of organization, and he started by going down the Route de Suresnes, which took us to the northern tip of the Lac Inférieur, a very popular spot. At the *embarcadère des canots* (the boat landing) people rent rowboats, and there is a small ferry to the island in the middle of the lake. That day the Lac Inferieur and the smaller Lac Supérieur were a happy panorama of rowboats and small sailboats that had the quality of an Impressionist painting.

We passed the exclusive Racing Club de France ("very chic if you are that sort of person," said Mac) and reached the Pré Catelan, a beautifully kept, smaller park within the Bois. There are playgrounds for children and the Jardin Shakespeare with an alfresco theater presenting the plants and flowers mentioned in the works of the Bard. (There are guided tours at 11:00 in the morning and at 1:30, 3:00, and 5:30 in the afternoon.) But the great attraction of the Pré Catelan is the almost two-hundred-year-old beech tree whose boughs are said to have the largest spread of any tree in Paris, covering a surface of 650 square yards. It's really very impressive. Yet there are other fine things at the Pré Catelan, especially the well-kept *pelouses*, carefully groomed super-lawns. Even if you are not that sort of person, you will like the Pré Catelan and its atmosphere.

Next, Mac took me to the polo grounds, where we admired the nervous small horses rather more than the players. Mac said it was all right to walk around for a while, "but let's not stay too long or some *type* may ask us what we are doing here." He indicated that the Bois was a democracy, *bien sûr,* but some spots perhaps were less democratic than others. So we rode to the very democratic *terrains de sports,* geographically outside the Bois but spiritually part of it. Groups of young people were playing soccer, rugby, and other games. Almost all wore the uniforms of their teams. When the French try to emulate the British, they often try too hard, whether it's with Savile Row, Scotch whiskey, or sports.

We went onto the Parc de Bagatelle, which turned out to be one of the best things in the Bois. The history of the Bagatelle (Mac defined the word as *"une chose frivole,"* of little importance) began in 1720 when the Maréchal d'Estrées built a small house there for his wife. In 1775 the Comte d'Artois, later King Charles X, bought the house, which, by then, was very run-down, whereupon his sister-in-law, Marie-Antoinette, teased him about his purchase. The Comte got mad and said, "Want to bet that I'll have a new house built here in less than three months?" It sounded absurd, but he won. The noted French architect François Bélanger designed the plans in twenty-four hours, and the house was completed within sixty-four days. They couldn't do it today. Thomas Blaikie, the well-known English gardener, designed the grounds in the style of the Parc Monceau.

The Parc de Bagatelle was saved from willful destruction during the Revolution when it was declared "a place of pleasure for the people." Napoleon knew a good thing when he saw it. In 1806, he took possession of Bagatelle with the idea of making a palace in it for his son, the appointed King of Rome. But history intervened, and the palace was never built. During the Restoration, the Parc de Bagatelle became the property of Charles, Duc de Berry. The last private owner was Sir Richard Wallace, an Englishman, who loved Paris and donated several fountains to the Bois. In 1905, the City of Paris bought Bagatelle from his heirs and made it semiprivate. One buys a ticket (one franc) to get in, which seems to keep out many people who don't like to spend one franc on a park (though they don't mind spending it on wine or gasoline—even on wine that tastes a little of gasoline). Actually, the visit is worth much more. There is the Petit Château Trianon with a fine *cour d'honneur,* and, above all, magnificent flower landscapes: the Miroir Japonais, the Orangerie, the Parterre Francais, the Jardin des Iris. All spring, one sees brilliantly colored crocuses and tulips, and beginning in June, there are many varieties of wonderful roses. Bagatelle is a sanctuary for people in quest of peace and privacy. I strongly urge you to go there, and one franc be damned.

If you prefer crowds and fun rather than peace and privacy, you'll find, at no extra cost, lots of people on the meadows near the Seine: city dwellers who, though it may be cold and rainy, immediately lie down on the grass. It's a good thing the Bois is no longer a preserve of the chic and the rich. Everybody goes there, especially people living in crowded districts of the capital. All over the *pelouse* there are families with picnic hampers, forming small islands, keeping to themselves, as in their homes. They would keep the shutters closed if they could bring them along. Only the children, blissfully innocent, break out of the small enclosures and run all over the lawn, looking like spring flowers in their bright clothes. There are young people in love (but they would never carry on the way they sometimes do in the parks of London) and old ladies enjoying the sunshine and busily knitting. It's all very French, very nice.

At the Jardin d'Acclimatation there are many attractions: the *jardin zoologique,* the swimming pool, and rides *pour les enfants.* For the grownups there is the Musée National des Arts et Traditions Populaires, where one may study "the daily life of traditional French society." The Galerie d'Etude offers large collections of costumes, agricultural tools, and pictures of the games played in rural France before the Industrial Revolution. (The museum is open daily except on Tuesdays, from 10:00 to 12:30 and from 2:00 to 5:00.)

Mac stopped the car at the edge of a small forest and pointed out a small brook. During the liberation of Paris in August 1944, he and his buddies in Maréchal Leclerc's Second Armored Division had spent seventeen days camping right there. "We had come into Paris by way of the

Boulevard Saint-Michel. There were a few *bagarres* (skirmishes), and eventually we reached the Palace de la République. I suppose they didn't know what to do with us, and we wound up here in the Bois. It wasn't as comfortable as the Ritz, but, believe me, we were happy to be back in Paris."

At a nearby clearing there were several *pétanque* games going. A sign at the upper end of the Avenue Foch states that it is forbidden to play *boules* and other games in the Bois, so the champions and their fans have moved to the edge of the Bois where the police seem to practice benign neglect. There was much excitement, with many bets and side bets; I was surprised at the large number of elderly women among the spectators. Mac said the best players are professionals who make good money and are much respected, because *boules* is an honest game. No one even tries to cheat; it's a matter of honor and skill. In summertime the games sometimes go on until two in the morning.

This part of the Bois is well lit. People who love the Bois indignantly deny stories that the park is not quite safe anymore after dark, but many admit, reluctantly, that it wouldn't be "prudent" to walk off the main roads into the dark woods. "It isn't as bad as Central Park at night," a Parisian who spends part of the year in Manhattan told me, "but I wouldn't advise you to get out of your car at night and into the trees, looking for company. The police have warned the population about the girls in the park, or rather about their 'protectors.' You'll find yourself minus watch and wallet."

There are several restaurants in the Bois, some of them chic and expensive: Le Pré Catelan, Le Pavillon Royal, the Pavillon des Princes, the Pavillon Dauphine. The best of them, gastronomically and architecturally, is La Grande Cascade at the Carrefour de Longchamp, where several roads meet. The restaurant is named after the nearby forty-foot-high waterfall, created in 1854 by Monsieur Alphand, the aforementioned engineer and miracle-maker. Hollywood during the 1930s (now wistfully remembered as the Golden Age) often made comedies set in Paris. Usually the would-be seducer would take the (virtuous) heroine for supper to Maxim's, or, rather, to a studio-made replica. The famous Belle Epoque restaurant was considered a real test of a girl's virtue. The film directors in Paris, who were somewhat more in touch with reality, would film similar sequences at lunchtime in the Bois de Boulogne, often at La Grande Cascade, built for Napoleon III, ostensibly as a private hunting pavilion, an authentic Second Empire jewel. But what would the Emperor hunt in the Bois? A delicate question that was much discussed by gossips in Paris, but it was generally agreed that the *pavillon de chasse* (hunting box) was the right place for the Emperor's very private hunts. A noted Paris historian tells me that there is surprisingly little known about the Bois then and now, "except the sort of story you read in police reports."

Fortunately the hunting pavilion survived the end of the Second Empire and the siege of Paris. In 1900, at the time of the Paris World's Fair, the French sensibly turned the pavilion into a restaurant. It is a rare specimen of a sumptuous style much admired nowadays, with its fine wrought-iron structure, glass roof, and gilt paint, with its blue silk-velvet curtains and candelabra-like lights, and with its large windows giving a fine view of the Bois. André Menut, the present proprietor, bought the place in 1964 and, at considerable expense, keeps it in impeccable shape. Nothing is changed. Monsieur Menut once worked for the great Jean Drouant, whose restaurant, in the Place Gaillon, is famous for its fish dishes and the annual *déjeuner* of the jury awarding the Prix Goncourt, the most prestigious among the too-many literary prizes in France. M. Menut knows that "the best guarantee of profitability is to give a place a certain style, fine food and good wines, and very good service, and then the customers will come back and bring their friends."

The formula has worked well. La Grande Cascade is open all year except from mid-December to mid-January, though only lunch is served during the winter months, when the Bois is often deserted. But last December even on bad days the restaurant always had at least fifty people for lunch. During the warm months lunch and dinner are served in the dining rooms and on the *terrasse fleurie*. On weekdays high-powered executives come out for lunch. M. Menut says, "It's easier to discuss difficult business problems when one feels surrounded by beauty and flowers, tranquility and good food."

There were no executives discussing business deals when we had *déjeuner* at La Grande Cascade on a Sunday. The atmosphere was *famille* and very French: small and large families with children and sometimes the small children of the grown-up children. Everybody seemed to be right at home, studying the large menu without bothering to look at the prices. Just as well. At La Grande Cascade it's easy to spend a hundred francs per person. Later M. Menut told me that some of the clients owned racehorses and would be at Auteuil in the afternoon in time for the first race. Somehow M. Menut has managed to keep La Grande Cascade as a restaurant where food, wines, and service are important. In the later afternoon and at night there are often large private receptions in the main dining room, called the Salon Napoléon III, and in the smaller Salon Bagatelle and Salon Saint-Cloud. Two intimate salons, Auteuil and Longchamp, are on the second floor.

"This afternoon we have a wedding reception for three hundred people," said M. Menut. "Caviar, *saumon fumé*, lobster, all that is needed. If the marriage works out as well as the reception, it should be a success."

M. Menut also owns the restaurant Garnier, across the Gare Saint-Lazare, which is well known in the quarter for its good fish and *fruits de mer* at relatively popular prices. La Grande Cascade offers a little of everything, but the emphasis is on the seafood. Lobster and *langouste* (spiny lobster) any way you like them, oysters and mussels, and clams and cockles and *oursins* (sea urchins). Fine specialties: *suprême de Saint-Pierre à l'oseille* (filet of John Dory with sorrel), *daurade rosé en papillote* (sea bream *en papillote*), and *sole soufflée en corail d'oursins* (sole with sea urchin coral). We had something one should order only in the very best fish restaurants, *turbotin grillé aux aromates* (grilled small turbot with herbs). Escoffier classes *turbotin* "among the most delicate fish." We were told we would have to wait fifty minutes, but the turbotin proved well worth it. It was grilled *à point*, deliciously flavored with herbs. Beautifully fresh, it had no need for a sauce, though two were served on the side. Later we were told by M. Menut that it had been caught the night before and had arrived in Paris only that morning. Earlier, we'd had the *salade Longchamp*, a *spécialité* of the house: thin slices of raw mushrooms and just-cooked thin green beans with a very light dressing of oil and vinegar. M. Emile Tabourdiau, the chef, certainly knows his business. He is from Anjou and worked at L'Escargot-Montorgueil and Ledoyen before he came to La Grande Cascade. The people at the neighboring table had a fine *selle d'agneau farcie au poivre vert* (saddle of lamb stuffed with green peppercorns) with *pommes sarladaises* (potatoes with truffles). They looked as though they owned a racehorse. I am not a dessert man, but the *pêches blanches des vergers de*

Gascogne flambées (flamed white peaches) looked nice, if you are the sort of person for whom a meal without dessert is *zéro*.

The wines were carefully selected and their prices rather low: a Charmes-Chambertin '53 (120 francs), a Château l'Angélus '69 (100 francs), a Château Cheval-Blanc '66 (300 francs, one of the finest, most expensive bottles, and worth every franc). But the sommelier encouraged us to have just half a bottle of 1971 Chiroubles, the *vin du patron,* for only seventeen francs. "Why shouldn't you have red wine if you like it?" he said, even though we'd ordered fish. It's that kind of place, proof that, contrary to widespread opinion, you can eat well in the Bois de Boulogne—even if you don't own a racehorse.

VIENNA

An Introduction

ONLY AFTER LIVING IN VIENNA for a long time can one begin to understand why the Viennese seem so often unable to separate reality from legend and truth from make-believe. The Viennese are essentially a baroque people. For over three hundred years, "baroque" has been a way of life in this city. In art, the term was originally used by critics as an expression of disapproval, to describe works of art that failed to conform to the "classical" standards of beauty. "Baroque" meant something elaborate and theatrical, grotesque and extravagant, bizarre and flamboyant. An imperfectly shaped pearl, for instance, was classified *barroco* by Spanish jewelers. After 1600, "baroque" came to describe a cultural epoch, the period following the Counter-Reformation. By the end of the century, the threats of Protestantism and of Turkish aggression, present for over two hundred years, had gone. Men were jubilant, yet humbly and gratefully aware of God's omnipotence. The contradiction was outwardly resolved by baroque exuberance. "Vienna reached its cultural zenith during the baroque, and remained baroque in its strangest and finest expressions of life," wrote Egon Friedell, himself a baroque mixture of philosopher, essayist, actor, and cultural historian.

Beginning, then, as an architectural style, baroque was later to influence all the other arts, finally to become a state of mind. There was baroque music, furniture, weapons, and interiors—even baroque coffins. The Empress Maria Theresa and her consort, Franz of Lorraine, are buried in sarcophagi with beautiful baroque ornamentation. The baroque appealed to the sensuous love of the Viennese for beauty and gracefulness and to their perennial infatuation with drama and music. Emperor Leopold I (1640–1705) remains the most popular Habsburg ruler of the baroque era because he loved music and was an able composer—ninety-seven pieces of church music, nine "theatrical festivities," one hundred and two dances, and a requiem for his wife performed also during his own funeral. Legend says that when he felt death approaching, he ordered his *Hofkapelle,* the Imperial Orchestra (founded in 1496 by Emperor Maximilian and thus the predecessor of the Vienna Philharmonic), to perform his favorite pieces in an adjoining hall, whereupon he died at peace. A great many Viennese would like to depart that way.

"The whole world is a giant theater," wrote the Hamburg critic Johann Mattheson in 1728. Life to the Viennese is nothing but a play. They often will tailor reality to fit their imagination. The playwright and critic, Hermann Bahr, a shrewd observer of the Viennese character, once said that for the Viennese life began at the theater. They think of their city as a vast stage where everybody performs a part while watching his own and others' performances. The Viennese is a born character actor who performs with considerable skill the part life has assigned him. Only foreigners are impressed by the polite manners of the Viennese. The natives know there is no conviction behind the charming smile. People fight, too, but are soon friends again—after all, they have only played a scene. In his verse play *Paracelsus,* Arthur Schnitzler wrote, "We all act parts, and wise is he who knows it." Schnitzler was the brilliant analyst of a decadent epoch of Vienna who transformed this disorganized portrayal of life into the sublime, bittersweet stage play where all the characters wore masks depicting themselves as well as their alter egos.

This baroque schizophrenia of the Viennese is the essence of their *Lebenskunst,* their way of life and their philosophy. In times of oppression and censorship, music and theater—the stage—are used to express the secret and true feelings of the people. When the prisoners in Beethoven's *Fidelio* sang their exciting "freedom" chorus for the first time, at the Theater an der Wien, on November 20, 1805, Vienna had recently been occupied by Napoleon, and French officers sat outraged in the auditorium. Later, in the *Vormärz* (pre-March) days, prior to the 1848 revolution, the theater once again became the mouthpiece for Vienna's poetic fighters for freedom. Unlike in Poland, Hungary, and Italy, no political leader inspired revolutionary feelings in Vienna; rather, it was the great satirical poet and playwright, Johann Nestroy, whose *Freiheit im Krähwinkel* was a typical Viennese mixture of wit, irony, and exultation ending in disenchantment. (One character in the play says, "Human beings start from baron upwards." This was not Nestroy's whim but an opinion often expressed by Austrian aristocrats at that time.) Again the stage was speaking the truth.

Life begins, and ends, at the theater. A Viennese will take nothing seriously—least of all himself. Since he performs only a part in a play, he experiences even disaster with a certain detachment. Nothing is really as bad as it seems; life may be hopeless but it is never serious. Many people have wondered what has made the Viennese the complex, fascinating, strange people they are. Franz Grillparzer, the great Austrian poet, playwright, and bitter, sardonic critic, created his characters from them, with all their contradictions. More recently, Helmut Qualtinger and Carl Merz let the Viennese look at "Herr Karl," the unprincipaled rascal with the irresistible charm. The Viennese have all met Herr Karl, the fellow who does not try to fight against an absurd fate but tries instead to outwit it by equally absurd means. No wonder. Their city has lived through an endless chain of disasters. Having had to learn the art of survival, a Viennese now considers himself a "born survivor." *Biegen, nicht brechen,* "Bend but do not break," is a popular Viennese saying.

Vienna is a romantic city—one of the last on earth. Its air vibrates with charm and sentiment, and often with mystery and a kind of despair. The poet Hugo von Hofmannsthal called Vienna "the wonderful, inexhaustibly magical city with its mysterious, soft, light-filled air." Here the haze is never harsh; even fog, that can be hostile and terrifying in the cold wet cities further north, is but a soft, friendly mist that seems to float along the banks of the Danube, to caress the green slopes of the hills. Climatically, Vienna may be a northern city; the heat is on in most houses for more than six months of the year. But emotionally it is a southern city. Gustav Mahler sensed it instinctively when a young *Kapellmeister* in cool Hamburg, missing the musical and *musiche* ("Muse-minded') warmth of Vienna while he waited for the call from "the god of the southern zones."

Vienna is a synthesis. The heroic and the *gemütlich,* the hidden and the ostentatious, the past and the present, the romantic and the modern are blended into a harmonious whole. Somehow the cheerless, gray streets of the ugly suburbs with their dark tenement houses and the noble baroque palaces and Gothic churches form a perfect composition, framed by the lovely hills of the Wienerwald. The city is surrounded by a permanent mist of clichés that obscure the outlines, but underneath the sugar coating of commercialized Vienna there is the genuine Vienna, not always so sweet. As in a well-mixed marzipan, the bitterness of the almonds rather than the sweetness of the sugar dominates the quality and the taste.

Vienna's very name inspires the imagination, excites the fantasy. *Ein gewisses Etwas,* "a certain something," seems to surround the sound of its name, creating magical associations. But this magic of Vienna is hard to define. Hofmannsthal wrote about Vienna's "magical air": "How beautiful is all this! How beautiful is beauty (*Wie schön ist Schönheit*)!" It is an improbable mixture of wistful charm and veiled eroticism. Long before Schnitzler—a doctor who understood the dark secrets of body and soul—dissected Vienna's sensuality, the town was notorious for its erotic passions. Hedonists called it heaven; moralists called it hell. Vienna's charm, a highly elusive element, is one of Austria's greatest hidden assets, though it never appears in the country's balance of payments.

The illogical German language, which distinguishes three sexes, makes "Wien" neuter (one says *"das* Wien"), but everybody who comes to Vienna feels it to be a very feminine city—capricious, charming, and utterly unreliable. It can be a dangerous city, *une ville fatale.* Detached, usually unemotional people have felt disturbing sensations as they walked down Ringstrasse on a mild evening in June. The scent of linden trees is very strong. An attractive woman I know, usually calm and composed, admits that the fragrance sometimes makes her *deppert;* in such a mood one might do something very foolish and later be unable to explain why.

She is not the only one. The Viennese mixture of scents—linden and lilac, jasmine and acacias—penetrates the skin, and, according to the poets, the heart and soul. The poets of Vienna are always searching for its "soul." All of them feel that Vienna *has* a soul though they cannot agree on where it is to be found: perhaps in the narrow streets of the old town, or between the trees in the Wienerwald (which, thanks to Johann Strauss, will always be known to the English as the "Vienna Woods"). Others find the soul of the city in the dreamy introduction to some of its great waltzes. But undoubtedly the soul is there, as is the Wienerwald, or the vineyards that form a tiara round the city's western outskirts.

The magic of Vienna catches you at unexpected moments. I once spent a summer afternoon in the Pfarrplatz (the church square) of Heiligenstadt, the western suburb where Vienna's migratory composer, Beethoven, came in 1802, and later in the summer of 1808, and then again in the spring of 1817, when he lived in a house near the baroque statue of Saint John Nepomuk. The afternoon of my visit there was an alfresco concert in the church square, a performance of Beethoven's Fifth and Sixth (Pastoral) Symphonies, two works that Beethoven had written there. In the brief pause between the second and third movements of the Pastoral, while a few violinists were furtively tuning their instruments, the birds were singing. An American friend and musician who was with me, a man blessed (and cursed) with absolute pitch, exclaimed softly, "Listen! They sing in tune!" He seemed flabbergasted, but I was not at all surprised. For not only were the birds singing in tune, so was the air around us, as was the ground on which we sat, and the façades of the old houses.

Sometimes this magic is purely visual—as when one is among the rose gardens in the Volksgarten. Here there are hundreds of varieties of roses, some very rare, all beautiful, each carrying a small wooden sign with the Latin name and the place of origin. In Vienna, blossom time lasts from early March until late November.

The magic is still alive in the dreamy suburban streets where the city dissolves into meadows, vineyards, and woods. The street names have bucolic sounds—Sommerheidenweg, Haubenbiglstrasse, Rohrerhüttenweg—and there is an idyllic mood in the sleepy squares that Moritz von Schwind, Schubert's friend, the Romanticist among Vienna's artists, caught accurately in his Biedermeier paintings. At the beginning of the nineteenth century, Vienna was still a town of garden palaces whose baroque façades artfully blended with the landscaped gardens, such as in the Palais Trautson or Schönborn. Later, the expanding metropolis devoured most of these gardens. Only the gardens of the Schwarzenberg Palais, the Belvedere, the Palais Starhemberg-Schönburg, and the Liechtenstein Palais have survived.

One of the most beautiful lies behind the Schwarzenberg Palais (and behind the tall monument of the Unknown Soviet Soldier, called "The Unknown Rapist" by the Viennese, pledged to remain there forever by an Austrian State Treaty of 1955). The German poet Joseph von Eichendorff sat there one day in June 1811, "on a concealed bench near the wall from where one looks onto the fields. Everything is lonely and quiet, only a few people are nearby, reading." The fields have become expensive building sites, but the garden is still loved by children playing their mysterious games and by old people in search of a place that is "lonely and quiet." For Vienna's public gardens are oases of tranquility in the heart of a hectic inner city. They are smaller, more intimate than the spacious parks of London or the carefully laid out pleasure grounds of Paris. As one steps from the noisy, traffic-jammed Ringstrasse into the Burggarten, one is transposed into a peaceful world where there are no screeching tires, no exhaust fumes. Trees look down upon a small lake, and children lie around the statue of Emperor Franz Joseph I. Young couples walk arm in arm in this beautiful garden. Here, it is easy to fall in love.

Oskar Kokoschka once reminisced about a "forbidden garden," separated by a high fence from the courtyard of the house where he lived as a child. The fence consisted of gilded lances with flashing bowls made of yellow, red, blue, and green glass that reflected even more colors as the sun went down. "At noon these burning reflections made our hearts sad, for the garden was forbidden territory for us children. At the beginning of autumn, the large soft lawn invited games, and the trees were heavy with fruit. But we were permitted to walk only in the courtyard, and behind the fence the garden kept its secrets, almost near enough to be grasped by our hands—making it more attractive, if that was possible."

From late spring until autumn, Vienna is a city of flowers. In front of Westbahnhof (the West Railroad Station) where most visitors arrive, they are welcomed by lovely flower beds. Several years ago the city arranged a magnificent flower show, with its gardeners transforming a former swampland near the Danube into a sort of Klingsor's magic garden. The show has long been closed, but the garden has remained and now makes life more bearable for the citizens of Vienna's drearier suburbs.

The magic of Vienna becomes more powerful as winter approaches, because most of the visitors and tourists have gone home. For a short time—which seems to get shorter every year—the town belongs to the Viennese. On these early winter afternoons a misty curtain of fog screens the noble decay of the Imperial city. The old districts, around Saint Stephen's, Freyung, and the Hofburg, are enveloped in silence and beauty and by a sense of timelessness. Soon, fresh snow will cover the scars that postwar poverty and the passage of time have inflicted upon the grandeur of the baroque palaces.

An old friend of mine, a retired *Hofrat* (court councilor), lives in a modest two-room apartment in the Leopoldine wing of the Imperial Palace. It is just below the richly ornamented rococo residence, with its Florentine mosaics and old tapestries, once inhabited by the Empress Maria Theresa, and now the official residence of Austria's federal president. It was provided, at a nominal rent, by the government, as a sort of consolation for his low pension. Other small apartments in the Hofburg were allocated to deserving opera singers, to influential bureaucrats, or to people "who know the right people." The *Hofrat*'s pension just enables him to pay his bills, buy some food, ride on the streetcar, and spend the afternoons at his favorite coffeehouse. He had to give up his subscription to the Philharmonic concerts, but once in a while he gets a free seat at the State Opera—where he knows the right people.

On early winter afternoons my friend loves to walk through the older parts of the inner city. He knows that "the best time of the year" has come, when saddle of venison and other game specialties appear in the better restaurants. He loves to study the menus displayed in framed glass cases next to the entrance. Sometimes he is tempted to enter, but then he remembers the business of tipping and walks on. In a Viennese restaurant, one seems obliged to tip not only the waiter who brings your food and the girl who brings your beer or wine, but also the "pay-waiter" (headwaiter) who writes your bill, the gnome called "piccolo" who brings your bread and rolls (they will appear on the bill), the hatcheck girl (usually a dignified lady in her late sixties), the cigarette girl (very pretty), the man who sells flowers, the fellow who plays on the piano (even if he is the owner), the doorman, who looks like a retired Bohemian admiral (and may well be), and the *Wagentürlaufmacher* (the man-who-opens-the-door-of-the-car). Karl Kraus, the Viennese satirist, once said that on the day of resurrection the first thing the Viennese will see is the outstretched hand of the *Sargdeckelaufmacher*, the man-who-opens-the-coffin-lid.

The *Hofrat* lost his savings four times in his life, considered "normal" in Vienna, but he does not think of this when he leaves for his regular afternoon walk, though the short distance from the Hofburg to the coffeehouse is filled with memories. He steps from his apartment into the inner courtyard, once the scene of the colorful mounting of the guard, always watched by "The Old Gentleman," Emperor Franz Joseph I, when he happened to be in town. The *Hofrat* likes to remember those good old days because what came afterwards were the bad old days. Now the guardhouse is empty and the courtyard has become a vast parking lot. The *Hofrat* walks through the pseudo-baroque gate built in 1890 on the site of the former Burgtheater; on some evenings the entrance is beautifully illuminated, and the *Hofrat* pauses briefly to look back. Now he is walking past Michaelerkirche where a requiem mass was read after his wife's death, years ago, and past Josefsplatz, Vienna's loveliest baroque square, with the magnificent façade of the National Library forming the backdrop. Alas, it is now another vast parking lot.

Nearby stands the old building where the *Hofrat* once had his office, with the dear and familiar sounds of cracking wooden floorboards, big white-tiled stoves, the musty smell of dust-covered files in the antechamber, where the "parties" were humbly waiting on him—citizens who needed the *Herr Hofrat*'s nod or his signature on an *Akt* (a file). The *Hofrat* dearly loved his files and kept them on his desk as long as possible before reluctantly affixing his signature and sending them on. He hated saying good-bye; a file signed was a file lost. The *Hofrat* talks about them in the same way that other people speak about their friends; the files seemed more alive to him than the "parties" they concerned.

On dark winter afternoons the local melancholy becomes as contagious as the common cold. Sometimes the streetlights have to be turned on soon after midday. In Vienna, streetlights are always turned on during state funerals, and on such a day people might ask hopefully whether anyone important had died, seeming somewhat disappointed to learn that it was just another dark winter afternoon.

We lived for years in the Thirteenth District, in Hietzing, where many houses have façades the color of egg yolk ("Schönbrun yellow"), indicating buildings that once belonged to the Imperial household. The old-fashioned gas lamps in our street took me back to my youth, when the teenage boys in my hometown used to hold spitting contests. One had to spit through a narrow hole in the lower rim of the lamp to blow out the gas flame. Healthy lungs and a careful aim were essential, and afterwards one might have to make a quick escape when the furious lamplighter or a policeman suddenly emerged out of the darkness.

I did not really enjoy this cold war that we boys were waging against the lamplighter, whom I secretly admired. He would walk through the streets at dusk, a lonely fellow, carrying his long stick on his shoulder, its end a flaming taper. The lamplighter would reach through the narrow hole and light the lamp. There would be a soft, muted explosion as the gas caught fire, and the mantle would begin to glow with a warm, soft light. The lamplighter has remained with me, a permanent association of my youth, as has the chimneysweep in his top hat, and the chestnut roaster at the windy street corner, who would snatch the hot chestnuts from the coals with his bare, blue hands, never burning his fingers—an astonishing feat I never tired of watching.

Alas, the lamps in our street were fitted with an automatic device that turned them on and off, and no lamplighter was needed. But on Saturday mornings a municipal employee, wearing a dark blue uniform without insignia of rank, would appear in the street, carrying a long ladder over his shoulder. He would lean the ladder against the lamp post, climb up, and carefully wipe the inside of the lamp with a clean cloth. Then he would get down again, take his ladder, and walk toward the next lamp. He was a quiet man with a Buster Keaton face, and he was surprised when I offered him an unopened bottle of wine at Christmas.

In Vienna one gives Christmas presents to many city employees, a habit, as so many others, imported from the *bakshish*-minded Balkans. Nowadays, most employees do not wait for their gifts but come to the house to collect them: the municipal garbage collectors, the street cleaners, the men working down in the sewers (they wear their rubber boots up to their thighs so that they cannot possibly be mistaken), the man who inquires every three months whether one has noticed "any rats, mice, or vermin" in the house. (The Viennese have remained rat-conscious since the Great Plague of 1679 that killed seventy thousand people.) Even the traffic policemen at certain intersections get beautifully wrapped wine bottles and other small gifts. The motorists know that a certain policeman is on duty at a certain intersection, and they hope he will be lenient when they make a wrong turn or pass through an amber light. The policeman knows that the wine bottle is a down-payment for favors to be returned later on—in fact, a bribe—but he considers it "acceptable" and places the bottle on the small heap of gifts in the middle of the street, saluting with his right hand while he keeps directing traffic with his left. Many of Vienna's traffic policemen are would-be Karajans conducting their symphony of horsepower. They give a cue to every car, creating forte and piano effects, silencing a noisy

Volkswagen with two fingers of the left hand, building up a black Mercedes with a very low number on its license plate (probably someone "important"), and providing stunning feats of traffic harmony. Foreigners often stand, in admiration, at the curb watching the policeman's performance. Some traffic conductors actually find time to greet each driver as he passes. One man, an imitator of the late Toscanini, would hold his right hand in a characteristic gesture in front of his chest, imploring the driver to proceed with more feeling. Years ago, when one of these popular traffic maestros was hit by a car and had to be taken to the hospital, his grateful admirers made a collection and presented him with a small car. Eventually his competitors and superiors got so irked by his popularity that they exiled him to the suburbs—more or less what happened to Karajan when he got too popular in Vienna.

My lamp cleaner, though, was surprised when I gave him the bottle of wine. He said he did not "rate" a gift. I did not tell him it was too late to give it to the lamplighter of my youth whom we had so infuriated. Later, the lamp cleaner would often come in for a chat. He was dedicated to his job. He did not aspire to be the mayor of Vienna or to become a millionaire, but he did want to be the finest lamp cleaner in Hietzing. He knew very well that his days were numbered. Progress was inexorable. Soon the modern lamps would be reaching our street, driving out the old gas lamps and the lamp cleaner. And one day they did.

On Christmas Eve Vienna becomes a silent city. Mariahilferstrasse, the big shopping street, remains a fairyland boulevard under its canopy of colored lanterns, bells, and emblems, but the lights in the shop windows are turned off, the cinema marquees are dark, and the side streets are deserted. In this Roman Catholic city, everything is closed on this holy night, including the restaurants, cafeterias, and coffeehouses. Even the "ladies," who ply patiently up and down the Kärntnerstrasse, have gone home for the evening (though one wonders what "home" means for them), and the State Opera is closed. Behind the windows are beautifully lighted trees, and one thinks of the people opening their presents. And there are burning candles in many, many windows, put there by people who lost someone "in the war," which in Vienna means both world wars. Around midnight, the streets become alive again with people going to their favorite church for midnight Mass.

A Catholic friend from Germany feels that Vienna's churches are "friendlier and happier" than the austere cathedrals of Germany. They also seem less severe than the cool dark churches of Italy or Spain where the women go to pray before breakfast for strength to see them through the working day. The Viennese step into their favorite church casually, as into their favorite pastry shop, for light spiritual refreshment. Everybody has "his" church, and "his" delicatessen, and "his" coffeehouse, and "his" hairdresser. "Here one owns everything," the Viennese say.

Perhaps the only cathedral in Vienna that no one claims to own is Saint Stephen's, though nearly everybody goes there once in a while. Vienna's oldest church is Saint Ruprecht's, a merry, intimate church in Romanesque style. Nearby is Sankt-Maria-am-Gestade, a fourteenth-century church with a seven-sided Gothic tower crowned by a small cupola, once the church of poor fishermen and later of the Czech population in Vienna. My own favorite is Minoritenkrche, which has a fine Gothic portal and is very warm and cozy with its profusion of old wood. Two nearby churches have an austere, forbidding touch—Augustiner-kirche near the Hofburg, the scene of many great weddings, and Michaelerkirche, solemn and dark, with candles burning at side altars, not exactly a place for easygoing sinners. But as you step out of the gloom, you see the elegant five-story building with the gold-lettered name above the entrance, flanked by three gold medals on each side: Demel's.

New Year's Eve, too, has its strict ritual in Vienna. The State Opera puts on a gala performance of Johann Strauss's *Die Fledermaus*. Everybody waits impatiently for the third act when Frosch, the jailer, makes topical jokes, which are sure to bring down the house. On this night only, Frosch enjoys *Narrenfreiheit*, a fool's immunity. He may, and does, attack sacrosanct institutions and sacred cows; anything goes. Recently, Austria's federal president and the cardinal archbishop of Vienna, representing the country's worldly and spiritual powers, sat in opposite boxes and laughed at this impertinent jailer; during the intermission they toasted each other with a glass of champagne.

Across the Ringstrasse, meanwhile, the waltzes of Johann Strauss are played at the New Year's concert of the Vienna Philharmonic. The pleasant ritual was introduced after the last war by the late Clemens Krauss, the elegant conductor and opera director. Viennese born and bred, and a former member of the Wiener Sängerknaben (the Vienna Boys'

Choir), he understood the musical soul of his city, where New Year would *not* be New Year without Johann Strauss. The Philharmoniker plays the great Strauss waltzes with warmth and sentiment, brio and buoyancy, and always with impeccable taste. Since Clemens Krauss's death, the concert is conducted by Willi Boskovsky, the orchestra's first concertmaster, also a true Viennese, who mounts the conductor's platform, fiddle and bow in hand, wearing the striped pants, patterned waistcoat, and morning coat typical of the time of Johann Stauss. Boskovsky conducts with his bow, but occasionally he will put his violin to his chin and play a beautiful solo melody. Everybody smiles happily, the old ladies behind their tears; their mothers had known Johann Strauss and had told them about the great Hofballmusikdirektor, the genius who wrote some of his finest waltzes in the morning, rehearsed them in the afternoon, and premiered them at night. And dear Willi Boskovsky looks and acts *exactly* like Strauss, swaying with the rhythm, holding the fiddle high and closing his eyes, as he loses himself in one of the immortal melodies. "How beautiful is beauty!"

I doubt whether Johann Strauss and his musicians played the waltzes as beautifully as Boskovsky and the Philharmoniker perform them in this age of musical precision—with subtle *ritardandi* and sudden changes of mood, with that ever-so-slight accent, after an inaudible pause on the second beat, which distinguishes a real Viennese waltz player from his imitator. Some horseplay is added, when the third percussion player dresses up in the mask of Johann Strauss to present Boskovsky with a golden wreath, or puts on a hunter's hat and fires off a couple of shots during the "Hunt Polka." The concert always ends with encores, followed by the encore's encore, "The Blue Danube." By this time some people are quietly crying. Others seem on the verge of jumping up and dancing in the aisles.

Like politicians shaking hands again in front of the camera for the benefit of reporters and readers, the Philharmoniker nowadays plays the *Neujahrskonzert* twice—on New Year's Eve for the Viennese, and the following morning for the largest television audience in the history of Eurovision (Western Europe) and Intervision (Eastern Europe). Last year it was planned to transmit the concert "live" via Telstar to America, but the time difference made this impossible. Still, an estimated four hundred million viewers saw Strauss-Boskovsky and the Vienna State Opera ballet. Somehow the elaborate showmanship did not kill the spirit of Johann Strauss. Perhaps it cannot be killed.

Like the city itself, all Viennese music has haunting undertones of sadness and sorrow. Even Haydn, the most optimistic of Vienna's great composers, had his melancholy moments. "For quite some time now I have had days of depression without really knowing why…," he wrote in 1791 to Mme Luigia Polzelli, his great friend. The sounds of sorrow are audible in almost every major Mozart opus; the tears and the smile are there both in his great G-minor String Quintet (which he wrote after the death of his father), and in his G-minor Symphony. The G-minor key expresses Vienna's ever present mixture of gaiety and sadness, euphoria and gloom, cheerfulness and resignation: Vienna seems a city in G-minor.

The most Viennese of all composers, Schubert and Johann Strauss, always blend lightheartedness and melancholy. Some of Schubert's finest songs are also his saddest; his "Heidenröslein" (after Goethe's "Sah ein Knab' ein Röslein steh'n") is so moving and beautiful that it has become an "anonymous" folk song. Johann Strauss begins some of his most exhilarating waltzes with a dreamy introduction and ends, in the coda, with a plaintive, wistful echo. Strauss well understood that the Viennese are not happy because something nice has happened to them—but in spite of it. For centuries, Vienna's favorite communal pastime has been *Raunzen*—a cheerful, paradoxical form of complaining often misunderstood by non-Viennese. In 1906 Hermann Bahr wrote, "The Viennese is unhappy about himself, hates his fellows but cannot live without them. He has no respect for but is often moved by himself. He gripes all the time, but wants to be praised all the time. He is unhappy—and happy to be unhappy."

The Viennese does gripe about Vienna, but he loves his city dearly. He finds everything wrong with it, yet he would never live elsewhere. He remains a loyal member of the family; though he himself is very critical of the family, he can get very angry with any outsider who expresses criticism. Any attempt to change the Viennese way of life is met with outright hostility. Robert Musil, the great Austrian novelist, whose gift for universality has been compared to Proust and Joyce, writes in his brilliant, satirical novel, *The Man Without Qualities:*

For it was not only dislike of one's fellow-citizens that was intensified into a strong sense of community; even mistrust of oneself and of one's destiny here assumed the character of profound self-certainty. In this country one acted—sometimes indeed to the extreme limits of passion and its consequences—differently from the way one thought, and one thought differently from the way one acted. Uninformed observers have mistaken this for charm, or even for a weakness in what they thought was the Austrian character.

What makes the Viennese such complex, contradictory people? The question has puzzled Vienna's satirists and moralists, writers and poets for over three hundred years, ever since an eighteen-year-old Augustinian friar, Abraham a Sancta Clara, came to Vienna from Swabia in 1662 to become the city's conscience and its greatest Catholic preacher. Like many "imported" citizens, he became more Viennese than the natives, knew them well, and wondered about them. In his rough rhymes and robust homilies, he preached against their sensuous enjoyment of leisure, their distrust for authority, their tendency toward muddling through, their occasional displays of courage and frequent displays of fickleness, their aversion to facing cold facts. Looking for the truth, Abraham a Sancta Clara found

> false talk, false writing, false coins, false wines, false gold, false silver, false flowers, false jewelry, false hair, false faces, false friends—yes, the whole world is false.... The portal of the church looks as if it were made of the finest Salzburg marble but it is only plaster made to look like marble.... The women are as beautiful as a bride but nothing is genuine about them—neither their hair, nor their pearls, nor their clothes, nor their teeth, not even their undershirt.

The outbreak of the 1679 plague had been preceded by "ringing trumpets and music resounding everywhere, making a noise as though a hole had opened in the sky," as Pater Abraham writes in *Mercks Wien* ("Take Notice, Vienna!"). But when the plague was over and the dead were buried, the sound of music was heard again in noblemen's houses and courtyards. The funerals ended, and the fun resumed.

But underneath this Viennese myth of waltz and wine, operetta and whipped cream, there is what Nestroy called "threadbare *Gemütlichkeit*," what Ilsa Barca calls "the legend of the Heart of Gold of the Viennese."

All winter long the Viennese—at least a considerable number of them—spend their weekends in the Wienerwald with their skis and sledges. There are ski trails within a short streetcar ride from many people's houses; it is only twenty minutes by car from the Opera to the snow-covered hills. (All distances in Vienna are measured by the time it takes to get to or from the Opera.) Even people who do not ski go to the Wienerwald for a walk in the snow; paths are cleared and beautifully marked. A day in snow and sunshine is considered a healthy antidote to dancing and merrymaking. In many families the older people skate while the youngsters go skiing. There are over fifty ice skating rinks in the city, among them some artificial ones of high quality. The Stadthalle's rink is used for the performances of the "Wiener Eisrevue," a world-famous ice show; the Eislaufverein's was the largest in Europe until it was sold to an American-owned hotel. Advanced skiers drive out to the Semmering, Vienna's "Hausberg" (private mountain), the Schneeberg, or the Raxalpe. On Monday morning the newspapers publish frightening tales of sporting accidents and broken bones. Everybody is shocked about so many accidents, and the next weekend they all go out again to be "in the snow."

Vienna's aristocratic palaces still dominate the image of the inner city. Many palaces, and many people who once lived in them, have seen better days. Both are slightly run down but keep up an elegant front. In Vienna the upper middle classes always imitated the *Lebensform*—the way of life—of the aristocratic class. It was important for a man to be a "Kavalier" (as the Baron Ochs von Lerchenau, who does not always behave like a "Kavalier" in *Der Rosenkavalier,* likes to emphasize).

Most of the palaces were given up by descendants of the former owners, who now live in bourgeois circumstances, or prefer the convenience of a modern, centrally heated apartment. Some of these palaces have the most magnificent baroque staircases—but bathrooms and plumbing are thoroughly inadequate. Once the owners of these palaces were exempted from taxes, civic duties, and military service, had their own seals, and held patrimonial courts—the privileges of a feudal aristocracy. Even during the liberal era, toward the end of the last century, the Habsburgs and the landed gentry, not more than eighty families, were the ruling elite, with inherited rights and prerogatives that could not be taken away. When a young aristocrat failed to pass his examination at the law faculty of Vienna's university, the professor said, "Count, I can't prevent your appointment as governor of Lower Austria, but I can at least postpone it for a year."

These privileges no longer exist. In the republic of Austria, aristocratic titles, though used and respected, are not legally admitted. Of this erstwhile glory only the houses remain, silent witnesses to a great era. They have survived the ravages of time and war with more dignity than the less exalted bourgeois buildings around them. Some have become schools, and others—Palais Starhemberg, Mollard-Clary, Modena, Prince Eugene—have become ministries. Only a few families still keep their palaces, among them the Harrachs who have some beautiful Breughels and Rembrandts in their private art gallery, and the Liechtensteins who rule over the sixty-two-square-mile principality in the Alps between Austria and Switzerland.

The oldest palaces were built after the victory over the Turks, toward the end of the seventeenth century; a second group was put up in the middle of the eighteenth century—the Palais Questenberg, Schönburg, Schönborn, Daun-Kinsky. At the time of the Congress of Vienna some wealthy foreigners, such as the Rasumofskys, built their palatial town houses in Vienna. Almost all are in the inner city; in Freyung (Palais Kinsky, Montgenuovo, Harrach), in Minoritenplatz (Starhemberg, Liechtenstein), Herrengasse (Wilczek, Modena, Trautmannsdorff). There was little space in the narrow streets; the old files often contain requests for permission to "build into the street"; and of course there was no room for elaborate balconies. But the entrance gate was always monumental, with the family coat of arms in stone relief.

Many of these old palaces are hardly noticed by the passersby in the narrow, dark streets. At night they disappear between the bright neon signs and the colored lights of the brash upstart buildings on both sides. The old palaces are reticent; they always were reluctant to give away their secrets. The thick, discreet walls never did reveal much of the fascinating life that went on behind them.

PERFECT SERVICE
London's Savoy Hotel, and Others

THE SEVENTY-FIVE WAITERS on the fifteen floors of the Savoy Hotel in London know two famous men called Heath. One is Edward Heath, the prime minister. At the Savoy, however, they are better acquainted with Royton E. Heath, who, until his recent retirement from the position of head floor supervisor, taught and tested and hired and fired the floor waiters—something that the prime minister could not do.

Royton E. Heath, sixty-four, a born-and-bred Londoner, was at the Savoy for thirty-seven years. Even during World War II when physically in uniform, he remained spiritually at the Savoy, where he arrived one day in 1935. He had studied catering and worked in Nice and at several once-famous nightclubs. "That was the era of the Duke of Windsor," he says with feeling—and that's about all he's ready to say. Noblesse oblige.

A trim, sandy-haired man with bright bespectacled eyes and an authoritative manner, Heath could be professor of service and catering at any university where they had enough sense to set up such a department. No one has done it thus far in England, so Heath organized his own courses at the Savoy. His trainees were well advised to study the book that he wrote on food service if they wanted to pass the difficult examinations.

Like so many of his colleagues, Heath pursues some extracurricular activities. He is one of England's leading authorities on Alpine plants and shrubs; he has written several books on the subject, including an encyclopedia of rock plants. He was elected a Fellow of the Linnean Society in 1959. Not bad for an ex-floor waiter! He paints roses, acts as a judge at flower shows, and conducts Alpine flower tours for connoisseurs.

Heath always had the right approach: He wanted to become a floor waiter's floor waiter. London stage actors cast as such, who wanted to perform with the authentic touch, have studied with Heath. He was a technical adviser when MGM made *Goodbye, Mr. Chips.* Heath knows that many waiters today consider their job a temporary embarrassment and think of themselves as future general managers. Most of them never make it and remain bad waiters, taking out their frustrations on their unfortunate clients. There is a widespread feeling now that to wait on people is less "dignified" than, say, to work on an assembly line. Apparently taking orders from a computer is more respectable than taking orders from a foreman or a customer.

"Before World War I," Heath says, "most waiters at the Savoy were Swiss. Later, the profession was dominated by Italians. In England, a fellow was not respected when he put on a black tie for work. Now travel has become Big Business. Some countries have built their new prosperity on the money spent there by foreign visitors. Large hotels have sprung up everywhere like mushrooms, and at the same time the pool of experienced staff gets smaller. The profession is not respected, because most travelers base their opinions on untrained waiters in second-rate establishments. The average man has a poor idea of hotels. I admit that a modern hotel manager must know his figures if he wants to stay in business, but the best hotels are still run by men who are *hôteliers* first and accountants second."

Several years ago Heath began sending his assistants to depressed areas of England to recruit young men who would be trained in London and might become first-rate waiters. "We tell them that we must keep up the image of the great hotels with genuine personalized service. If not, we'll wind up with plenty of executives and no service, like an operetta army with lots of generals and few privates!"

To cope with the shortage of experienced personnel, many big hotels have introduced systems of central service: "The guest dials room service. His order is transmitted to the special department, sent up, and served by the first available waiter. It may work out—provided the order is simple and the waiter efficient. But if the guest stays for weeks and occasionally wants something special, he doesn't like to see new faces all the time. He wants the same floor waiter who knows his likes and dislikes. Otherwise he always feels as if he is in a strange house, not at home. We try to anticipate the client's wishes. That is our idea of perfect hospitality. Believe me, it's harder to install than electronically run elevators."

The new luxury hotels have smaller staffs and, instead of personal service, offer color television, temperature control, and other technological gadgets. But *real* luxury is still personal, quiet, efficient service, given with tact and understanding. "I taught my students that breakfast is important," says Heath. "It sets the mood of the day. If the coffee is bad, the toast cold, and the guest didn't get his favorite morning paper or, even worse, he got a paper he dislikes, he is off to a bad start." I said they didn't have that problem in New York City; there isn't a large choice of morning papers. "At the Savoy a guest can expect the paper he likes," said Heath. "They make a note of it, to be sure." There you are.

The Savoy's floor waiters serve about twelve thousand meals a month, not to mention drinks and snacks. Some guests are so happy in their suites overlooking the Thames that they never go down to see and be seen at the Savoy Grill. Mr. Heath kept an extensive card index with the wishes and preferences of thousands of customers in his office. He compared the daily arrival list with his cards and started the wheels rolling. When the guest appeared and walked into the sitting room of his seventy-five-pound-a-day River Suite, he found his special brand of whiskey and his favorite mineral water on the private bar. How did they remember? The guest had been there only once before, nine years ago.

"Well, that's what the Savoy tries to do, twenty-four hours a day," Heath explained. "I said, 'Welcome home!' to people I knew. That's the sort of thing even a rich man cannot buy. He feels he is wanted, which is rare in this age of aggression. We don't hate him. We like him."

In his courses Health emphasized "the three Cs" that make a first-rate floor waiter: cleanliness, courtesy, capability. Cleanliness is taken for granted. Courtesy already poses problems. Some waiters find it hard to smile or to say, "Yes, Sir." Others don't want to learn that the guest is always right, even if he or she isn't. And capability cannot be taught, only acquired by experience. One never stops learning: a good waiter must cope with every situation instantly and efficiently. That sounds easy but is difficult when one deals with blasé clients. Years ago, Heath made simple translations of the important French culinary expressions for his floor waiters so they wouldn't confuse a *hollandaise* with a *béarnaise* or *mouton* with *moutarde*.

"If a restaurant waiter forgets to serve something, he quickly goes back to the kitchen to get it. But if the floor waiter serves a saddle of lamb and forgets the mint sauce and red currant jelly, the result can be catastrophic. By the time he has telephoned down and fetched the things from below, the guest has eaten his lamb without the sauce or complained to the management. He's angry. I don't blame him."

Each course is served separately, "exactly as in the restaurant." At the Savoy it couldn't happen that the hors d'oeuvre, main dish, and dessert arrive at the same time, as in some of the new luxury hotels. And a good floor waiter knows what to serve with various dishes, but just in case, Heath drew up a comprehensive list of "adjuncts," which his waiters had to know by heart. At the Savoy, oysters are served with slices of brown bread and butter, lemon, chili-flavored vinegar, Tabasco, and mignonette. If a guests wants a cocktail sauce, it is made with tomato sauce, lemon juice, and a dash of Worcestershire sauce. Plovers' eggs are served with brown bread and butter; cucumber with salmon. Irish stew ("always serve in a soup plate with spoon") comes with Worcestershire, corn on the cob with hot melted butter and a finger bowl. The recipe for Russian dressing is also on the list, he says, with slightly raised eyebrows, because "it is a favorite with a large number of American visitors." The "normal" (and presumably proper) dressing at the Savoy is made "from a little English mustard, salt and pepper, three parts oil and one part vinegar, the whole mixed well together."

I said it sounded like a lot to ask from a floor waiter. Heath ignored this frivolous remark. "The Savoy serves *everything* in the rooms. The men must be expert carvers, prepare crêpes Suzette, mix the hotel's standard dry Martini (four-fifths gin and one-fifth dry vermouth). Nothing is refused. During the long run of *Mame*, Ginger Rogers wanted a special cranberry cocktail. We got six bottles of cranberry juice. Just routine."

I'd heard rumors that Mr. Heath was usually on duty on the rare occasion when the Queen.... He lifted his right hand with the outstretched palm. "One might say," he said, deliberately, as though he was dictating an important communique, "that I have personally supervised private parties for members of the Royal Family on numerous occasions."

It's been a long time since the happy nightclub days of the Duke of Windsor, but it's still noblesse oblige with Royton E. Heath.

At the Gritti Palace in Venice—one of the most beautiful hotels in Europe—the individual flower arrangements reflect the colors of the rugs and curtains. Guests of long standing may find their own furniture in their rooms. Ernest Hemingway called the Gritti *"casa mia."* He always stayed in 115-116 (which, along with 117, is now known as the Hemingway Apartment), and there he wrote *Across the River and into the Trees,* which established the Gritti's place in literature. Two doors away, in 112-114 (the Maugham Apartment), W. Somerset Maugham would write, look at the Grand Canal, or meditate, doing *piccolo punto,* petit point. *"Ah, c'est bien, Madame, toujours la même chose,"* he would say to Signora Cosima Giandomenici, the first *governante,* the Gritti's head housekeeper. She would make sure that it was "always the same thing" before Maugham arrived—the red carnations, a certain pink rug he liked, some other little things that made all the difference between a hotel room and the warmth of a home. No wonder Hemingway and Maugham gave Signora Giandomenici many of their books with grateful dedications.

The Signora was fond of Hemingway. "He had such *dolce,* soft eyes," she told me one recent morning. "A sweet man. Every morning at ten, he would ring for caviar and champagne, and that was just the beginning. There would be more champagne, and later there would be whiskey. He would sit up in bed, propped against the pillows. He liked the windows open, and he would write while looking out on the Canal." Just underneath his windows, the *gondolieri* hung up a Madonna and set up a landing place; today, there is a regular crossing service at that location. The *gondolieri* were (and are) enthusiastic and noisy; even when they had an amiable conversation, one would think it was a life-or-death argument. The hubbub didn't bother Hemingway, who would sometimes send them some wine, after which they got even noisier.

Signora Giandomenici was born in Venice. Richard Wagner had died there in 1883 at the Palazzo Verdramin-Calergi; Signora's parents, ardent Wagnerians, called her Cosima, after Wagner's widow. The housekeeper is a frail, dark, soft-spoken woman who learned about hotels from her late husband. Prior to World War II, they had run a first-class hotel in Addis Ababa. When the Italians had to leave Ethiopia, she and her husband returned to Venice and started all over again. In 1947, the CIGA chain remodeled the Gritti, then a not particularly elegant *dépendance* of the Grand Hotel. Mrs. Giandomenici was hired with other key people.

"The place looked terrible," she remembers. *"Brutto, brutto.* So much work and money were needed to turn it into our jewel." Raffaele

Masprone rebuilt the old palace (named after Andrea Gritti, 1455–1538, the sixty-seventh Doge of Venice, whose portrait can be admired downstairs). Since then the Gritti has become a hotel beloved by many—"a fantasy, a feeling, a state of mind." From the canal it looks less imposing than many other *palazzi;* understatement and quiet elegance are the cardinal rules. The Gritti has always had a special attraction for writers: John Ruskin wrote part of *The Stones of Venice* in an upstairs room. Charles Dickens came here, as did George Sand and Richard Wagner. In more recent years, Sinclair Lewis, John Dos Passos, Noel Coward, Sir Winston Churchill, Georges Simenon, and John Gunther were among many who found peace, and perhaps even some inspiration, at the Gritti.

The lovely hotel was reopened in June 1948. By that time Signora Giandomenici had hired the members of her invisible staff: valets and chambermaids (who work in teams of two) and the people who work in the *guardaroba,* the laundry room. Almost all the employees came from Friuli, the region between Venice and Udine that was not then industrialized. The Friuliani were the best workers; Venetians didn't want to work in hotels. Signora Giandomenici believes that the employees' morale, the team spirit, was what made the Gritti. The super morale-builder was Raffaele Masprone, CIGA's unforgotten *grand seigneur* who turned the Gritti into the "Kohinoor diamond" of his chain, with the help of some crucial people—Signor Lis, the concierge; Signor Gava, the maître d'hôtel; and Signora Giandomenici. She is very proud of a letter from Masprone saying, "Without you, the Gritti would not have succeeded."

It was not easy. For twenty years, she would get up at five-thirty in the morning, take the *vaporetto* from her house at the Lido, and arrive at the Gritti at seven. And often she was there until nine in the evening. She went home only to sleep; on Sundays she would see her daughter and her grandchildren. "I gave my best years to the Gritti, *con amore*. It was always a living thing," she said to me as we walked through a corridor. "Look! Every room is occupied, and some are being made up now, but there is not a sound. *Il silenzio di palazzo.*"

Mrs. Giandomenici's day begins with the situation report. She checks arrivals and departures and makes up a list with mysterious signs and symbols. Many people are marked "F" (flowers) while some have special remarks, such as the guest who gets "a blooming anthurium plant on her bedside table." Next, she walks from floor to floor, giving precise instructions. She trusts her employees, most of whom have been there for the past twenty years, but they must be controlled to assure *perfetto servizio*. This is possible only in a not-too-big hotel. The Gritti has only ninety-one rooms and ten suites. Each year ten rooms are completely redecorated—new tapestries, new curtains, new rugs. When I visited her in her small office I saw samples of brocade and other materials awaiting final selection by Dr. Natale Rusconi, the Gritti's *direttore,* and Signora Giandomenici. Rusconi, a suave, civilized gentlemen who supervises the Gritti, says, "Mrs. Giandomenici *is* the Gritti."

Occasionally, the hotel is obliged *not* to be forgiving. One of Rusconi's predecessors was once called into the dining room, where a slightly intoxicated and not-so-slightly irritated English guest had offended the maître d'hôtel because the *pollo alla cacciatore* had tarragon in it. The manager explained quietly that the usual Italian version contains no tarragon but that the Gritti makes the dish in the classical French style, described in the *Larousse Gastronomique* as having finely chopped tarragon. The Englishman never got into the Gritti after that.

The Gritti's management has a top-secret rating system, ranging from ordinary VIPs to especially recommended VIPs; and there are also VVIPs and even a few select VVVIPs. Don't even try for the top rating; only Charles de Gaulle and Gianni Agnelli of Fiat have earned it, though Hemingway and Maugham would have made it were they still alive. Truman and Vice President Nixon were only VVIPs. The guest book of the Gritti reflects changing times. In the early 1950s there were members of the Italian nobility and top movie stars: Clark Gable, Bette Davis, Greta Garbo, Robert Taylor, Ronald Colman as well as Margaret (who signed "Princess of Great Britain and Northern Ireland") and "Edward" and "Wallis Windsor." Gradually, the Italian aristocrats dropped out and were replaced by Dean Acheson, Nathan Milstein, Herbert von Karajan. Later, there were Wallis (who then signed "Duchess of Windsor"), Charlie Chaplin (who drew the picture of the beloved tramp), Richard Burton, and "Elizabeth Taylor Burton." A recent page read, "Mrs. Spiro T. Agnew, Washington, D.C."

Mrs. Giandomenici has seen them all and noted their idiosyncrasies and special wishes in her little book. No detail is unimportant enough to be neglected; she knows that it is the details that make a great hotel. "Our work is never finished," she says. On the first of July, Madame

Valentina Schlee, the designer, will arrive on the *wagon-lit* from Paris and will go shortly thereafter to her room, as she has every year since 1951, always on the same date. She will find her own furniture, lamps, breakfast napkins, china, books, and paintings. In five minutes, or maybe even sooner, she will be "at home."

"We have many such clients," says Mrs. Giandomenici, quietly and modestly, "and they have many special wishes. There is, *naturalmente,* no special charge for such extra service." Naturally. Try that elsewhere!

Quite a few people who love ships have tried to get one of the few staterooms on the port side of the sundeck on the SS *France.* Before booking, they always make sure that Robert will be on duty. They don't know his family name; shipboard etiquette accords the cabin steward only his first name.

I didn't know my good luck when I left on the *France* one day last fall in S-20 ("Provence"), a luxurious apartment decorated in provincial style, but I soon found out. When I stepped into S-20, a slim French steward came in, said *"Bonjour, Monsieur, je suis Robert, votre garçon de cabine,"* took my coat and briefcase, handed me some forms to sign, asked whether he might unpack, and turned off the small radio, having noticed my irritated glance—all this in less than five seconds. Perhaps you'll understand why I consider S-20 the finest hotel room in the world.

Robert was polite without being subservient, cheerful but never familiar. He carried himself better than most first class passengers. ("I eat only once a day. I have a young wife and two children.") He had pride in himself and his work. He liked what he was doing. He didn't want to be the president of the French Line but "the best cabin steward on the *France,* or on any other ship afloat." He was pleased because M. Edmond Lanier, the president of the French Line, another civilized man, always travels in "Provence," instead of in the overwhelming splendor of the grand-luxe suite below.

No wonder. Robert was always around, though often invisible. I rarely had to ring for him. He simply anticipated what was needed, from fresh towels to fresh water for the flowers. When I said I liked strong coffee in the morning, he said that I would get it. He made the coffee himself in a machine in the small pantry, which he shares with his colleague André, who is in charge of the starboard staterooms. The coffee was strong, the toast was warm, and the *omelette nature* still fluffy when Robert took the cover off with a flourish—though the kitchen is six floors below.

One evening I asked a few friends to dine with me in "Provence" to see, for once, how the other half lives (more exactly, the other half percent). Robert told me that most of his steady clients had many of their meals in their staterooms. "We've served everything up here, even a soufflé, and it hadn't collapsed by the time the people ate it."

He proved it. The caviar, in a large bowl with ice, was excellent. Robert had made sure that a new tin was opened for us downstairs. The baked Idaho potato was hot. The vodka glasses had a light frost; Robert had put them in his small *frigo*. He and André worked as a team during dinner. Everything was fine, including the wines, and there was the added luxury of privacy. I suppose that's the way to live, if you are the president (of the French Line or the French Republic), or at least a second-rate millionaire.

Such perfection is, of course, the result of hard work. Robert Tromeur, fifty-one, comes from the small fishing village of Térénez, near Morlaix, in Brittany. Térénez has less than fifty houses, but among the crew on the France, three men come from there; once there were as many as six. Most people in Térénez are small-scale fishermen, going out in the morning, coming back at night; or they work on ships. "We have wonderful *belon* oysters in our deep waters. We sell the best varieties and eat the less expensive ones." Robert started as a *mousse* (cabin boy) at the age of fourteen on the SS *Champlain,* later worked on the *Normandie* and the *Ile de France.* Then came World War II. "I did all sorts of things," he said, smiling. After the war, he worked fourteen months as helmsman on a *petrolier* (oil tanker). In 1949 he was *garçon* in the dining room of the new *Ile de France,* worked as cabin steward on other French Line ships, and was assigned to the *France* prior to her maiden voyage on February 3, 1962. He's been there since, always assigned to the deluxe suites.

Later, I heard that he'd been a high-ranking man in the Resistance in Brittany. ("Robert?" says Raymond Cordier, the barman in the Riviera Lounge. *"Oh là là!* He was terrific.") Another man remembers that he heard the captain of the *Flandre* being addressed with the familiar *"tu"* by Robert, a steward. When he asked Robert how he dared, Robert smiled. "He served under me during the war." He calls himself "a Breton, not just a Frenchman," and he speaks Breton, a sort of Gaelic. Many Bretons from the Finistère region work in Manhattan restaurants; most return to Brittany after they retire. Once I asked Robert if he would like to go back to work on the bridge. He shrugged. He had a family to support, and a sailor doesn't make enough money. "There is nothing wrong with being a steward, Monsieur, provided you are a *good* steward."

"A cabin steward is more than a waiter," he said. "The waiter sees the passengers all dressed up. We see them, so to speak, in their underwear. A man may be nice to his wife in the dining room but here, *c'est la vérité.* People tell you things they wouldn't tell the barman downstairs." Robert thinks no man can be a good cabin steward before he is forty-five. It takes time to learn the psychological side of the *métier.* "One learns to listen to confidences but never to utter one." Then there is the problem of women traveling alone. *"On reste toujours le garçon de cabine."* The profession has strict ethics.

People often misplace things and ask him, "Didn't you see my diamond ring, by chance?" with a funny gleam in their eyes. "One must not show one is offended," says Robert. "After a while they find the ring and apologize to you. And it's important not to be around too much. One enters discreetly; when somebody is getting dressed, one pretends not to see anything. Remember that people come here to be away from it all, to enjoy privacy almost as newlyweds on a honeymoon."

Robert takes a good look at a new passenger. When he meets a couple, he soon learns which is in charge. (*"C'est souvent la dame qui mène la boutique."*) He is always nice to Madame. "Monsieur will follow. In bad weather I prefer to have Madame sick. Gives Monsieur a chance to be strong and look after her. But when he is sick, and she isn't, you've to be very tactful, because he is miserable and she tries not to show that she is having a very good time."

A good steward must also be a good sailor. "Most of us served in the French navy. We've taken courses as firemen, and there is continuous training in security and lifeboat service so that we know what to do in case of fire or disaster." Robert was aboard the *Ile de France* when she reached the sinking *Andrea Doria.* The crew of the *Ile de France* put the shipwrecked passengers in warm blankets and served them hot food.

Many were separated from wives, husbands, children. "Only after they arrived in New York did the terrific tension subside."

Despite serving rich and famous people for many years, Robert has not become a cynic. Most people nowadays appreciate good service. "The Americans are the nicest; they remember that there are other people aboard who expect to be served. They often behave as though they were invited guests, not paying passengers. Europeans are more demanding, but one learns to keep a straight face when a man wants his coffee very hot and the milk with it very cold. One must be attentive. When someone wants 'soap' one must not bring him *soupe*. Celebrities are often very easy. Pablo Casals and his wife never asked for anything special. Salvador Dali: *très gentil*. Madame de Gaulle: a great lady." Jean Anouilh, the playwright, rarely left "Provence," telling Robert, "I like my little village on sun deck. No use going downtown."

Sometimes Robert works twelve hours a day. In harbor he stays aboard to clean, while the waiters go ashore and have fun. He thinks that "we French are less formal than the British stewards, but less relaxed than the Italians." Nowadays, few young people want to work in the *métier*. "They don't like to serve, they don't like to be called adventurers because they go out to sea, and, if they are married, their young wives don't want to spend many months each year by themselves."

"In ten years or so...." He gave a shrug.

"In ten years, Robert, perfect service will only be a memory?"

He nodded.

Perfect Pitch

THE VIENNA STAATSOPER
A Question of Reverberation

AN OPERA HOUSE IS JUDGED by its acoustics, and the men responsible for the reconstruction of the bombed and burned-out Vienna Staatsoper—a project that got under way almost ten years ago and has been completed only in the last week or two—have worried all along about how the result of their labors was going to sound. So have the one million seven hundred thousand citizens of Vienna, all of whom consider themselves joint owners of the opera house, even though some of them would never think of going to it. Opera was first heard in Vienna more than three hundred years ago, and it has played a singularly prominent part in Viennese life since at least 1666, when Emperor Leopold I celebrated his marriage to Margaret Theresa of Spain by sponsoring the world's first great opera festival. It lasted for the better part of two years, and its highlights were a production of Marc Antonio Cesti's *Il Pomo d'Oro,* with a cast of a thousand singers (and a deficit of a hundred thousand gulden), and an alfresco ballet entitled *La Contesa dell' Aria e dell' Acqua,* in which the emperor himself appeared, along with most of his court. Four hundred different operas were produced in Vienna during Leopold's reign, and for that reason, among others, Austrian historians have always spoken well of him.

Over the intervening centuries, Vienna has never been without at least one opera house (sometimes it has had three houses running year round, and even during the last ten years the Staatsoper company has been performing regularly in two theaters), but its greatest and largest has been the Staatsoper—or the Hofoper, as it was known from 1869, when it first opened its doors, until the end of the First World War, when it was officially renamed. The famous directors and conductors associated with this opera house—Johann von Herbeck, Wilhelm Jahn, Hans Richter, Gustav Mahler, Felix von Weingartner, Franz Schalk, Richard Strauss, Bruno Walter, Wilhelm Furtwängler, Hans Knappertsbusch, Clemens Krauss, Karl Böhm, Josef Krips—have always been more popular with the Viennese than emperors, statesmen, or generals. The private lives of the great singers who have appeared there—Emil Scaria, Amalia Materna, Hermann Winkelmann, Theodor Reichmann, Rosa Papier, Pauline Luca, Marie Renard, Anna Bahr-Mildenburg, Marie Gutheil-Schoder, Erik Schmedes, Richard Mayr, Leo Slezak, Selma Kurz, Alfred Piccaver, Emil Schipper, Maria Jeritza, Lotte Lehmann—have always been regarded as public property. The most exclusive club in town is the Wiener Philharmoniker, whose hundred and five members make up the Staatsoper's orchestra; they have a reputation for being as temperamentally difficult as they are artistically competent, and the Viennese call them, not without respect, "the hundred prima donnas." The signing of the Austrian State Treaty last May 15 was a great event for Austria, but in many ways the reopening of the Staatsoper on Saturday night, November 5, will be a greater one—something on the order of a nationwide housewarming or, as some people have been saying, "Austria's Coronation Day." The opera is to be Beethoven's *Fidelio,* and the house has been sold out, of course, for weeks, even though good seats went for as much as two hundred dollars apiece.

Most of the people who have set themselves up as consultants on matters of acoustics contend, not unnaturally, that by applying certain laws of physics and using certain testing devices they can determine in advance how hospitable to sound a new auditorium will be. The fact is, however, that several auditoriums built in Germany recently under the guidance of consultants who presumably applied the laws of physics and used the testing devices have turned out to have dreadful acoustics. (When Berlin's new concert hall at the Hochschule für Musik, which was hailed in advance as Germany's finest auditorium, opened last year, it proved to be an acoustical atrocity; in some seats, disconnected noises seemed to be bouncing off the rear wall of the hall, in others multiple echoes closed in from all directions, and in still others practically no sound at all could be heard. Although years of acoustical study had gone into the design of the building, it was discovered after the first few concerts that the ceiling and the side walls were all wrong in relation to one another and to the size of the room, and the only thing the technicians could do was put up floor-to-ceiling hangings on the walls and hope that they would not only absorb the unwelcome noises but spread the music around more evenly. This has been helpful, but the acoustics are still far from satisfactory.) The sad truth is that while scientists in many fields can foretell with unvarying accuracy what will result from a combination of known factors, those who specialize in acoustics seem to be on no surer footing in making their forecasts than meteorologists are in making theirs. From the evidence, it appears that no one can say for certain what the acoustical qualities of an auditorium will be until it is finished, furnished, heated, and filled with musicians, music, and listeners. And if the qualities turn out to be disappointing, it will very likely be expensive to correct them—if it can be done at all.

In times past, the designers of opera houses perhaps knew little or nothing about the science of acoustics, but a few of them, aided either by instinct or plain good luck, produced auditoriums in which the acoustics are fine—notably, Milan's La Scala, Venice's Teatro Fenice, New York's Metropolitan, and Barcelona's Liceo. Until the afternoon of March 12, 1945, Vienna's Staatsoper could have been added to this list. The Staatsoper, or Hofoper, which was built conveniently close to the Imperial Palace, was a blending of Venetian and Spanish Gothic with Florentine and French Renaissance, designed by Eduard van der Nüll and August Siccard von Siccardsburg. The house took eight years to build, from 1861 to 1869, and neither architect lived to hear an opera in it. While it was under construction, they were mercilessly lampooned— by some people for being too unoriginal, by others for being too revolutionary, and by still others for being merely eclectic. A popular ditty of those times went:

Der Siccardsburg und van der Nüll,
Die haben ihren eignen stul.
Ob griechisch, römisch, Renaissanz,
Das ist den beiden alles ans.

(The Siccardsburg and the van der Nüll,
They have their own style.
Greek or Roman or Renaissance,
It's all the same to them.)

The criticism proved too much for van der Nüll, and in 1868 he committed suicide. Von Siccardsburg died soon afterward—of a broken heart, many Viennese said. In later years, both men were widely and extravagantly praised by qualified authorities as the creators of one of the finest buildings on the Ringstrasse—the Hapsburg monarchy's Via Triumphalis.

On the afternoon of March 12, 1945, American planes dropped five bombs on the Staatsoper, setting fire to the stage and the auditorium. The city's water supply had been knocked out by previous bombings, and every able-bodied member of the Vienna fire department had been drafted into the Volkssturm, so there were neither the means nor the men to save the building. It burned all the rest of that day and through the night, while throngs of Viennese looked on, many crying with despair and frustration and none of them able to do a thing about it. At two o'clock in the morning, the roof of the auditorium collapsed. Ever since that night some Viennese have looked upon the burning of the Staatsoper as their greatest collective tragedy of the war. It had never occurred to them that their opera house might be bombed; in their eyes it was a sort of sanctuary, mystically immune to the destructive forces of war. Practically everybody who had ever been associated with the Staatsoper—and a great many people who hadn't—had stored musical instruments, jewelry, personal documents, and other valuables in the building's large cellars, where, it was agreed, they would be absolutely safe. All these possessions were destroyed by the fire, along with the sets for a hundred and twenty operas, and more than a hundred and sixty thousand costumes. There were no casualties, for nobody was in the building at the time of the bombing; the autumn before, the Nazis had closed theaters of all sorts, and the Staatsoper had not been used since June 30, 1944, when Hans Knappertsbusch conducted *Gotterdämmerung* there. Belatedly, the Viennese noted the prophetic significance of Brunnhilde's line "The dusky twilight closeth on us." By the time the fire had burned itself out, only the massive walls and the lobby were left; the stage and the auditoruim were a giant, burned-out shell.

Many of the Viennese who watched the opera house burn had been bombed out themselves and had no prospect of finding a home in the foreseeable future, but they never doubted for a moment that one of the city's most pressing jobs was to restore the wrecked Staatsoper to its former splendor. Few of them, however, could have guessed that it would take ten years and ten million dollars to do this—a longer, costlier job than the construction of the original building. At first, there was some talk of starting from scratch and putting up a brand-new opera house, but this idea didn't get very far; after all, the French Renaissance façade and the main lobby, with its marble pillars, its large frescoes, and its magnificent candelabra, were intact, and an overwhelming majority of the Viennese preferred to preserve what they could of the old house, which was rich in tradition and a constant reminder of the city's past grandeur. The actual work of reconstruction was somewhat slow in getting started, for five thousand tons of rubble first had to be removed, along with a hundred and fifty carloads of twisted girders. The walls had to be reinforced, and a temporary roof installed. From time to time during the years of rebuilding, work came to a standstill for lack of money or materials. Most of the money was provided, bit by bit, by the government, hard-pressed though it was for funds, but the last hundred million schillings—four million dollars—was raised by an issue of seven-percent bonds that was enthusiastically oversubscribed by the public.

During the first nine years of its reconstruction, the Staatsoper, which stands in the very heart of Vienna, was screened from the eyes of curious passersby by a high wooden fence, but many tantalizing stories drifted out about the magnificence of the new house, and the facilities it would have—air-conditioning, elevators, a vast stage, and so on. Reassuring as all this was the Viennese have been uneasy from the start about one thing: how is the new house going to sound? Musicians, acoustical experts, and the public at large have been arguing this question for ten years, and they are arguing it to this day. Some say that the acoustics will be the same as they were in the old house, since the basic form of the building has been retained. Others gloomily liken the old house to an old violin, attributing its warm, luscious, sweet, "Viennese" sound to the aged wood of its fixtures, and pointedly observing that new violins aren't in the same class with instruments that have been mellowed by time. Pessimism has been especially widespread among singers; the new house, it has been whispered, will prove to be a deathtrap for all but the most powerful voices—and how many really powerful voices are left, anyway? These fears have been accentuated by the fact that since the end of the war the Staatsoper company has made its home in much smaller quarters—the venerable Theater an der Wien, which was four years old when Beethoven's *Fidelio* had its premiere there, on November 20, 1805.

(It was a failure.) In contrast to the new building's capacity of about two thousand the Theater an der Wien is a lovely, intimate house, seating only nine hundred and fifty, and its acoustics are warm and somewhat muted—ideal for Mozart and parlando-style operas, like *Der Rosenkavalier,* but something less than ideal for works by Verdi and Wagner, in which power and brilliance of sound are essential. Some singers, having grown accustomed to the limited requirements of the Theater an der Wien, aren't looking forward to adjusting themselves to an auditorium of nearly three times the area. They are not necessarily reassured by a prediction from Heinz Keilholz, a well-known German acoustics engineer who has been hired as a consultant by the opera management. The new house, he says, will have "the bright, modern sound that people have come to admire in high-frequency recordings."

A few weeks ago, in the midst of all the acoustical suspense, I walked into the office of a friend named Wolfgang Teubner, who is a member of the engineering staff at work on the opera building. I've known Teubner since the late twenties, when we met regularly in the Stattsoper's fourth, and topmost, balcony. The fourth balcony, which offered the best acoustics, or so I thought, as well as the cheapest seats, was frequented by *Opernnarren* (opera fools), including the members of the claque, a group of impecunious young men with callused palms and uncompromising artistic standards, to which Teubner and I belonged. The members of the claque were contemptuous of the moneyed people in the stalls and boxes down below, where, we firmly told ourselves, the hearing was awful. (I sat downstairs a few times, at the invitation of a generous uncle, and I had to admit to myself that the hearing wasn't at all bad, but I never dreamed of confessing this to my fellow claqueurs.) Teubner and I were in the fourth balcony almost every night. He was studying engineering, to please his parents, and singing to please himself; I was studying law for my family and the violin for myself.

I knew that in the old days Teubner had had a fine tenor voice, and as we renewed our acquaintance in his office, I asked him how he had made out with it. He replied that he had become a *Heldentenor* in the thirties, after I left Vienna, and that no sooner had he embarked upon his singing career than the war began. When it was over, engineers were in greater demand than *Heldentenore,* and Teubner had taken a job as a *Baurat,* or building surveyor, in Austria's Ministry for Commerce and

Reconstruction; the pay didn't amount to much and promotion was slow, he said, but he did have old-age security and an official title. As a *Baurat,* Teubner was promptly assigned to the opera project—one instance, at least, in which bureaucracy has succeeded in filling a round hole with a round peg.

A slim man with a milk-white face, blond hair, thick glasses, and a deceptively soft voice—he can raise it to a startling *fortissimo* in the "Schmiede-lieder" from *Siegfried*—Tuebner told me that at the moment, as I might have suspected, he was pretty much preoccupied with acoustics. "To judge by the latest coffeehouse rumors, everybody in town is convinced that the acoustics are going to be sour," he said. "Naturally, we won't know for certain until opening night, but we hope to get some indication next Monday at the first full orchestra rehearsal in the new house. Ever since the beginning, we've kept our fingers crossed and prayed for the best. One thing the coffeehouse critics forget is that high-frequency recordings have made people's hearing more sensitive than it used to be. Why, only a few years ago the highest frequency you would find on recordings was five thousand *Hertz,* or cycles per second—about four octaves above middle C. Now they're making recordings at frequencies up to fifteen thousand *Hertz.* When we first heard these, we all said they sounded too sharp—perhaps a semitone high in pitch—but now we've accepted them, because they reproduce actual sounds more exactly than ever before. And they have taught us to hear more of the overtones of music. You only have to listen to an old Caruso record to realize how far we've progressed in a short time. Our problem is to meet this modern challenge, and to do that we've got to make the acoustics of the new house not only as good as they were in the old house—though many people say we can't possibly do that—but better. It's largely, of course, a question of reverberation. The reverberation in the old house was one and three-tenths seconds. That's much too short. The Theater an der Wien isn't really much better; we love it because it's so *gemütlich,* but it has a reverberation of only one and thirty-eight hundredths seconds. Much too short, too."

I asked Teubner what he meant by reverberation. "Well," he said, "in the sense that I'm using it, it's a standard of acoustical measurement. In an auditorium, sound should bounce off the walls, the ceiling, and the floor until the whole place is uniformly filled with it. If the source of sound stops, the sound remains audible for a while—sometimes for as long as three seconds. That is called reverberation—the prologation of sound after it has left its source. Reverberation strengthens sounds, and it is desirable up to the point where it starts to interfere with succeeding sounds. The length of time that a sound can be heard after being originated is used as a measure of a room's reverberation. If the reverberation is too short, the sounds we hear are muffled, dead. If it is too long, the sounds jostle one another; syllables and phrases are hard to understand, and tones flow into one another and get confused. The most favorable reverberation count for an average-size opera auditorium has been found to be from one and a half to one and eight-tenths seconds, or even longer. The sounds in the Theater an der Wien, with their short reverberation, lack brillance; too much is swallowed up by the upholstery. Personally, I think the Festspielhaus at Bayreuth has nearly perfect acoustics. For one thing, it's funnel-shaped, and that's a great advantage, because parallel walls often create dangerous reflections. Then, it has no boxes, which is all to the good, too, for boxes have a way of absorbing sound instead of reflecting it. You can hear every word at Bayreuth—small voices seem to grow, and singers never have to strain. Bayreuth has a very long reverberation—two and four-tenths seconds. That's even longer than the two and two-tenths seconds of the auditorium of the Gesellschaft der Musikfreunde, which to my mind has better acoustics than any other hall in Vienna—so far, anyway."

Jotting down Teubner's comparative figures, I noticed that the Theater an der Wein was considerably closer to the ideal figures he had cited than were the Gesellschaft and Bayreuth, and I asked him why, in view of this, the acoustics of the first should be so poor and the acoustics of the others so good.

He gave me a pitying smile and replied, "Both the Gesellschaft and Bayreuth are large auditoriums, and the bigger the house is, the longer the reverberation may be without blurring the enunciation. Mind you, I say *may* be." I began to see why acoustical engineers have sleepless nights. Teubner, however, went on as if he had written "Q.E.D." on his thesis. "Even Cherubino's aria from the *The Marriage of Figaro* sounds good in the Gesellschaft, and I consider that a real test," he said, and began to sing "Non so più cosa son" at high speed. Despite the exaggerated allegro, I could make out each syllable, but his voice certainly seemed to lack brilliance. Teubner apparently noticed this, too, for he stopped abruptly, with a shrug of disgust. "This office is soundproofed," he said. "No reverberation whatsoever. But to get back to the subject. Every listener absorbs sound—men, in their woolen suits, a little more than ladies, in their silk dresses—and no opera house sounds the same when empty and when it contains two thousand living sound-absorbers. In the perfect auditorium, which doesn't exist yet, the seats will be upholstered in such a way that each one will absorb the same amount of sound when it is empty as a person does when sitting in it. Well, we haven't figured out how to manage that yet. Some people suggested that the Staatsoper be rebuilt along the lines of Bayreuth—funnel-shaped and without boxes—but tradition won out, as it always does in Vienna. So the auditorium is still shaped like a horseshoe, and we still have boxes and galleries. Another advantage of Bayreuth is a covered orchestra pit, but that wouldn't work here, either. Several of the world's leading conductors were consulted, and every one of them opposed the idea. One of my colleagues remarked that conductors might welcome the acoustics of a covered pit if it had a Plexiglas dome through which the conductor would be visible to the audience."

Teubner chuckled, but his manner was tense. "It's one compromise after another in this business," he went on. "There's always a battle between the designers, who want to install elegant heavy silks, velours, and brocades—all highly sound-absorbing—and the acoustics experts, who don't care how a hall looks, as long as it sounds right. In this case, we reached our compromise after a great many long-winded round-table conferences. It was decided that no heavy fabrics would be used. The backs of the seats were to be covered with a hard velvetlike material that absorbs almost no sound, and the walls of the boxes lined with a hard artificial-silk damask, which reflects sound instead of swallowing it up, the way the velour tapestries did. Oh, sure, the velours gave the auditorium a sort of feudal dignity, but to hell with feudal dignity. You can't have everything."

Teubner paused thoughtfully after this mild outburst, and before we started talking again we were joined by another member of the Reconstruction Ministry staff—a tall, diffident-looking man named Josef Krzisch, who, for all his reserve, has earned the reputation of being an able expediter. A couple of years ago, he was placed in charge of the opera job, with instructions to finish it as swiftly as possible. I asked him if there was any danger that everything wouldn't be ready for opening night. "We'll be ready, no matter how many last-minute bottlenecks we run into," he replied. "For months, people have kept asking why we don't speed things up by hiring more men. As it happens, we've had a lot more men working here than we originally planned, and besides, there's a limit to everything. You've heard the story of the general who was told that it would take two hundred men three weeks to build an airfield and who then ordered three thousand men to build one in a day. Well, I don't know how the general made out, but I do know that we couldn't have worked that way here. We couldn't put in the seats before the floor was ready, and we couldn't put in the floor before the wires were laid, and we couldn't lay the wires—" Krzisch threw up his hands, and turned to Teubner. "And how about you?" he asked. "Will the orchestra be ready to rehearse next Monday morning?"

"At ten sharp," Teubner said, and added, as if he were talking to himself, "Then at least we'll begin to know where we stand acoustically."

"I thought you knew already," Krzisch said, with a slight grin.

"Of course. Of course we know," Teubner said. "No doubt about it, we *do* know."

Shortly before ten on Monday morning, I made my way down Kärntnerstrasse to the Staatsoper's stage door, which, before the fire, was used only by the male members of the company. (The ladies used a door on Operngasse, around on the other side of the house.) This stretch of sidewalk is covered by an arcade, and back in the days when I was a member of the claque, my associates and I would meet under it every day at noon to receive our orders for the evening from our boss; then we would hang around picking up backstage gossip and paying our respects to our favorite singers and conductors as they showed up for rehearsals. We also had our girlfriends meet us there, hoping to impress them with our connections. There was a park bench under the arcade, and in the summertime retired singers would sit on it, staring wistfully at the younger people going through the stage door. The great Wagnerian *Heldentenor,* Erik Schmedes, who in his time had been Europe's finest Tristan, was one of the bench sitters—still, in those days, an imposing, if somewhat pathetic figure, always impeccably dressed in bowler, cutaway, striped trousers, and gray spats, with a white carnation in his buttonhole and a silver-knobbed cane in his hand. Schmedes would sit there for hours, talking grandiloquently about the past and commenting sardonically on the opera's current leading *Heldentenor*. (He used to say the man had the voice of a railroad conductor.) Sometimes the great basso Richard Mayr would relax on the bench between rehearsals. Mayr was no has-been; he sat there, he said, because he liked park benches, and especially park benches that weren't in a park.

There was a pile of lumber where the bench had stood, and part of the arcade was boarded up. From somewhere under my feet came the noise of pneumatic hammers. I went through the stage door and at once became aware of an unfamiliar odor. In the old days, there was always the mausoleum-like smell of dust and marble—an odor I could still identify anywhere on earth. Now there was a smell of paint and linoleum. People were hurrying about with boxes and packages, and there was a sort of exuberance and tension in the air that reminded me of an ocean liner an hour before sailing time. The elevators I had heard about were there all right—four of them—but they weren't running yet, so I walked up a flight of stairs and went down a dimly lit corridor, hoping it would lead to the auditorium. But I was lost in this new setting, and I was relieved to run into Ernst August Schneider, one of the Staatsoper's half dozen artistic directors, who function as upper-echelon factotums. He is a tall man with silvery hair and the savoir-faire of a diplomat, which comes in handy in his job. Ordinarily, Schneider looks aloof and imperturbable, but just then his face showed signs of strain. I asked him if he, too, was worried about the acoustics.

"That's the only thing I'm not worried about," Schneider said "I've been so busy lately I haven't had time to ask myself whether there will even be any acoustics. Not only have we been giving operas every night at the Theater an der Wien, but we've been putting on regular performances at the Volksoper and occasional ones at the Redoutensaal. That means three complete casts. Then everybody gets sick, and I have to telephone all over Europe to find ersatz Lohengrins and Aïdas. And as if that weren't enough to drive a man crazy, everyone comes to me with complaints about the new house. Yesterday some members of the chorus were squawking about their new dressing rooms. At the Theater an der Wien, they get dressed in a hole in the wall, and it's a miracle that they don't fall down those rickety stairs on their way to the stage. Here they have big dressing rooms and rehearsal rooms, to say nothing of elevators and canteens, but all they do is grumble." Schneider told me he was going to the auditorium, so I went along with him. He led me down another corridor, where workmen were laying linoleum and we had to pick our way along some planks, and presently we came to a boarded-up door. Schneider had a couple of the workmen open it, and there we were in the auditorium.

For a second, I had a sharp feeling of disappointment. Perhaps I had unconsciously expected to find the old house again—a symphony in slightly faded ivory and gilt, the ivory the shade of an old billiard ball and the gilt with the reddish patina of age. At any rate, I wasn't prepared for the brightness and newness of the vast room. The boxes were decorated with gilded-stucco leaf designs that shone like a jeweler's shop-window display. The curtain showed Orpheus and Eurydice in an angular, stylized setting, and they didn't look as if they belonged there. Still, I was relieved to see that no effort had been made by twentieth-century copyists to re-create the baroque paintings that formerly ornamented the ceiling; in their place was a simple, modern pattern of gilded-stucco rays. The seats were not yet in place; scaffolding surrounded the upper tiers of boxes and men and women in white smocks stood on it energetically applying gold leaf. The whole room was illuminated by a garish white light provided by several powerful bulbs suspended from the ceiling, for the chandelier had not yet been installed. The place smelled of damp mortar, and while there was only a touch of chill in the air outside, here it was definitely cold—a bone-penetrating cold. From the fourth gallery came the sound of hammering.

The members of the orchestra, in their hats and coats, were in the pit, standing around and chatting. Schneider and I sat down on a couple of wooden crates off to one side of the room just as the curtain went up; a number of singers were wandering about uncomfortably, the men with scarves around their necks and the ladies in furs. Near the pit were several large black boxes, stenciled in white with "WIENER PHILHARMONIKER" and all but covered with hotel stickers from Spain and Portugal, where the orchestra had recently been on tour. Two women in black aprons appeared and began to lift musical instruments out of the boxes, dust them off, and put them on the floor, while the musicians, one by one, straggled over and picked them up. Then Dr. Karl Böhm, who has been the director of the Staatsoper, and its leading conductor for the past year, came down from the rear of the house, surveyed the scene dourly, and asked Schneider why there was no heat in the auditorium. Schneider said he guessed the heating system wasn't working yet. A diva strolling by overheard the remark, and she turned on Schneider and said, "Do they really expect us to sing in this icebox? And the cold's not the only thing wrong with this place. All this talk about the finest opera house in the world! Oh, yes! Plenty of gold leaf for the public, but no private showers for the soloists!" She glared at Schneider. He glared back and said, "Don't blame me. I didn't build the house."

Rudolf Moralt, one of the conductors who work under Böhm, came by and sat down on a crate beside Schneider. "I'm terribly excited," he said. "I'm so happy to be here today. There were times when I just about gave up hope that this day would ever come."

"I'm glad somebody feels that way," Schneider said. "Everybody else seems to be just cold and angry."

"They're all excited, even the ones who don't show it," Moralt said. "Anyone who isn't excited today doesn't belong here. But they do complain a lot, don't they? Talk about being cold! You didn't hear them complain back in the winter of '47, in the Theater an der Wien. In those days, you could see their breath when they sang."

Taking another look around, I saw Teubner standing in the rear of the auditorium, and I walked back to join him. "I wish they'd begin," he said nervously, rubbing the palms of his hands against his jacket. He pointed toward the top balcony and said, "Remember?" I did, of course, but even more vividly than our adventures in the claque, I remembered the last time I'd visited the Staatsoper. It was on a bleak winter day in 1947, with the reconstruction barely under way, and when I looked up to see what had become of the top balcony, I found nothing but a gray gash. "We've done away with the pillars and the arches that obstructed the view of the stage from the fourth balcony, and there's no reason why the acoustics up there shouldn't be as good as they ever were," Teubner said. "Do you remember how bad the third balcony was acoustically—just as bad as the fourth was good. Well, now it's a bit higher than it used to be, and we've put in some sound reflecting material behind the seats. That should make quite a difference."

As we spoke, workmen began lugging rolls of heavy fabric out onto the floor of the auditorium and draping the stuff over chunks of wood, in an effort to approximate the sound-absorbing potential of a house full of seats and people. A horn player came up to us and complained that it was terribly crowded in his corner of the pit; he wanted to know why the pit wasn't larger. Teubner told him it was the largest opera-house pit in the world—and at least a third larger than the one in the Theater an der Wien, where he had never heard the horn players complain. "Some people will never be satisfied," he said to me as the horn player walked away. "Below the auditorium we've installed a large, air-conditioned tune-up room for the musicians with built-in, velvet-lined closets shaped to fit their instruments. They've got their own washrooms, and a private stairway leading directly to the pit. They've got a smoking lounge of their own, too. At the Theater an der Wien they have to go outside in the street to smoke. We've tried to please everybody, but it sometimes seems as if we're going to wind up pleasing nobody."

Apparently, Teubner's chronicle of the luxuries about to be bestowed upon the unappreciative musicians momentarily took his mind off the imponderables of acoustics. He seemed more cheerful than he had been during our meeting the week before, and he began telling me of some of the other things that have been done to make the new house an improvement over the old. Most of the basement space used in the old days for workrooms and storage had, he said, been turned into rehearsal rooms for the orchestra, ballet, ensembles, and soloists. Carpenters, painters, and other workmen engaged in building sets had been transferred to the old Imperial Armory, and the sets now are stored there. The smaller workshops for costume makers, milliners, and bootmakers are located in a nearby building, formerly occupied by the Ministry of Social Affairs, and linked to the opera house by an underground tunnel. All the dressing rooms have been wired for sound so that singers can follow the performance, which should soothe their nerves as they wait to be called on the loudspeaker. The opera house is to be heated by radiators supplied with hot water from boilers in the Imperial Palace, where they will be less of a fire hazard than the old ones in the basement were. And the whole house is to be air-conditioned; fresh air will be pumped into it from the gardens of the Imperial Palace, which should make a pleasant contrast to the exhaust fumes that used to float in from the Ringstrasse. The pit, which holds a hundred and ten musicians, has three platforms, each equipped with a raising and lowering mechanism to amplify or minimize the sound coming from it. Moreover, there are special sound-absorbers to mute the efforts of the brass players, who so often dominate the strings, and these, in turn, have the added benefit of sound-reflectors. On the sixth floor of the building, just below the roof, is an organ with thirty-two registers and more than twenty-five hundred pipes; it has two keyboards—one right beside it and the other in the orchestra pit. The visible stage can be eighty feet wide, and a hundred and sixty-four feet deep—obviously, all that vast expanse will seldom, if ever, be used at one time—and the cavern over the stage is a hundred and forty-eight feet high. Like the pit, the stage has platforms that can be raised and lowered independently, so that sets can be put up while a performance is in progress. Some of the seats in the auditorium are to be equipped with headset amplifiers, for the hard of hearing, and others are to have reading lamps, for those who want to follow the score. There is an amplifying system with invisible loudspeakers inside the ceiling, and at either side of the proscenium, to transmit such sound effects as rain and thunder. "But the amplifying system will not be used to strengthen weak voices, no matter what rumors you may hear," Teubner said sternly. "Böhm would never allow canned music in this house."

After letting that sink in, Teubner relaxed once more and continued his happy recital. "You remember the small boxes in the rear, above the emperor's box? They have been turned into control rooms for the producer, the technical director, the chief electrician, and the radio and television engineers," he said. "And the emperor's box, as you can see, is gone, and so are the court suites, the salons, the emperor's reception hall, the festival hall, the archduke's box, and the incognito box. Latecomers, who since the days of Gustav Mahler have never been permitted to enter the auditorium during the overture, will now be able to hear it over loudspeakers in the lobby, and that's something that should make for better dispositions all around."

A small, wizened, mustached man in a blue beret came limping up to us on a cane and, with a curt nod to Teubner, said gloomily, "Are you ready for your Waterloo?"

"I beg your pardon, Professor?" Teubner said politely.

"It's all wrong," said the professor, pointing his cane at the musicians, who were now tuning up. "The reverberation is much too long. The phrases will be blurred. You'll hear nothing but noise. It will be a national disaster. Don't say I didn't warn you." With that, he stumped off, muttering to himself. Teubner told me the Professor was a prominent opera connoisseur, whose word meant a lot in Viennese musical circles. Then he fell silent.

A perturbed-looking baritone came up and said to Teubner, "I hear the stage is a hundred and sixty-four feet deep and a hundred and forty feet high."

"A hundred and forty-eight feet high," Teubner corrected him grimly. "The stage is higher, and deeper, and wider than the auditorium."

"God Almighty!" the baritone exclaimed. "How am I going to sound in such a cave?" He stared in dismay at the stage, then sighed and walked away.

The orchestra was still tuning up. Teubner told me that Keilholz, the German acoustics expert, was due in from Berlin at any moment and would conduct some scientific sound tests in the opera house that evening. If I'd care to return around midnight, Teubner said, he'd let me know the results. Just then, Böhm took his place on the podium. The tuning and talking stopped, but the hammering in the balconies went on. Somebody shouted at the carpenters from the stage, and finally there was silence. Böhm, a short, tense man given to abrupt gestures, made a brief speech to the orchestra. He spoke softly, but we could hear every word from where we stood. "When I was a youngster, getting my first taste of grand opera up there," he said, pointing toward the top balcony, where the carpenters, in their overalls, were now looking down over the rail, "I never thought that one day I would be the director of this new opera house. None of us ever thought that the old house might perish. Well, it was a great house, and we'll work hard to make the new one great. I've been asked to christen the house with the prelude to *Die Meistersinger,* but we haven't got the music, and some of you musicians tell me that you don't think you know it well enough by heart. So we're going to start with the first act of *Wozzeck.* No symbolic meaning whatsoever should be attributed to the fact that the opening words to be sung in the new house will be 'Langsam, Wozzeck, Langsam' ['Slowly, Wozzeck, slowly']."

Mild applause and a flurry of not very mirthful laughter greeted this little joke. Böhm raised his baton. The house grew extremely quiet; for perhaps a minute, it seemed that no one was so much as breathing. Even the stagehands, who had been watching the orchestra and the singers with the indifference common to their kind in backstage life all over the world, were now looking on attentively. Then Böhm lowered his baton to signal the beginning of *Wozzeck,* and after a short orchestral introduction—just a few bars, *fortissimo*—the tenor singing the role of the Hauptmann began, "Langsam, Wozzeck, langsam." I heard Teubner sigh deeply. It was, I knew, a sigh of relief, for the acoustics were undeniably brilliant—perhaps a bit too brilliant for some people's taste. One could hear the softest pianissimo of the solo violin. Presently, Böhm interrupted the orchestra to correct a mistake, and excited whispering broke out all over the house. Moralt came up to Teubner and shook his hand warmly. "Congratulations," he said. "It will be perfect."

"I hope so," Teubner replied. "So far, so good, anyway. The sound is bright and still somewhat young, like new wine. The reverberation is almost two and a half seconds. But when all the seats are installed, and the walls of all the boxes covered, and the house is full of people, it should come very close to one and eight-tenths. Then we will have the warmth and roundness that many Viennese love so much. It may even suit the Professor. Personally, I wouldn't mind if the acoustics stayed just as they are today. This is *modern* sound."

The diva who had complained to Schneider about the lack of showers sauntered up. "There's too much metal all over the place," she said. "In Hamburg, they put so much iron and steel into the auditorium that everybody had to shout. It was a tragedy. Almost all the singers ruined their voices. Thank heaven I didn't ruin mine."

Teubner bowed to her coldly. "Let's go up to the top balcony," he said to me.

We left the auditorium and walked through the main lobby, which looked exactly as it had twenty-five years before, with its old marble staircase, its lovely frescoes by Moritz von Schwind, and its lyre-playing angels. Here the familiar smell of old stone still prevailed, and I inhaled deeply. There was the same long corridor where Teubner and I used to queue up for hours on end, waiting to get in. We made for the stairway that I had run up so many evenings, taking two or three of the low steps at a time, holding my ticket in my left hand and my overcoat in my right. There were a hundred and fifty-five steps, and in the race for a good place to stand—we in the claque had to be content with standing room—youthful sprinters could elbow their way past less nimble people who had been much farther up in the queue. One night, I made those steps in exactly twelve seconds, but even so, faster *Opernnarren* were ahead of me, and by the time I arrived, gasping for breath, the best spots were taken.

Now Teubner and I, no longer young or in a hurry, climbed slowly up to the top balcony, found a couple of chairs, and sat down gratefully to listen. Up there, the acoustics left almost nothing to be desired. The sound of the orchestra was lucid and sensuous; I could hear the dynamic nuances, and I had no trouble distinguishing the various groups of instruments; the singers sounded as though they were standing right next to me. Teubner, I could see, was feeling better all the time.

After the first act of *Wozzeck,* the Hauptmann came up and joined us. "It's terrific!" he said. "Your voice comes back to you. You're not singing in a vacuum, as you are in the Theater an der Wien. You know what you're doing. It's my guess that this house will amplify beautiful singing and point up mistakes as well. It will be a challenge to work here."

There was a short break in the rehearsal, and then Böhm conducted the beginning of Richard Strauss's *Die Frau ohne Schatten,* which calls for a larger orchestra than *Wozzeck,* The house was filled with sound, as is a Gothic cathedral when the organ is being played with all the stops out. In the old house, the soloists usually tried to sing their arias from one of two spots at the sides of the stage, where the acoustics were said to be best, but now the singers were moving about all over the stage, and wherever they moved, we could hear them well.

The Hauptmann left us, and a few minutes later we had two more visitors—a portly man with a reddish face and carefully brushed blond hair, and, hobbling along behind him, the professor. The newcomer was Keilholz, who said his plane had just got in from Berlin. After listening attentively to the music for a few seconds, he closed his eyes and seemed to breathe in the sound; he sampled it much as a French wine expert judges a rare vintage.

"Two and four-tenths seconds," Keilholz said presently. "Maybe one-tenth of a second more than that. Some corrections may be necessary, but not many. What do you think, Professor?"

"I think it's a tragedy," the professor replied. "I hear only noise."

"But we haven't even begun to put in the sound-absorbent material," said Keilholz, with a puzzled look at Teubner, who raised his eyebrows warily.

"The polyphonic structure is lost," the professor said. "The people of Vienna won't stand for this sort of sound." He banged his cane on the floor to emphasize his point, and then turned and limped away.

Keilholz seemed saddened by the professor's harsh verdict. "I've had similar arguments over and over again in Germany," he said. "Mostly they're with elderly gentlemen who play chamber music at home and love the muted, intimate, soft sound they achieve there. They don't like our new, bright-sounding halls. But the truth is that many chamber groups are coming to prefer medium-size, bright-sounding halls to the small, intimate ones they used to like to play in. It's all pretty much a matter of what one is accustomed to, I suspect."

When the rehearsal was over, I took my leave of Teubner and Keilholz, who had begun arguing hotly over some esoteric point of acoustics, and went to pay a call on Böhm in his private music room, next to his office. "I liked the acoustics the moment we started to play," he told me. "The tone was full and round. The musicians say that they can hear both themselves and the others. Just a little muting here and there, and a little less sound around the brass section, and we'll be in excellent shape."

A telephone rang in Böhm's office, and he went to answer it. When he came back, he said angrily, "Again! Someone can't sing tonight. All of them work too much, sing too often, strain their voices. They give four performances a week, work for the radio, make recordings, and travel all over the place, and then they're surprised to find themselves losing their voices while they're still young. It's nothing new, though. I once had an uncle in Berlin, a well-known tenor, who could sing every one of the high Cs in *William Tell*. He got so carried away by the sound of those high Cs that he would sing them all day long, starting in the morning while he was shaving. He was through at the age of thirty-two. I warn my singers that their most valuable capital is what they have in their throats, not in their bank accounts, but they won't listen to me."

When I returned to the Kärntnerstrasse arcade shortly before midnight to find out about the tests, the stage door was locked. I rang the bell, and presently an old watchman showed up, carrying a big bunch of keys. I asked him whether Herr Teubner and Herr Keilholz were still at work inside. "They're here, all right," he said grumpily. "And maybe you'd say they're at work, considering how crazy everybody is around here. All I know is they've got some loony sitting in the pit and shooting off a pistol. This used to be an opera house, not a penny arcade!"

Sure enough, as I walked down a deserted corridor, I heard a shot, and then another, and another. There was no need to worry about getting lost this time; the shots led me directly to the auditorium, and there, in the middle of the pit, under the glaring lights, sat a man who was firing away with a toy pistol. Keilholz and Teubner were standing on the stage just above him, surrounded by a half dozen sleepy, bored-looking stagehands. Teubner explained to me that he and Keilholz had placed microphones in acoustically strategic spots around the house in order to record the reverberation time of the shots. Then he led me to a room backstage where some weird pieces of apparatus had been set up on a broad table; among other things, there was an electro-acoustical "mute-writer," with a sensitive needle that inscribed an alarmed jiggle on a roll of paper every time a shot rang out and recorded the rate of "sound decay," and a small black machine, with wires running from it and a dial that showed the decibel intensity of the sound in various parts of the house. An assistant in a white jacket, who seemed more interested in a ham sandwich he was munching than in the tests, kept watch over the machines and entered figures in a notebook after each shot; Teubner bent over the notebook and studied it as a musician studies a score. Everything was going well, he said; the figures were just the ones they had hoped for. I asked why they used a pistol, instead of musical instruments or human voices, to find out whether or not they had a good opera house. "Because our testing apparatus needs sounds that are at once extremely strong and extremely staccato," Teubner said. "Shots provide the most accurate gauge of reverberation, and there's nothing like them for ferreting out dead spots."

Keilholz came in and took a look at the notebook. "The boys who originally designed this building knew what they were doing," he said. "I wish our modern architects knew as much. I sometimes think there's too much so-called pioneering going on these days. When this house was built, nearly a hundred years ago, people didn't go in for pioneering. They'd studied the designs of the great Italian opera houses, and they built another along those lines. Fine. Until we learn more about the science of acoustics—and we're just beginning—we ought to stick to proven formulas."

I waited to hear what Teubner, with his admiration for the funnel-shaped hall in Bayreuth, had to say about that, but just then one of the stagehands came to the door and asked if he and his companions might go home. It was getting late, and they had to be at work early in the morning.

"I've got to be at work early in the morning, too," Teubner said. "But go on home, if you want to." As the stagehands vanished, he remarked, "When I look around at all the technological wonders of this new house and then hear people—singers and musicians, too, not just stage-hands—complain about late hours and other inconveniences, I can't help thinking of the fine performances this same outfit put on at the Theater an der Wien in the years just after the war. There was no heat, no food, no money, no costumes, no material for sets. The stage machinery was creaky, the lights were forever going out—everything was on a makeshift basis. In fact, we had nothing but enthusiasm and talent—but that seemed enough. And now..."

While Teubner was speaking, he had walked to the door, and with his last words he made a sweeping gesture toward the immense stage outside. I followed him out onto it, and he sat down at a piano that had been left standing near the footlights. He played a few chords and hummed a few notes, and then, gradually, his voice grew stronger and he began to sing Cavaradossi's aria from *Tosca*, "E lucevan le stelle." He listened to the sound of his voice—clear and resonant there in the empty auditorium—and nodded with satisfaction.

Keilholz came out of the testing room and walked to the rear of the auditorium. "Well, how does it feel to sing here?" he asked Teubner after listening for a while.

"Wonderful!" Teubner answered. "I'm giving it less volume than when I sing in my living room. No strain at all. How does it sound back there?"

"Fine!" said Keilholz.

Teubner swung over to the "Schmiede lieder" from *Siegfried*.

The old watchman came out of the wings, still dangling his ring of keys. "Well, what do you know!" he said, shaking his head. "Who'd have thought that the *Herr Baurat* was a *Heldentenor!* And a good one, too! Any night the regular tenor gets sick, the *Herr Baurat* can take over."

Teubner was singing "Nothung, Nothung, neidliches Schwert" in full fortissimo, and there was a contented smile on his face. It seemed to me that for the moment, at least, he not only sounded, but looked more like a *Heldentenor* than a *Baurat*. And for the moment, too, no one was giving a thought to acoustics.

THE BUDAPEST STRING QUARTET

ONE EVENING IN 1918, when I was eleven years-old, my Uncle Bruno, the most enterprising organizer of string quartets in our home town, in what is now Czechoslovakia, drafted me to take over the second-violin part of Beethoven's Opus 18, No. 4, because his regular second fiddler, a surgeon, had to hustle off to perform an operation. Ever since that night, I have been a passionate player of chamber music, and I find myself in complete agreement with Henry Peacham, a seventeenth-century British essayist, who wrote of it, "I dare affirm, there is no science in the world, that so affecteth the free and generous spirit, with a more delightful and inoffensive recreation, or better disposeth the mind to what is commendable and virtuous." The performing of chamber music—"the music of friends," it has been called—engenders an atmosphere of warmth and a degree of psychological rapport that are unknown to most virtuosos, prima donnas, or members of large orchestras. For them, music is ordinarily a competitive business, a race that goes to the fastest or to the loudest. Not so with chamber music. It is based on give-and-take; it is civilized and egalitarian; it is a garden of musical fellowship from which the law of the jungle has been banished and in which egotism simply cannot thrive. But if chamber music is noncompetitive, it is far from lukewarm, and nothing could be more wrongheaded than the view that chamber music players are austere and bloodless esoterics, as anyone can attest who has watched a chamber music group in action, soaring to the heights of happiness when a movement comes off, and plummeting to the depths of despair when, as happens more often, it doesn't. Chamber music players are compelled to tolerate imperfection; they do not tolerate the slightest lack of zeal.

Chamber music has no hard-and-fast ground rules, and even its most polished practitioners show a surprising degree of spontaneity, but it does observe certain conventions. The number of players varies widely, for instance, but there have to be at least two, and there should not be more than eight or, at the most, ten. Pianists are welcome—though not pianists who insist on banging away and drowning out everybody else—and so are flutists, oboists, and clarinetists. Primarily, however, the instruments of chamber music are the strings—violin, viola, cello—and the most popular combination is the string quartet, with the string trio and the string quintet strong runners-up. When Heifetz or Oistrakh, Primrose, or Casals, or the overworked second violinist of a symphony orchestra wants to put his chores of the day behind him and have real fun, he plays with a string quartet. Versatile as string groups are, they have their limitations, and if you like your music flamboyant, full of tone, color, strong rhythms, and dramatic effects, chamber music is not for you; you had better listen to opera companies, military bands, and symphony orchestras. If, on the other hand, you like economy of means, a balanced ensemble, subtlety of texture, and clarity of expression, chamber music is your best bet—and particularly the string quartet, surely the most sensitive musical instrument of all, and one of the supreme achievements of Western civilization.

Like so many great achievements, chamber music started off unobtrusively, and its origins are obscure, but the experts agree that it was first composed in the sixteenth century, and that from the beginning its essential characteristic was the scoring of individual parts for several instruments, to be played at the same time. The name indicates that this sort of music, unlike church music or opera, was intended to be performed in a chamber, and in the early days the chamber in question belonged to an aristocratic patron. In at least one case, the patron was also the composer, Henry VIII of England, who acquired every worthy instrument he could lay his hands on—lutes, virginals, organs, recorders, flutes, cornets, guitars, and horns—wrote some chamber music and liked to play it with his courtiers. Perhaps the first mention of chamber music in literature was provided by the Spanish writer Jorge de Montemayor, in his pastoral novel *Diana Enamorada,* published in 1559 (the instruments involved were four wooden cornets and a sackbut), and the first time the phrase "chamber music" appeared in English was in 1630, when the composer Martin Peerson published what he called "Mottects or Grave Chamber Musique…All Fit for Voyces and Vials, with an Organ Part." For a time, the viol—a relatively large and clumsy instrument, which was held between the knees—was the central instrument of chamber music, but then, early in the seventeenth century, the violin emerged, and soon its long and continuing reign began, in spite of the spirited opposition of die-hards like

Anthony Wood, an Oxford man, who claimed that gentlemen "esteemed a violin to be an instrument belonging only to a common fiddler, and could not endure that it should come among them, for fear of making their meetings vain and fiddling." With the violin in the ascendant, a good deal of pioneering in chamber music was done during the seventeeth and early eighteenth centuries by Vivaldi, Gabrielli, Frescobaldi, Vitali, Corelli, Purcell, Buxtehude, Dall'Abaco, Handel, Bach, and others. All of them wrote music for several instruments, and many of them cultivated the trio sonata, usually for strings, but none of them hit upon the string quartet as we know it today. That astonishing invention was left to Joseph Haydn.

In 1755, when he was twenty-three, Haydn was invited to spend some time in a country house in Weinzierl, Austria, as the guest of a patrician music lover named Karl von Fürnberg. There the young man played the violin at chamber music evenings, and there he composed his Opus 1, No. 1—now generally regarded as the world's first string quartet. When Haydn left Weinzierl, early in 1756, he had written at least six quartets, calling them *divertimenti, castaziani,* or *notturni.* By modern standards, they were rather naive and simple, being dominated, like most chamber music of the time, by the first violin, but Haydn's ideas were developing, and in Opus 20, written in 1772 at the East Austrian home of Prince Nicholas Esterhazy, he let the four voices participate on equal terms, with the cello singing out the opening theme—something that had never been done before. And from then until his death, in 1809, Haydn kept turning out masterpieces, each in a different mood but all rich in invention, vibrant with feeling, full of beauty. Altogether, Haydn wrote eighty-four quartets, in which he brought this noble art form from birth to full maturity—an almost incredible accomplishment.

With his first quartet, Haydn inaugurated what is now called the classical period of chamber music, which ended with the death of Beethoven in 1827. During that period, Mozart wrote his twenty-five quartets and Beethoven his seventeen, and these, with Haydn's, form the permanent gold reserve of all good string quartet players. In dedicating some of his quartets to Haydn, Mozart wrote that they were "the fruit of a long and arduous toil." You would never think so; they are divine music, seemingly written without any effort whatever, and a splendid example of Mozart's genius. And Haydn recognized that genius. "Before

God and as an honest man," he told Mozart's father, "I tell you that your son is the greatest composer known to me." (The Irish singer Michael Kelly, who performed in Vienna in the 1780s, mentions in his *Reminiscences* about a quartet evening at which "the players were tolerable." The players were Joseph Haydn, first violin; the composer Karl Ditters von Dittersdorf, second violin; Wolfgang Amadeus Mozart, viola; and the Viennese musician Jan Baptist Wanhal, cello. As for Beethoven, his early quartets—the six of Opus 18—occasionally betray the influence of his predecessors, but by Opus 59 he was very much on his own, and his style gave rise to grave doubts in contemporary musical circles. The violinist Radicati, who, at Beethoven's request, worked out the fingering for Opus 59, wrote, "I told him that surely he did not consider these works to be music." Beethoven replied, "Oh, they are not for you, but for a later age." In 1824 Prince Nicolas Borissovitch Galitzin, a Russian amateur cellist, who lived in Vienna and commissioned Beethoven to write three quartets said, in a letter to the composer, "Your genius is centuries in advance." Any four string players who have attempted to bring off the late Beethoven quartets will devoutly agree.

But if we string players have forbidding tasks, we are also very lucky. Some of the greatest composers have written some of their finest works for us. The "literature," as we call it, may not be very large, but it is extremely distinguished. In addition to the quartets of Haydn, Mozart, and Beethoven, there are about a hundred and fifty important trios, quartets, and quintets by Schubert, Mendelssohn, Schumann, Brahms, Franck, Saint-Saëns, Tchaikovsky, Borodin, Taneyev, Glazunov, Smetana, Dvořák, Grieg, Gade, Sibelus, Kodály, Dohnányi, Bartók, Verdi, Hugo Wolf, Bruckner, Debussy, Ravel, Hindemith, Reger, Prokofieff, Martinù, Schönberg, Webern, Berg, Kreneck, Milhaud, and others, past and present. All these composers were fascinated by the challenge of saying something important with the bare essentials, and since the bare essentials quickly expose any shoddiness or trickery, what they produced had to be well made and uncompromisingly honest. There are plenty of phony symphonies and operas; there are few phony string quartets.

It was early in the nineteenth centry, while Haydn and Beethoven were still producing their spectacular creations, that chamber music broke out of the chamber and into the concert hall, and one of the men who propelled it, though perhaps inadvertently, was another patron of Beethoven's—Count Andréas Rasumovsky, the Russian ambassador in Vienna. At first, chamber music groups had been assembled rather casually, from the best amateur and professional talent at hand. Then, in 1809, Count Rasumovsky decided to form a regular quartet to put on a series of musical soirées at his home, and he asked Ignaz Schuppanzigh, a virtuoso who was an admirer of Beethoven, to recruit one. For a time the count himself played with the group as second violinist, but the other men were professionals, and when Rasumovsky dropped out, they made up their minds to stick together, and got hold of a fourth professional. At first, the Schuppanzigh Quartet played in noble houses, but before long, to the horror of purists, it began going on tour and performing in large auditoriums for listeners who paid to get in. The present-day professional quartet was born.

There have been many professional quartets since Schuppanzigh's: the four Koella brothers; the four Mueller brothers, who performed Haydn, Mozart, and Beethoven all over Europe in the 1840s; the famous quartets founded by, and called after, their first violinists—Joseph Hellmesberger, Sr., Joseph Joachim (his was probably the most celebrated nineteenth-century quartet), Arnold Rose, Frantz Ondřiček. The Kneisel Quartet, which lasted from 1885 to 1917, was the first famous group in America, though it was rivaled by the Flonzaley Quartet, sponsored by Edward de Coppet, a Wall Street broker who lived in the Villa Flanzaley, beside Lake Geneva in Switzerland. Since then, many fine quartets have been heard here and abroad—to name only a few, the Kroll, the Busch, the London, the Gordon, the Kolisch, the Lener, the Coolidge, the Perolé, the Roth, the Amadeus, the Smetana, the Claremont, the Curtis, the Hungarian, the Végh, the Paganini, the Griller, the Juilliard, the Hollywood, the Alard, the LaSalle, the Loewenguth, the Koeckert, the Berkshire, the Barylli, the Wiener Konzerthaus, the Janáček, the New Music, the Pro Arte, the Fine Arts, the Musical Art, and the Quartetto Italiano.

Chamber music devotees are a frankly prejudiced and contentious breed, split into more factions than the old French Chamber of Deputies, but most seem to agree that, of the professional quartets now appearing in this country, the Budapest String Quartet is outstanding. Certainly, it is outstanding for staying power; as quartets go, it has reached a venerable age, having been founded in Budapest thirty-eight years ago by three Hungarians and a Hollander. One by one, over the years, the founders dropped out and the current members came in: Joseph Roisman, first violinist; Alexander, sometimes known as Sascha, Schneider, second violinist; Boris Kroyt, violist; and Mischa Schneider (Alexander's brother), cellist. Roisman was the first of them to join the Budapest, in 1927, and Kroyt the last, in 1936; the Schneider brothers were enlisted in the early 1930s. All four men are Russian-born Jews and naturalized Americans who received their musical education in Russia and Germany—Kroyt, at sixty-two, is the eldest, and Alexander Schneider, at fifty-one, the youngest—and the only one who has ever set foot in Budapest is Kroyt. They are all multilingual, but they know no Hungarian, and their Hungarian admirers have learned that it is hopeless to come backstage and try to strike up a conversation in the old tongue. During the Second World War, when Hungary was allied with Nazi Germany, the members of the Budapest wanted to change its name to the Roisman String Quartet, but the group's management, the recording people, and almost everybody else vehemently opposed the idea, and after a while it was dropped.

The Budapest has probably performed for more people than any other quartet in history. In its first couple of decades, though, the going was hard, for chamber music was in a severe slump, and the group spent the twenties and most of the thirties roaming about Europe, playing for small groups of cultists, and struggling along on very little money. Then, in 1938, after several preliminary tours of America, the quartet settled down here, and shortly afterward there was a remarkable rebirth of interest in chamber music, which the Budapest no doubt had some part in kindling; in any event, the group's progress has been phenomenal ever since. Nowadays, the Budapest has something it would never have dreamed of in the old era of chasing around Europe—a permanent headquarters. This is the Library of Congress, in Washington, where it plays ten concerts every fall and ten more every spring in the Coolidge Auditorium (established by the late Mrs. Elizabeth Sprague Coolidge, a wealthy lover of chamber music), using the library's own instruments (donated by Mrs. Gertrude Clarke Whittall). In addition, the quartet makes about a hundred appearances a year on tour. It could easily play to a full house every night of the year, and as it is, its performances are almost always sold out long in advance. Chamber music audiences are ordinarily small, a thousand being considered a large crowd, but in 1956 the Budapest performed for thirty-five hundred people at the Teatro Colón in Buenos Aires. It has appeared in most countries where Western music is played, though not in Russia, and has made five tours of Indonesia and two of Japan. Its fee is now a thousand dollars a night—the highest ever paid to a string quartet. Before the Budapest, quartets never made money; they might achieve a *succès d'estime*, but their members always had to do something else—teach, perform as soloists, play in an orchestra—to make a living. The members of the Budapest can afford to play chamber music and do nothing else.

The Budapest's total record sales are now over two million, which makes it incontestably the world's best-selling quartet. Since April 1940, when it signed an exclusive contract with Columbia Records, it has recorded the complete string quartets of Beethoven and Brahms, the so-called "ten famous" Mozart quartets, and many works by Haydn, Schubert, Dvořák, Sibelius, Grieg, Ravel, and Debussy. Its most successful records have been the Beethoven, Mozart, Debussy and Ravel Quartets, and Schubert's "Trout" Quintet, performed with the pianist Mieczyslaw Horszowski. The four men recorded the complete Beethoven quartet cycle on 78 rpms in the early forties, repeated it on LPs in the early fifties, and are now rerecording the whole thing in stereophonic sound. Often, when a new Budapest offering is ready, Columbia Records announces the fact in full-page advertisements—a rare honor indeed for a string quartet.

String quartet devotees who care little about bigness and business admire the Budapest String Quartet for its beautiful tone, its perfect integration, its impeccable taste, its careful phrasing, character, and style, and above all, its depth of interpretation, power, and sweep. The Budapest is never satisfied merely to perform music with a well-polished surface; the four men do not just play music, they make it, which is a different thing altogether. Their ensemble work is miraculous. The slightest *rubato* of one player is instinctively followed by the other three. Even their vibrato and bow pressure seem synchronized. But although the four instrumental voices are perfectly blended, the individual work of the performers is always clearly discernible, and this is something that the quartet, collectively and man for man, takes great pride in. The four members of the Budapest are equally good, and they are fully aware that no one of them is superior to the others. Chamber music ensembles made up of celebrated soloists seldom are well integrated, because great soloists often cannot subdue their personalities and mannerisms; each tries to overshadow the group, and sometimes wrecks it thereby. So deeply do the members of the Budapest believe in ensemble playing that three of them refuse to perform as soloists. (The exception is Alexander Schneider, and he goes all the way to the other extreme; he loves to perform the Bach sonatas for unaccompanied violin—perhaps the most ingenious and demanding violin music ever written.) String quartets, unlike soloists, play sitting down, and recently Roisman, upon being asked to perform as a soloist, exclaimed, "You mean I should walk out there without my colleagues and play *standing up?* Never!" Mischa Schneider once performed a Rachmaninoff sonata at the Library of Congress, with Artur Balsam as pianist, and he was so nervous that he says he will never solo again. And Kroyt, who was brought up as a soloist, now says that the quartet is his musical religion.

One evening not long ago, I met the four members of the Budapest at an enormous birthday party given for Alexander Schneider in the New York studio of the photographer Gjon Mili. It was attended by two or three hundred of Sascha Schneider's closest friends, a diverse group—including Pable Casals and Leonard Bernstein—united by their love of chamber music and their admiration for the guest of honor. As a birthday gift, they had set up the Alexander Schneider Fund, to pay for the education of talented young musicians. Alexander Schneider has his own orchestra of about thirty members which takes on various projects when the quartet is not busy, and the whole crowd turned up with their instruments and performed one of Bach's Brandenburg Concertos. At one point, Casals, carried away by the party spirit, seized the baton from Schneider, whereupon Schneider seized a violin from one of his violinists and played with the orchestra. Mischa Schneider and Kroyt were playing with the orchestra, too. Roisman sat smoking his pipe and quietly enjoying the fun.

This party was one of the rare occasions when the four members of the Budapest Quartet and the wives of the three of them (Alexander Schneider is not married) have appeared together at a social gathering, and everybody commented on it. Except at rehearsals and concerts, the four men rarely see each other; they have a long-established policy of personal nonintervention. They make out a powerful case against togetherness; in fact, they say that the reason they are still together is that they try to be together as little as possible. String players are sensitive people, who get on each other's nerves, and string quartets often have short, tempestuous lives, bursting apart under the stress of wild disagreements—artistic and financial. The Budapest has had its disagreements, too, but its members have learned to fight shy of as many sources of conflict as possible. They have their separate friends, separate hobbies, separate ways of life. On tour, they often take different planes or trains, or, if they take the same one, they don't necessarily sit together. Mischa Schneider spends his free time on tour visiting art museums; Roisman takes long, meditative walks; Kroyt goes looking for hardware stores and buys gadgets for his house; and Alexander Schneider is preempted by the local chapter of the Friends of Alexander Schneider. Once, the sight of the Budapest members eating lunch at separate tables at the Russian Tea Room on Fifty-seventh Street, would create rumors that the Budapest had split up; now people know that as long as the men eat apart they will play together. The three married members of the quartet, who all live in Washington, even discourage their wives from excessive mingling, though the ladies are not expressly denied the right to talk to one another when they cannot help meeting—for instance, backstage during intermissions at the Coolidge Auditorium. The wives are not permitted to attend rehearsals, however. The Budapest never rehearses in a member's home, but at the Coolidge Auditorium or, on tour, in hotel rooms. One winter years ago, during a grim blizzard, Mrs. Kroyt and her young daughter found themselves locked out of their house. Cold and desperate, Mrs. Kroyt went to the Library of Congress and interrupted the rehearsal to ask her husband for his key. The explosion that followed is still well remembered; Kroyt is said to have been the angriest of all.

The nonintervention policy derives partly from the different personalities of the four players. Roisman is reserved, competent, bald, and elegant; he looks more like a Morgan partner than a fiddler. Alexander Schneider is wiry-haired, vivacious, gregarious, erratic—the quartet's *bon vivant* and raconteur. Kroyt is small, heavyset, soft-spoken, good-humored, relaxed, and wise—its elder statesman. Mischa Schneider is gray-haired and solid, serious, and conscientious—its paterfamilias and worrier. No photograph exists of the Budapest Quartet in which all four men are smiling; at least one is always frowning. A fitting description of the Budapest String Quartet can be given by the tempo of the four movements of one of its favorite quartets, Beethoven's Opus 59, No. 1. It consists of an *Allegro,* a mood and tempo made to order for Roisman; an *Allegretto vivace e sempre scherzando,* which characterizes Alexander Schneider; an *Adagio molto e mesto,* which sums up Kroyt; and a *Thème russe: allegro,* a musical thumbnail sketch of Mischa Schneider.

Different as the four men are, they have learned to accept one another's convictions, idiosyncrasies, nervous spells, and emotional difficulties. Gone are the days when they had terrific fights about women, food, politics, and practically everything else, and when the future of the Budapest String Quartet was often up in the air. The group still has its arguments, but now they are confined to musical matters. The two Schneiders and Kroyt will shout at one another in English, Russian, German, and French, while Roisman acts as moderator. Goddard Lieberson, the president of Columbia Records, who for some years was recording director of the Budapest String Quartet sessions, recalls violent quarrels in the studio. "I'd be thinking that they would never speak to each other again," Lieberson says, "and then they'd sit down and play heavenly music." These arguments, which are often settled over a bottle of champagne (all four, fortunately, like their champagne *brut*), generally have to do with the composer's intentions. If the composer is still alive, they may appeal directly to him; otherwise they seek the answer in the score. When the Budapest members listen to the playback after making a record, their reactions are likely to vary sharply. Mischa Schneider often claims that the performance was "very, very good." Kroyt may say it was "almost all right." Roisman may shake his head and say, "I don't like it." And Alexander Schneider may be disgusted, "Terrible! There is no life in it." There are long debates about the balance of sound. If one player says he couldn't hear himself, the others are sure to disagree violently; they heard him very well indeed, they say. During a three-hour recording session, it is not unusual for the men to spend two hours arguing, but somehow, to everybody's surprise, they get their job done in the final hour. "They never agree on anything," Howard Scott, Columbia's current recording director for the

Budapest, said recently, "but when you hear the recording, they seem to agree completely."

The four members arrive at the recording studio in characteristic Budapest Quartet style—singly. Roisman is there half an hour before starting time, pacing about with his fiddle under his chin. Mischa Schneider arrives ten minutes later, sits down, and begins meticulously tuning up his cello. The two men don't speak. Another ten minutes pass, and Kroyt arrives; he talks to everybody, and doesn't touch his viola. Alexander Schneider comes in breathless one minute late, and immediately stirs up a violent musical argument. On occasion, however, he can be very helpful. At a recent session, when the group was recording the third movement of Beethoven's Opus 18, No. 5—a beautiful theme and variations—the four players, after listening to the playback, agreed that the fifth variation (which Scott compared to a German military march) did not have enough life in it. Alexander Schneider began to wander discontentedly about the studio. Against one wall he found a large bass drum and a set of cymbals, both with pedals. He brightened. He lugged the bass drum over to his chair, and Kroyt, getting the idea, fetched the cymbals. Then the Budapest played the fifth variation again, this time with drum and cymbals. When they had listened to the playback, they were so inspired that they ran through a few Russian folk dances. Everybody was in great form now, and when they recorded the variation once more—without drum and cymbals—it came off wonderfully, with plenty of life in it.

While I was at the birthday party, I spent some time chatting with Roisman; he invited me to take a plane with him to Washington the next morning and to attend a Budapest rehearsal at the Library of Congress in the afternoon and a concert in the evening. The quartet would be playing the Beethoven Opus 18, No. 4—the first piece I had played with Uncle Bruno—and the Brahms A-Minor Quartet, Opus 51, No. 2, a very beautiful composition with flowing melodies and great lyrical sweep. As the finale, there would be an added pleasure; the violist Walter Trampler would join the quartet for a performance of Mozart's String Quintet in G Minor. I naturally accepted Roisman's invitation, and when I arrived at LaGuardia Airport, I found him at the head of a line of people waiting to board the plane. We shook hands, and Roisman told me that his wife and Mrs. Kroyt were staying in New York for a few hours more to do a little shopping. He had come to the airport early, he went on, to get good seats. This was a characteristic move, for Roisman likes to plan things carefully and hates improvisation and last-minute changes. He was dressed in quiet gray, had an unlit pipe in his mouth, carried a small briefcase, and radiated composure, reticence, and reliability—precisely the requisite qualities for a quartet's first violinist. (Roisman and Mischa Schneider, the other conservative of the quartet, addressed each other for ten or twelve years as "Mr. Roisman" and "Mr. Schneider.") Roisman said that when he had left the birthday party, shortly after midnight, his three colleagues were still there. Mischa Schneider and his wife had planned to take a night plane to Washington, because they wanted to have breakfast with their children. Kroyt hadn't been sure whether he would take a train or a plane, and Alexander Schneider hadn't been sure about anything. "Mr. Alexander Schneider may even come on our plane," Roisman said, and added, with a smile, "If he does, he'll arrive a second before we take off."

As it turned out, both Kroyt and Alexander Schneider took our plane. Soon after Roisman and I had found seats in the middle of the plane, Kroyt came aboard, nodded to us, and made his way to a seat up front. He was presently joined by a slim man in his early forties, carrying a viola; Roisman told me that this was Walter Trampler. A few minutes later, just as the ground crew was preparing to remove the steps, there was a commotion at the door, and Alexander Schneider, hatless and unshaven, rushed in. He waved to us vigorously and sat down in the rear of the plane, where he at once fell into animated conversation with his neighbor, a stranger.

When the flight got under way, Roisman began quietly talking about the quartet's and his own past. Geographically, he said, the Budapest is split between Odessa, in Southern Russia, where he and Kroyt were born, and Vilna, in the North, in Lithuania where the Schneider brothers come from. "My sister Rosalia played piano in concerts with David Oistrakh when both were kids in Odessa," Roisman told me. "Rosalia is still in Odessa and still giving concerts." Roisman himself, who was born in 1900, was one of the many local *Wunderkinder* and was playing the violin quite well at the age of nine. His father, a moderately well-to-do haberdasher, died when the boy was ten. The Roisman children studied at the Odessa conservatory, and then, as proteges of the town's leading musical patroness, the wife of a wealthy tea importer, settled with their mother in Berlin, where Roisman studied violin with Alexander Fidemann. At the outbreak of the First World War, the family went back to Odessa. Roisman resumed his studies at the conservatory, won several competitions, and played with string quartets for pleasure and with the local opera orchestra for money; conditions in the opera house were quite primitive, and Roisman remembers a terribly cold winter when the musicians played indoors wearing gloves with the fingertips cut off.

During the Revolution, Odessa was overrun first by the White Army and then the Red, and afterward musicians were often sent to play at collective farms and in factories. On such a tour in 1923, Roisman happened to be near the Polish border, and he managed to slip across. Making his way to Prague, he got a job with the Czech Philharmonic and met a Hungarian girl named Pola Kvassay, whom he soon married. Then, in 1925, he moved on to Berlin. There, he ran into Boris Kroyt, a friend from back home who had also studied violin with Fidemann, and the two Odessa men spent their days talking wistfully about string quartets and their evenings playing the fiddle in cinemas and cafes. For one brief spell, they both worked in an eighty-piece orchestra at a movie theater called the Ufa-Palast am Zoo, under a Hungarian conductor named Erno Rapee. Years later, they ran into Rapee again in New York, where he was conductor at Radio City Music Hall.

For two years, Roisman drifted from job to job in Berlin, and then, early in 1927, when he was earning a decent salary playing in a café, he had to make a momentous decision. The Budapest String Quartet had turned up in Berlin, too, and its second violinist, Imre Poganyi, had just resigned. Roisman was offered the job, with the frank understanding that there was little money and practically no future in it. It was a question of trading the Toselli "Serenade" and regular pay for Beethoven and financial insecurity. Roisman talked it over with his wife, and she encouraged him to choose Beethoven. "Best advice I ever had," he said to me.

The Budapest knocked about Europe, playing where and when it could, and then, in the spring of 1930, with Mischa Schneider newly taken on as cellist, it made its first American tour, performing at Cornell University and in a dozen Eastern and Midwestern cities, winning considerable critical applause, but few paying customers. Back in Europe, in

1932, Emil Hauser, the first violinist, resigned to tour with a harpsichordist, and Roisman was naturally expected to become first violinist. Roisman himself was not so sure; a modest man, he suspected that he was not right for the job. The celebrated quartets of the past have all been dictatorships, usually with the first violinist as the boss; Roisman did not believe in dictatorship and dreaded the idea that no one would dare contradict him. Eventually, he did take the job, but only after he had made it quite clear to his fellow players, who now included Alexander Schneider as second violin, that the Budapest Quartet was going to be a democracy. And that is what it has been. If Roisman, with thirty-two years in the Budapest behind him, ruins a phrase, he is lambasted by his fellow democrats in the language—forthright, colorful, and rich in invective—of quartet players, whether amateur or professional.

"We decided early that we would share everything, good and bad, that goes with performing as a quartet," Roisman told me. "Responsibilities are equally divided, and so is money. All arguments about tempo, fingering, bowing, phrasing, rhythm, and so on, are settled by majority vote. If the vote is two to two, we negotiate and maybe compromise. Fortunately, we all have similar musical tastes. Otherwise, we couldn't have stayed together all these years." Roisman was silent for a moment, and then said thoughtfully, "Nothing is ever definite, least of all in a quartet. When I listened to some of our early recordings, I am puzzled. We used to play Hugo Wolf's 'Italian Serenade' very fast, in bravura style. Now we play it slowly. We *feel* that it should be slow. The exuberance of youth is behind us, I suppose. Still, I hope we will never become academic and dull. As long as we follow our instincts, we'll be safe. If you are sure of your musical tastes—and if you aren't, you have no business performing professionally—you feel that there is a definite character, tempo, and mood for each piece of music. We try to play the natural way; you could compare us to a singer who has a sound technique and sings his phrases with no effort. Sometimes we change the tempo a little to see how it will sound, but when we do, we usually find that our original tempo was right. Once, we tried to play the Debussy quartet in the French manner, with light bowing, little force, and great elegance. It didn't work. It wasn't French nor was it Budapest. Now we play it the way we feel it, and let the French play it their way, which is inimitable. There is room for all."

Roisman had a bad scare in August 1952, when the Budapest toured Japan. The episode is still remembered by the rest of the quartet as The Night We Lost Roisman. "One night, we were peacefully walking down a little street in a town called Okayama on our way to a rehearsal," Roisman told me, "when all of a sudden I fell into a ditch." The fall, as it turned out, had broken his left wrist. He was taken to an American army hospital where his bones were set, but the job wasn't well done, and three weeks later, in Washington, he had to have the wrist broken again and reset. Late in September, when the cast came off, he was unable to lift his violin. His wife had to put it under his chin and hold it up. And the fingers of his left hand pointed stiffly upward. "It was terrible," Roisman said, looking out into the clouds. "I had to start from scratch, and the Budapest had to play as a trio. I practiced etudes and scales for four months, til January 1953, and then, finally, my hand was all right." Roisman lives with his wife, his violins, and a collection of meerschaum pipes in an apartment on the eighth floor of a tall building on F Street in Washington. "You must come and have a look at my pipes," he said. "Some wonderful specimens among them. I always try to pick up a couple of new ones while we're on tour."

As we got off the plane at Washington National Airport, Alexander Schneider edged over to us. Roisman looked him up and down disapprovingly. "You look terrible," he said. "What time did you leave that party?"

"Four-thirty," said Schneider, fingering his stubbly chin. "I played some Italian arias for Gino, the old Italian waiter. He wept. I couldn't leave him, could I? Anyway, I did get some sleep. One hour and forty minutes, to be exact."

"Well, get some more before the rehearsal," Roisman said.

We were joined by Boris Kroyt and Walter Trampler, and the five of us walked over to the gate. A taxi stopped, but Alexander Schneider waved it on. He was still in a birthday mood and had ordered a black Cadillac limousine for us all. By the time we arrived, we had picked up two more passengers—violin-carrying members of the American Federation of Musicians, who were friends of Schneider's. Downtown, we split up. Trampler and the two hitchhiking violinists were dropped off at hotels; Roisman and Kroyt went to their homes, and Alexander Schneider accompanied me to my hotel, where I deposited my bag.

Then he and I set out—by cab this time—for Mischa Schneider's house, where Alexander stays when the quartet is playing in Washington. On the way, Alexander remembered that he had had nothing to eat since five-fifteen that morning, and he told the driver to go to the Occidental Restaurant instead. There he was welcomed like a major lobbyist and given a choice table. He ordered oysters with Chablis and roast beef with Beaujolais. "And don't bring everything at the same time," he said to the waiter. Both laughed, and I gathered that this was a standing joke.

Alexander Schneider leaned back and began to reminisce. There had always been music in his family's home in Vilna, he said. The father, who was a construction man and an enthusiastic amateur flutist, decided that his eldest son Mischa was going to be a cellist, that Sacha, four years younger, would be a violinist, and that a daughter, Manja, would be a pianist. "Manja died in Dachau," Schneider told me. "She was a good pianist. Mischa and I have a brother named Grischa. He revolted. He wouldn't play music and insisted on going into father's business. Now he works in iron construction in Toronto." There is a distinct advantage in having a good cello player in the house—there must be at least fifteen violinists for every cellist—and the Schneider family had its own quartet. Mischa and Sacha went to the Vilna Conservatory and later to conservatories in Germany, where they completed their musical education. Afterward, Mischa worked in Cologne, playing with a string quartet until he joined the Budapest, and Alexander got a well-paid "lifetime" job in Hamburg as concertmaster and program adviser of the local radio orchestra. Then, in 1932, as it grew obvious that the Nazis were coming to power, Alexander decided the job might not last a lifetime after all, and he handed in his resignation and began to make plans for getting out of Germany. Fortunately, the Budapest, which had just moved to Paris, was looking for a second violinist, and on Mischa's recommendation, Alexander got the job.

"Life with the Budapest was no bed of roses, believe me," Alexander Schneider said as he tackled his oysters and Chablis. "Right after I joined, we went on a tour of Scandinavia—big towns, tank towns, all kinds of towns. Everywhere we holed up in a hotel room and worked. Six hours, eight hours, nine hours a day. Sometimes we'd spend a whole day getting half a dozen bars into shape. After weeks of practice, we would give a concert that netted each of us four Norwegian crowns—a dollar. There was no demand for the Budapest String Quartet. Today I know this was just as well. It gave us time to study the literature, and it proved that we had what it takes. Each of us could have made much more money striking out for himself, but we decided to stay together because we loved chamber music. Even in the first few months in America we travelled in buses, stayed in cheap hotels and ate in cafeterias." As if to reassure himself that things were better now, Schneider ordered another half dozen oysters.

The second violinist has always been a string quartet's most delicate human relations problem. It is his sad fate to live much of the time in the shadow of the first violin, performing da-da-da triplets or endlessly repeating pom-poms while the first plays lovely lyrical melodies. After a few years, some second violinists become resigned to this life; others rebel. Alexander Schneider rebelled, and one day in 1944 the small world of chamber music was rocked by the news that he was leaving the Budapest String Quartet. For years, so the story went in knowledgeable circles, he had wanted to branch out into other forms of musical activity, while his colleagues had insisted that he confine himself to playing with the quartet. Now he took up a new career as a soloist. Among other things, he undertook to perform Johann Sebastian Bach's three suites and three sonatas for unaccompanied violin. "I played all six of them one night in Toronto," Alexander told me. "It almost killed me, but I did it." In 1944, he organized his chamber orchestra, and in 1950 he became Pable Casals's lieutenant for the various festivals in Prades, Perpignan, and Puerto Rico. Two years ago, Casals had a heart attack shortly before the beginning of the Puerto Rico festival, and Alexander Schneider took over his post as conductor, with great success. Alexander has led his orchestra in summer concerts in New York's Washington Square and Christmas Eve concerts at Carnegie Hall. He has also, of course, rejoined the Budapest.

When he quit, his place was taken first by Edgar Ortenberg, who resigned because the pace of travel was too much for him, and then by Jack Gorodetsky. Then, in January 1954, while the Budapest was in New York, Gorodetsky had to resign because he was ill, and Roisman wired Alexander Schneider, then on tour in Buffalo, for help. He joined the quartet the following day, played that night, and has been with the Budapest ever since. "I suppose we all learned a few things in those years," he said to me. "I learned that a quartet cannot go one man's way, it must go the way of all four. They learned to take me the way I am. Now they let me pursue my outside activities as long as these don't interfere with the schedule of the quartet, and I've promised they won't. Oh, we've learned many things. We've learned that after rehearsing for four or five hours, you need something to break the tension, or the tension will break you. I remember one day when we were rehearsing a difficult modern work. Everybody had begun to act like a nagging woman, and I suggested that we change instruments and play an early Haydn. Kroyt played first fiddle, my brother Mischa second, Roisman viola, and I cello. We didn't make beautiful music, but we sure had fun. The tension was gone in a minute."

Alexander Schneider is a rare phenomenon in chamber music—a first-rate violinist who doesn't mind playing second fiddle. He now plays it by choice, not out of necessity; he knows that he could play first any time. The Budapest Quartet is endowed with the ideal combination of violinists—two first-class artists, each with a definite personality. This is especially important for the performance of certain modern works, in which the two violin parts are equally demanding. Alexander Schneider has accepted the strict discipline of quartet playing, and the other members of the quartet not only have accepted his outside activities but sometimes even take part in them. Between tours of the Budapest Quartet, its second violinist usually heads for faraway lands. He is a restless man. In a tiny village of Provence, he has an old farmhouse with lots of beds, an out-of-tune player piano, no telephone, and an old wine cellar installed in a nearby cliff. Alexander Schneider spends about six weeks a year in this second home, and leaves the key for any friend who happens to pass through. Once, he threw the village into confusion when he received a phone call from Puerto Rico at its one café. "They couldn't get over it," he says. "They weren't sure any such place even existed." Alexander Schneider wouldn't dream of living in Washington; that city is too somnolent and too well-scrubbed for him. He loves New York, with its noise, dirt, and exhaust fumes, and spends the greater part of the year in an apartment in Greenwich Village.

Mischa Schneider lives with his wife and two sons—Gregor, eleven, and Mark, eight—on a quiet, tree-shaded street in Bethesda, Maryland. When Alexander and I arrived, he came out on the porch to greet us.

There is a certain facial resemblance between the brothers, but in temperament and manner they are as different as two men can be. Alexander is dynamic and outgoing, Mischa is quiet and introspective. Alexander is an optimist; Mischa, a pessimist. In addition to playing the cello in the Budapest, Mischa functions as its business manager, cashier, corresponding secretary, and historian, and when Alexander went upstairs to take a nap before the rehearsal, his brother let me in on some of these activities. The quartet, he told me, has always been handled by Friedberg Management on West Fifty-seventh Street, but he defers judgment on all business details and, only after informal discussion—usually during rehearsals with the other three—makes the final decision regarding concert dates and programs. These days, he said, the Budapest is so much in demand that he has to spend a lot of time appeasing those whose offers must be turned down. I gather that he is aided in his tasks by a cautious outlook on people in general, and on ones connected with the music business in particular.

After we had talked for a while, and I had discovered that Mischa was quite voluble on the subject of the quartet, while reticent about himself, he took me into his music room, which proved to be filled with books, scores, and various instruments, including not only a piano, but also a clarinet, played by his older son. He showed me "the book"—a diary in which he notes down the date of every performance. During a fairly typical two-week period last year, I saw that the Budapest gave thirteen concerts on consecutive nights, in Washington, Boston, Hartford, Northampton, Wellesley, New Haven, New York, Pittsburgh, Akron, Pittsburgh again, Cleveland, Utica, and finally back in New York. The fourteenth day was Thanksgiving, "A real day of thanksgiving," Mischa Schneider said, with feeling.

The Budapest's most famous achievement is its Beethoven cycle, Schneider told me, and it performs the seventeen quartets ("The Bible of Music") on five consecutive evenings almost every year in New York (alternately at the YMHA and the Metropolitan Museum), and in other cities that can afford the luxury of five or six all-Beethoven recitals. It has had less success with similar cycles of the celebrated quartets and quintets of Mozart and Brahms. The usual Budapest concert program consists of three works—often one classical and one romantic, with a modern work in the middle. Because the Budapest is most famous for its performances of Beethoven and the other classics, it is considered somewhat conservative in avant-garde circles, where life begins with Schöenberg, Křenek, and Webern. But actually the Budapest has performed more modern works than practically any other chamber music group. It plays modern works out of conviction, however, and not in conformity with various trends. Every year, the quartet spends a few days sight-reading new compositions, but for its repertoire, it will accept only works that all four men like, and that means perhaps two new pieces every year. "It mounts up, though," Mischa said, and went on to tell me that within the past ten years the Budapest has performed, among the contemporary works, seventeen quartets by Darius Milhaud; Bartók's First, Second, Fifth, and Sixth Quartets; four quartets by Paul Hindemith; three each by Dohnanyi and Heitor Villa-Lobos; two each by Kodaly, Arnold Schöenberg, Ernest Bloch, Serge Prokofieff, Dmitri Shostakovich, Frederick Jacobi, and Vittorio Rieti, and single works by Samuel Barber, Alexandre Tansman, Louis Gruenberg, Norman Lockwood, Nikolai Nabokov, Bohuslav Martinu, Walter Piston, Quincy Porter, Lukas Foss, Benjamin Lee, William Denny, Igor Stravinsky, Ralph Vaughan Williams, Georges Enesco, John Alden Carpenter, Daniel Gregory Mason, Ernst Křenek, David Van Vactor, Albert Roussel, Alberto Ginastera, Nikolai Lopatnikov, and Easley Blackwood.

"The Budapest's repertoire is larger than the average soloist's," Schneider told me. "At one time or another, we have performed almost every important work in the literature. In Washington alone, we play at least thirty different works every year. The four of us love all the music we play; each naturally has his favorites. Roisman is particularly fond of Mozart; Kroyt and Sascha like Beethoven; and I like Mozart's quartets in D major, B-flat major, and F major, Beethoven's Opus 59, No. 1, and Haydn's Opus 20, No. 6." All the pieces he named as his favorites, I noted, have exciting cello parts.

Conscientious historian that he is, Mischa Schneider not only keeps the "book" but covers the top margins of his cello scores with notations showing when and where each piece was played. He showed me Beethoven's Opus 18, No. 4, which the Budapest was going to perform that evening, and his notations, in tiny script, covered the tops of four pages, reaching far into the *Scherzo*. The Budapest had performed the quartet back in 1931, in Arendal, Norway. Subsequently the group had played it in Kristiansand, Stavanger, Bergen, Oslo, Copenhagen, and Hamburg; Buffalo and Baltimore; Perth, Adelaide, Melbourne, and Sydney; Paris; Providence, Louisville, Chicago, Washington, San Francisco, San Antonio, and Denver; San Salvador, Rio de Janeiro, Buenos Aires, Guadalajara, and Mexico City; Holyoke, San Diego, Sacramento, and Vancouver; and many, many other places, including, of course, New York, where it was played in 1938, 1939, 1940, 1941, 1943, 1944, 1945, 1946, 1948, 1949, 1951, 1952, 1954, and 1959.

Once in a while, the Budapest branches out and plays piano quintet with Rudolf Serkin, the group's favorite pianist. Other artists who have played with the quartet are the violists Milton Katims and William Primrose; the cellists Bernard Heifetz, Frank Miller, and Howard Mitchell; the pianists Claudio Arrau, Clifford Curzon, Myra Hess, Egon Petri, and the late William Kapell; and the clarinetists Benny Goodman, Simon Bellison, Mitchell Lurie, and David Oppenheim. The Budapest has also performed, in Buffalo and Detroit, with orchestra accompaniment, works by Elgar and Martinů. During a concert in 1957 in Louisville, Gregor Piatigorsky, the cellist, came to the quartet's dressing room. "Somebody suggested that Piatigorsky play with us," Mischa recalled. "He sent for his cello, and instead of the last quartet on the program, we played the beautiful Schubert Quintet, Opus 163, for two violins, viola, and two celli. No rehearsal. The audience loved it, though. The four of us know the music so well that it plays itself. One evening a couple of years ago, we were about to go onstage at the Library of Congress to play Beethoven's Opus 59, No. 3, when we discovered that the program said Opus 59, No. 2. It was a printer's error. Anyway, we played No. 2 without a rehearsal. We have never had a real catastrophe that made us stop in the middle of a quartet, but I remember an awful evening years ago when we performed a difficult modern work—I've forgotten which one. We started out at the same time and ended at the same time, but in between, we were chasing each other." Mischa Schneider smiled and said, "No one in the audience noticed anything. That's one beauty of modern music."

I took a cab to visit Boris Kroyt, who lives with his wife in a pleasant little house in a quiet section of northwest Washington. When I got there, Kroyt was working in a small, well-kept garden, and before ushering me into the house, he proudly showed me a fountain of Mexican tiles that he had built himself. Kroyt is always installing some new appliance in the house or tinkering away at his car, and his basement is filled with tools and do-it-yourself equipment. Mrs. Kroyt, a friendly, Russian-born woman who had just arrived from New York, told me that her husband had eight cameras, ranging from a Baby-Pathé to a Polaroid, and added, with a mock-reproachful look at him, that he was shopping around for a ninth. The Kroyts have one daughter, Mrs. Yanna Marya Brandt, who is a television producer and magazine writer in New York. When Kroyt joined the Budapest, Yanna, then a baby, became the mascot of the quartet. She traveled with it to Indonesia and Australia and almost got more publicity than the musicians. The Budapest broke its strict rule of personal nonintervention by playing at her wedding.

Kroyt and I sat down in the living room, and I had a chance to take a good look at him. He is a stocky man with broad shoulders, gray hair, and very gentle eyes. As the oldest member of the quartet, he is considered its *doyen* by his colleagues. They rely heavily on his advice in musical, financial, and homebuilding matters, and they have become rather proud of his struggles with the English language; after more than two decades in America, he still speaks with a heavy accent. A few years ago, Roisman had told me, the Budapest performed at a Midwestern college, and the college authorities asked that Roisman or some other member of the quartet make a few introductory remarks on each composition to be performed. The Budapest had a vigorous argument about whether or not to comply, with Roisman, a follower of the let-the-music-speak-for-itself school, dead set against the spoken word. He was voted down three to one. The two Schneiders refused to speak, though, and finally Kroyt volunteered. "No one understood what he was talking about," Roisman said, as if to prove that he had been right in trying to veto the whole idea. "There was a big blank stare in the eyes of all the people."

Leaning back and crossing his legs, Kroyt now told me that he had played the fiddle well when he was eight, had conducted a children's orchestra in Berlin at age eleven, and had learned to play the viola—in three days—at the age of twelve, when his teacher, Alexander Fidemann, who had his own quartet, needed a replacement in a hurry. Fidemann gave Kroyt a viola, which the boy could hardly hold up, but when concert time came, Kroyt played so well that he was invited to join his teacher's quartet. He has been in love with chamber music ever since, and with the viola—a noble instrument which, as he likes to remind his fellow players, was the choice of Mozart and Beethoven, when *they* performed string quartets.

At seventeen, Kroyt was concertmaster of the opera house in Görlitz, Germany. Later, he, too, had to look for work in cafes and cinemas, but eventually he made a name for himself as a soloist in Berlin. Richard Strauss liked the versatile young artist and, in 1926, upon becoming director of the Vienna State Opera, asked Kroyt to join him as assistant concertmaster. But Kroyt, who had just been having considerable success playing sonatas and chamber music with Artur Schnabel, was hoping for a brilliant career as a soloist, on both violin and viola. His finest hour came one night when he performed with the Berlin Philharmonic, first playing the Brahms Violin Concerto and then the solo viola part in the Berlioz concerto-like *Harold in Italy*. Playing the violin and the viola on the same evening is a difficult feat. The viola's fingerboard is longer; the fingers have to be spaced wider, and the pressure of the fingers on the bow is heavier. The proper intonation may be lost if a man switches suddenly from violin to viola. Apparently, it wasn't that night in Berlin.

Kroyt loves such stunts. One day, he told me, the Budapest recorded Milhaud's Quartets Nos. 14 and 15, which, though separate compositions, are so written that when played simultaneously, they form a string octet. After recording No. 14, they put on earphones and, while listening to the playback, recorded No. 15. Afterward, the engineers superimposed the two recordings. Since then, Kroyt, a man of Talmudic intellect, speculated that he might have performed six different parts in the octet, by recording the first and second violin parts, in addition to the viola parts that he actually played, and letting the engineers put them all together. "I could also have played both the violin and the viola solo parts of Mozart's Sinfonia Concertante," he told me, "conducted the accompanying orchestra besides, and had *everything* superimposed on the same record."

Kroyt went on to say that he has played in string quartets for as long as he can remember, but that the Budapest is the only one he has ever been devoted to full time. In Berlin, in 1919, he joined the revolutionary Anbruch ("Beginning") Quartet, which, living up to its name, specialized in contemporary music. In 1924, he formed his own group, the

Kroyt Quartet, and in 1926 disbanded it to join the Guarneri. Meanwhile, of course, he was pursuing his career as a soloist, and one day—he does not remember the year—he took a train to Budapest and gave a violin recital there. Kroyt managed to stay on in Berlin for some months after the Nazis took over, and during that uncertain period, he organized another Kroyt Quartet. Meanwhile, in Paris, the Budapest lost its last Hungarian, and Roisman was determined to have Kroyt as replacement. The only trouble was that Roisman had no idea where his boyhood friend was, and it took a long search before he managed to track Kroyt down, with the aid of mutual friends in Germany, and invite him to Paris. Finally, over coffee and *croissants* in a Paris café, the two men had a long talk, and Kroyt then and there agreed to join the Budapest.

Kroyt told me he has never regretted giving up his career as a soloist to join the Budapest. "As a soloist, you are always asked to play the same eight or ten concertos—Beethoven, Brahms, Mendelssohn, Tchaikovsky, and the rest," he said. "Think of the wonderful choices we have in chamber music. The Beethoven quartets alone are almost inexhaustible. Playing the Beethoven cycle is a string quartet's greatest responsibility and achievement. They form the heart and soul of the repertoire, the same exhilarating experience for a string quartet that Hamlet is for an actor. But the most difficult composer is Mozart. If Mozart isn't done exactly right, it goes awfully wrong. When we do Mozart well, I always think I hear the angels sing."

Kroyt practices "just a little" at the beginning of each session, he told me, and "very rarely" during the rest of it. He cannot remember ever practicing more than two hours a day. He follows a piece of advice that Fritz Kreisler once gave him—never to practice on the day of the concert. "He told me to take the instrument and improvise a little instead," Kroyt said. "It's bad enough to rehearse on the day of a concert, but I'm really sorry for those poor devils who are so nervous they have to practice up to the very last moment."

As Kroyt walked me to the door, I asked him whether the Budapest had ever considered playing by heart, as some of the younger groups do. "We had great admiration for the Kolisch Quartet, which always played by heart," Kroyt replied. "They even played Schöenberg by heart—terribly difficult. But we decided it just wasn't worth the effort. Playing by heart is especially difficult for the two middle voices. In the earlier

Haydns, the viola and the second violin have to play "pom-pom" for thirty-seven bars on end. I admit that playing without the score makes for a great effect on the audience. But"—Kroyt's eyes flashed—"the Budapest doesn't go in for that sort of effect."

After leaving Kroyt, I headed for the Library of Congress, where I had arranged to call on Dr. Harold Spivacke, chief of the library's music division, half an hour before rehearsal. When I got to his office, he said he would take me to see the instruments that the Budapest would play that afternoon and evening. They were in the Whittall Pavilion, a large, beautifully furnished room, with indirect lighting and air-conditioning, that is a memorial to a generous woman's love of fine stringed instruments. Mrs. Gertrude Clarke Whittall, the widow of a rug manufacturer from Shrewsbury, Massachusetts, has been a lifelong admirer and collector of such instruments; in 1935 and 1936 she gave the Library of Congress five outstanding stringed instruments and five fine bows, and established the million-dollar Gertrude Clarke Whittall Foundation for their preservation and use. Dr. Spivacke led me up to a glass case, opened it, and stepped back to let me have a look. Inside were three violins, a viola, and a cello, all made by Antonio Stradivari, and five bows by Francois Tourte, of Paris, who has been called the Stradivari of bowmakers. The most famous of the violins is the Betts, made in 1704 and named after a London violin dealer who once acquired it for twenty shillings; it is now worth between fifty and sixty thousand dollars. The two other violins are the Castelbarco, made in 1699 and named after Count Cesare Castelbarco of Milan, a nineteenth-century collector of fine instruments, and the Ward, a beautiful, orange-varnished one, made in 1700 and named after its first recorded owner, an Englishman. The viola is the Cassavetti, from 1727, when Stradivari was eighty-three years old, and named for an early owner. The cello, made in 1697, is also named for Castelbarco.

"Instruments like these must be played regularly or they will deteriorate, as Mrs. Whittall knew very well when she arranged this gift," Dr. Spivacke said. "Like other lovers of such things, she had long been saddened by what had happened to Paganini's Guarneri del Gesu; it is kept in a glass case in the Municipal Palace of Genoa, rarely played, and people say it has lost most of its power and beauty. So although Mrs. Whittall stipulated that the Strads must never leave the library except for restoration and repair, she also stipulated that the income from her foundation must be used to pay prominent artists to come here and perform on them. All the same, the instruments gave us a lot of trouble at first. Not many artists cared to play them after only a few short rehearsals. String players always need time to get used to another instrument. Among a number of quartets we invited for single concerts was the Budapest; it gave its first in December 1938, shortly after its members had decided to settle in the United States. They played well, but it was the old story—they didn't like to perform on unfamiliar instruments. So we did a little thinking. Suppose we had a quartet in residence here, and the players had time to make friends with these beautiful instruments. This looked to us like the answer, and the following year we offered the Budapest a contract to play a total of twenty concerts at the library in spring and fall. It has been here ever since, and the scheme has worked out well for everybody. The Budapest loves to perform on the Strads; the library is certain to have the quartet for twenty concerts a year; and each season the people of Washington hear thirty chamber music works played by this great group. The Budapest always plays to a full house. Tickets cost twenty-five cents—it's only a service charge, really—and people form long lines to get them on a first-come, first-served basis. But even if the price of admission were ten times what it is, I bet we'd never have an empty seat. By the way, you'll see Mrs. Whittall herself at the concert. She's ninety-two and slightly deaf, but she wouldn't miss the Budapest for anything."

While we were talking, Roisman and his colleagues drifted in—one by one, of course—to pick up their instruments for the rehearsal. The violinists sometimes switch from one of the three violins to another, and on this afternoon, Roisman chose the Ward, which has a soft, flexible tone, and Alexander Schneider chose the harder-sounding Betts. On tour, the members of the Budapest play their own instruments. Roisman has a Pietro Guarneri, a Guarneri del Gesù, and a Montagnana. Alexander Schneider has a Guarneri del Gesù. Kroyt has a viola made by Michael Deconet, an Italian who was very likely a pupil of Montagnana. And Mischa Schneider has a Gofriller cello.

Dr. Spivacke went back to his office, and I followed the four musicians into the Coolidge Auditorium which, with its small stage and a mere five hundred and twenty-seven seats, struck me as just the right size for chamber music. The members of the Budapest took their places on the stage—first and second violins on the left side, as always, facing the viola and cello. Roisman kept his jacket and tie on; he sat down and immediately began to practice scales. Across from him, Kroyt hung his coat over the back of his chair, loosened his tie, and began to tune his viola; then he drew a few long tones from the lower strings, clearly enjoying the deep, mellow sound. Mischa Schneider wearing an open-necked sports short, carefully adjusted the pegs of his beautiful cello, his head slightly tilted to one side. Alexander Schneider, in a white shirt, suspenders, and tie wandered all over the stage with his violin under his chin, playing the beginning of Bach's E-Major Partita and then switching abruptly to a gypsy air.

I sat down in the fourth row. No one paid any attention to me except Alexander Schneider, who enjoys an audience even if it is only an audience of one. Having slept a couple of hours, he was well rested and full of pep.

"You're going to have the treat of your life," he announced to me from the stage. "There are two outfits in this country that will never let you down. The Budapest and American Tel & Tel." He played a number of brilliant arpeggio passages. "Listen to that fiddle!" he said. "Aren't the overtones terrific?"

"All right gentlemen," Roisman said mildly. "Let's get on with the Beethoven."

Alexander Schneider sat down instantly. In a few seconds, when everybody was ready, Roisman began with the upbeat, an open-string quarter-note G, and I recognized the dearly familiar beginning of Opus 18, No. 4. But any similarity between these four and Uncle Bruno's group stopped with the next few notes they played. Most amateurs and many professionals need a while to "play themselves in," but the Budapest was completely integrated from the very beginning, and the qualities that have made it famous were all there—the warm tone and incisive bowing, the rhythm and dynamics, the temperament and the spontaneity, the balanced sound and the crystalline clarity. The four men played with great intensity. They were enjoying the music and they conveyed their enjoyment to me.

Technically, it was a brilliant performance. When the Budapest played a sudden *forte-piano,* all four men reduced their bow pressure at the same instant. After Roisman had brought off a magnificent semiquaver passage, Mischa Schneider looked up at him approvingly, and Alexander shouted, "Bravo, Joe!" Kroyt tapped his right foot (he was the only one who did any foot-tapping, and he didn't do it at the concert) and sat bent forward, cocking his left ear toward his viola as he played. All scores are divided into more or less arbitrary sections, marked by letters or numbers, and in this one there is a short stretch right after the letter "L" where the second violin carries the theme. It is a famous trap for inattentive second fiddlers, but it wasn't so for Alexander Schneider, who jumped up from his chair, held his violin high in the air, and played the passage with exaggerated *schmaltz,* like a street fiddler in Naples. Kroyt, always the perfect partner, stopped playing and started singing a Russian song, sounding a little, but only a little, like the late Chaliapin. Mischa Schneider thereupon performed a number of stupendous triads on his cello that would have much impressed coffeehouse audiences in his native Vilna. Only Roisman went quietly on with his part, untouched by the pandemonium around him, playing Beethoven with his noble tone and elegant bowing. Before long, his impeccable performance in the midst of bedlam stopped the others, and Alexander Schneider laughed so hard that I began to fear he might drop the Betts.

"Joe, you're killing me," he said.

"Are we rehearsing or aren't we?" Roisman inquired in a sad voice.

"All right," said Mischa Schneider. "Once more, nine bars before 'M.'" They started again.

"You are not together, gentlemen," Mischa Schneider told the violins, and stopped playing. "Nine bars before 'M.'"

From there on, things went smoothly until the middle of the second movement, when Mischa Schneider called, "More lightly, please. Just touch it!" In the third movement, he and Kroyt had a short argument while both continued to play. The members of the Budapest Quartet are able to play a difficult passage, carry on a running conversation, and point out a musical accent in the score simultaneously. They played only excerpts from the last movement of the Beethoven, but they rehearsed the entire Brahms A-Minor Quartet. They attacked it with gusto, almost as they would at a concert, and the illusion would have been perfect if Alexander Schneider hadn't sung out the notations—"*Dolce,*" "*Sempremezza voce e grazioso,*" "*Lusingando,*" and so on. The *Andante* was superbly done. In the third movement, *Quasi minuetto*, Alexander Schneider took advantage of a short rest in the middle part, *Allegretto vivace*, and danced a *czardas* around Roisman's chair, but he was back in his own chair in time for his cue and didn't miss a note. Roisman brought off his delicate *spiccato* passages with virtuoso facility, and both Alexander Schneider and Kroyt shouted *"Bis! Bis!"* All of a sudden, Brahms was forgotten and the four members of the Budapest were demonstrating brilliant *spiccato* runs on all strings, each trying to outdo the others.

At length, order was restored by Roisman, and the quartet went on again. Then Kroyt played an open string note in a solo phrase, and Mischa Schneider objected vehemently.

"That sounds awful, Boris. An insult to my ears."

"I was playing that open-string note when you were still a baby," said Kroyt.

"I wouldn't remember," Mischa Schneider said coldly. "I wasn't brought up a *Wunderkind*, Herr Kroyt."

"That's been oblivious to me for some time," said Kroyt.

"You mean obvious," said Alexander Schneider.

"Obvious *and* oblivious!" shouted Kroyt.

"Gentlemen! Gentlemen!" said Roisman.

A few minutes later, Walter Trampler, carrying his viola, came down the side and slipped into the seat next to me. We listened happily as the Budapest played the wild, syncopated finale of the Brahms with terrific power. At one point, Trampler sighed deeply. "They are incredible," he said. "You would think they all exhale in the same rhythm." He nodded his head and said, as if to himself, "Yes, that's it, they *do* exhale their phrases together."

Trampler's arrival had a stimulating influence on Alexander Schneider, who could now perform for an audience of two. Toward the end of the movement, he abruptly slid into "O Sole Mio." Kroyt at once chimed in with the second Kreutzer *étude* (the theme made famous by Jack Benny on the radio), and Mischa Schneider plucked the strings of his cello. At that point, even Roisman broke down, and began playing his fiddle between his knees, like a cello. Poor Brahms went down ingloriously.

Trampler dissolved into laughter. "You know, they are really smart," he said at last. "They know that monotony is the worst enemy of a quartet rehearsal. Anything to beat monotony. They have fun and they argue about musical matters, but they are beyond bitter, personal fights. They have learned to compromise. This is the fourth season I have played with them. We've done lots of recordings—Mozart and Brahms. Recording sessions are always tough, because you have to repeat so many things, but they made it easy for me from the very beginning. I never had to prove anything. I just went along with them and all was well. There is never that awful strain that has broken up so many groups. And everything they do has artistic conviction. When they feel instinctively that they have to play a *piano* a little louder, they will do it, and usually they are right. Their *piano* is never too soft, and their *fortissimo* has tremendous volume. I know fine quartets, but I know no other group whose personalities merge so completely and happily." He paused and said thoughtfully, "Haydn would have liked them. Mozart would have liked them. Even Beethoven—and you know how gloomy he could be."

On the stage, a violent argument in Russian and German had broken out between Kroyt and Mischa Schneider over an esoteric musical question in the finale of the Brahms. They would shout at each other until they ran out of breath, and then Alexander Schneider would say "*Messieurs, faites vos jeux!*" Roisman shook his head sadly but kept silent. Then, as Kroyt and Mischa Schneider shouted louder still, he said, in his gentle voice, "Gentlemen, *please!*" and almost immediately the argument faded away. The four men repeated the end of the last movement.

"Without Roisman there would be no rehearsal at all," Trampler remarked. "He rarely speaks, but when he does, they all listen to him."

Roisman suggested that they play the beginning of the finale once more. All went well for a while, and then Alexander Schneider motioned furtively to his brother and Kroyt, and the three of them gradually played more and more softly, until they were just going through the motions and only Roisman was audible. The rehearsal ended on a note of general merriment. I asked Trampler whether it was always like this.

"Anything goes at rehearsal," he said. "That's the rule."

After the Brahms, Trampler unpacked his viola and joined the others on the stage. The five men began to play the Mozart G-Minor Quintet, one of the greatest chamber music works of all, and Trampler's instrument blended in as if he had played with the Budapest all his life. Later, the two violists played a passage together, and then the two violinists, while the others looked up and commented. This interlude was followed by a long and thoughtful discussion of how Mozart had meant a particular passage to be played. Presently, Alexander Schnieder announced that the tempo of the quintet would have to be stepped up that evening, because he had to catch the eleven o'clock plane back to New York. There was no more comic relief during the Mozart, and when it was finished, Roisman sat back, looked at his fellow players, and said he thought it was all right.

Alexander Schneider nodded. *"Es sitzt,"* he said.

Suddenly everybody was in a hurry. The men took the instruments back to Dr. Spivacke, and within two or three minutes the artists had all gone off in separate directions.

I arrived at the Library of Congress shortly before eight-thirty, and found the corridor in front of the Coolidge Auditorium densely crowded. When I got inside, I spotted Dr. Spivacke. He took me over to the rear of the auditorium and introduced me to Mrs. Whittall, a silver-haired lady of graceful dignity, who sat in a chair equipped with a special hearing aid. "I'm looking forward to the lovely Beethoven quartet," she said. "I never get tired of it."

There were a few minutes left, and Dr. Spivacke took me backstage. Kroyt, who was filling a cup at the watercooler, looked happy and relaxed. Roisman sat in the dressing room with his pipe in his mouth and his fiddle in his hand. The Schneider brothers were in the narrow corridor outside; Alexander was playing a scale and looking eager to go out and perform, and Mischa, carrying his cello, exuded that solid, rocklike quality that makes a great cellist the foundation of a string quartet. I caught Alexander Schneider's eye. "Don't forget," he called out to me. "The Budapest will never let you down!"

Dr. Spivacke and I went back to the auditorium and took our seats. A few seconds later, the wings of the door at the center of the stage were opened and the four members of the Budapest Quartet came in, led by Roisman. They sat down; Roisman played the first note, and the beautiful opening theme of Beethoven's Opus 18, No 4, filled the air.

STRADIVARI
Ne Plus Ultra

NO ONE KNOWS when and exactly where Antonio Stradivari was born. Almost nothing is known about his childhood. His grave no longer exists. "These questions, we fear, can never be answered," the Hill brothers wrote in 1902 after years of thorough research. It doesn't matter. Mozart's grave is unknown, but his music will survive all but the apocalypse of mankind. Stradivari's instruments assure his immortality.

The Stradivari family—variously spelled Stradivarto, Stradilvertis, Stradivertus, Stradaverta—lived in and around Cremona since the twelfth century. There is a record in the city archives, dated December 7, 1176, about one Lanfranco de Stradilvertis, *"iudex constituttus a consulibus iustitiæ Cremonæ."* Various records also mention Johannis Stradivertus, *"sindicus Cremonæ,"* in 1220; Giuliano, *notairus;* Tebaldino, Isacco, Pietro, Balzarino, and Gasparino, all in the fourteenth century. Professor Renzo Bacchetta, today the great Stradivari authority in Cremona, believes that the family came to Italy with the Goths and that the name means "leader" in the Gothic language. E. J. Payne assumes that the name derives from *"Stradiere,"* a customs officer posted on the *strada* (road). Professor Astegiano, who catalogued the rolls of the ancient community of Cremona, derives the name "Stradverta" from *"strada aperta,"* open road. The Hills quote Signor Mandelli, a former mayor of Cremona, who found a record dated August 30, 1622, of the marriage of Alessandro Stradivari to Anna Moroni at the parish of San Prospero (Alessandro was born on January 15, 1602). Three birth certificates were later registered in that parish: Giuseppe Giulio Cesare in March 1623; Carlo Felice in September 1626; Giovanni Battista in October 1628.

Since no record mentions his birth, the first official document concerning Antonio Stradivari is the certificate, dated July 4, 1667, of his marriage to Francesca Feraboschi, also spelled Ferabosca, the widow of Giovanni Giacomo Capra. On June 3, 1680, according to an existing deed, Antonio Stradivari, "son of the late Alessandro," bought a house from the Cremonese family of Picendair for seven thousand imperial lire. The house was No. 2, Piazza San Domenico. Today a modern building stands on the site, now known as No. 1, Piazza Roma. Stradivari lived and worked in his home until he died.

During the seventeenth century, Cremona underwent several disasters: there were military campaigns in Lombardy, a terrible famine in 1628 and 1629, and the plague in 1630. The violin maker Hieronymus Amati, his wife, and two of their daughters died that year. (In Brescia, Paolo Maggini died of the plague in 1632.) Two-thirds of the population of Cremona was wiped out; the town had "the appearance of a wilderness." A parish priest in San Vincenzo reported that "many citizens have left Cremona to live quietly in other towns...rich people have by this time (1630) been reduced to such a state of poverty, caused partly by the billeting of soldiers in their houses, and partly by the heavy taxes imposed, that, were it not for the shame of it, they would go begging." François Joseph Fetis, the French nineteenth-century writer and authority on Stradivari, concludes that many archives in Cremona "were stolen, concealed or even destroyed." The Hills assume that Antonio Stradivari may have been born not in Cremona but in a nearby town or village where his parents went to escape hardship, persecution, and disease. Yet a search of parish registers in the vicinity turned up no clue.

The label in an early Stradivari violin reads "...Alumnus Nicolai Amati, Faciebat Anno 1666"; it is the oldest documentary proof of his existence, preceding his marriage record by one year. How then can we think we know when he was born? Again, his labels are helpful. In his last years, Stradivari was justifiably proud of being able to make fine instruments at such an old age, and about half a dozen times he added his age to the date on the label. Among these are a violin dated 1732, "de anni 89" ("at age eighty-nine"); another dated 1735, "d'anni 91"; a cello dated 1736, d'anni 92"; a violin dated 1737 (the last year of Stradivari's life), with the notation "d'anni 93," the notation probably added by Stradivari's son, Omobono. The old man was perhaps no longer able to write. All these labels were seen by the Hills, who wrote in *Antonio Stradivari* in 1902, "We may therefore conclude that...the matter [of the year of his birth] may be finally placed beyond controversy."

Yet the controversy continues. In 1950 Renzo Bacchetta published the *Carteggio* (diary) of Count Cozio di Salabue (1755–1840), the Piedmontese nobleman who lived in Casale Monferrato. He had inherited a Nicolò Amati violin dated 1668; he fell in love with violins and became the greatest collector in violin history. After acquiring many of the finest instruments, Count Cozio in 1775 bought from Stradivari's youngest son, Paolo, a magnificent collection of Antonio Stradivari's memorabilia— letters, designs, tools, perhaps even a formula for making varnish. Paolo, a textile merchant, was not interested in violins. Cozio then began to write his *Carteggio*, which contains invaluable material about the Cremonese and other masters, exact measurements of famous instruments that he owned or saw elsewhere, information about other owners of important instruments. Gradually the collector became also a dealer and a shrewd businessman.

Cozio admits in his *Carteggio* that he made several alterations on the labels of Stradivari and added notations to the dates of some labels with his own hand ("...*e manuscritto sotto di mio carattere come el 31 il datta biglietto pure de...d'anni 92*" [Written below in my handwriting is "age 92," the same as in the inscription on ——'s violin, also of the 1731 period]). According to René Vannes, Antonio Stradivari is listed in the "*Stati anima*" (census) of the Cremona archives as twenty-nine and thirty-three years old respectively. Bacchetta believes that Stradivari was born in 1648; he proved this thesis brilliantly in an essay, "Stradivari Was Not Born in 1644." Vannes, in his *Dictionnaire Universel des Luthiers*, believes that Stradivari may have been born in 1649 and that, at his death in 1737 (this date is recorded), he was eighty-eight or eighty-nine and not ninety-three. Thus the matter remains confused. It seems more important to remember that during the last years of his life Stradivari made some magnificent instruments which, two hundred years later, were the concert violins of celebrated violinists. Kreisler owned the "Lord Amherst" of 1734 and another violin dated 1733, on which Heifetz later performed. Heifetz also owned a Stradivari, made in 1734. Menuhin still performs on the "Prince Khevenhüller," made in 1733. Efrem Zimbalist played the "Lamoureux," made in 1735. What difference does it make whether Stradivari was in his late eighties or early nineties when he made these magnificent violins?

After his marriage in 1667, Stradivari lived first in Casa del Pescatore, in the parish of his bride, Francesca Ferabosca Capra, who was four years younger than he. Her father was a noted mathematician. Though her first marriage had ended with her husband's suicide. Stradivari seems to have been happy with her; they had two girls and three boys. Two of the sons—Francesco, born in 1671, and Omobono, in 1679—later learned their father's art and became his only assistants.

The house in Piazza San Domenico which Stradivari bought in 1680 and where he worked all his life was sold in 1777 by Antonio, his grandson, to Giovanni Ancina. It remained unchanged until 1888, when it was bought by the owner of the adjoining "*caffè con bigliardo*" to enlarge his establishment; he modernized the façade, for no one in Cremona thought to preserve the house where the city's most celebrated inhabitant had lived and worked for over fifty years. During the Mussolini regime, Piazza Roma, as it was now called, was modernized and Stradivari's house disappeared altogether. Again no one raised his voice.

Stardivari's house had three floors. The workshop occupied the ground floor; passersby might see Stradivari there, surrounded by his apprentices, working at his bench. Many people came to see him: friends, colleagues, and customers who wanted to commission or buy an instrument. On the roof was a flat terrace (*seccadour*) where Stradavari hung up his freshly varnished instruments for slow drying. During the warm season he worked there for its light and fresh air. When the house was rebuilt in 1888 workmen found blocks of wood, shavings, and other valuable relics—everything was thrown carelessly away.

Almost nothing is known about Antonio Stradivari's private life and personal habits. After the death of his teacher, Nicolò Amati, in 1684, Stradivari was the most famous violin maker in Cremona. Twenty years later, after he made the famous "Betts," at the age of sixty, he was admired all over Europe. More important, he was acknowleged as first by his own peers, the prominent violin makers of Cremona. But almost nothing was written about him; no attention was paid to the absolute ruler of the violin world. There were a few exceptions: in 1720, Don Desiderio Arisi, a monk in Cremona, wrote that "Stradivari's fame is unequaled as a maker of instruments of the finest qualities." Perhaps Stradivari was not personally very interesting. He lived a quiet, busy life; there were no scandals, no crimes. Much more is known about Guarneri del Gesu, for that erratic genius was always involved in some trouble.

There are only two letters written by Stradivari (both are reprinted in facsimile in the Hills' book). The great genius of the violin seems to have had a sketchy education; if he began his training at Nicolò Amati's workshop at age twelve or fourteen, usual in Cremona, he hadn't spent much time in school. In his letters, Stradivari makes many mistakes in spelling, omits articles, uses the wrong vowel, *"solo"* for *"sole,"* *"mane"* for *"mani,"* and also uses the Cremonese dialect, *"vallio"* for *"valgo,"* *"prumisso"* for *"promesso,"* *"tedare"* for *"tediare."* The style is unsophisticated and humble. In one letter, Stradivari asks for one *filippo* (a Lombardian silver coin now worth perhaps five dollars) for repairing and varnishing a cracked violin. He writes that the work "...is worth more, but for the pleasure of serving you, I am satisfied with this sum." The other letter ends, "...I will now finish, not wishing to weary you further, kissing your hands and making obeisance—Your Excellency's most humble and devoted servant, Antonio Stradivari." At that time Stradivari was perhaps seventy years old, wealthy and famous, aware of his standing in the town. In 1729, looking for a burial place, he purchased a tomb from the heirs of Francesco Villani, member of an old, noble Cremonese family. It was located in the Chapel of the Blessed Virgin of the Rosary, in the Church of San Domenico. Instead of ordering a new tombstone, Stradivari had the inscriptions around the sides and the coat of arms in the center effaced, his own name and inscription substituted. This tombstone, the only relic of him that still exists, suggests that Stradivari liked to be prepared for everything ahead of time, even death, and that he didn't like to throw money around, even for a new tombstone.

Some historians assume that Stradivari may have been Nicolò Amati's godchild, but there is no proof of this. The guild rules in Cremona were strict about accepting an apprentice: master and apprentice appeared before a notary, and a contract drawn up. Among violin makers the standards of professional ethics were high; it is unlikely that a man of Nicolò Amati's standing would benefit unfairly from the work of his apprentices and assistants, nor would the younger men dare take advantage of their master's reputation. Although Stradivari could have got more money by selling his early violins under the name of "Nicolò Amati," this was out of the question. A violin maker's apprenticeship lasted six years but he was expected to make a violin himself after three years. The earliest known Stradivari violin is dated 1666; assuming he was born in 1644, Antonio was then twenty-two (or eighteen, if he was born four years later); in any case, he was probably already a young assistant, not an apprentice.

Some experts have wondered exactly when Stradivari's originality began to assert itself—when it would be correct to call a late Amati "an early Stradivari." They claim to detect evidence of Stradivari's hand in some late Amati violins; but a fine violin must be considered in its entirety if it is a work of art, and a work of art embodies the spirit of its maker. If a late Amati breathes the spirit of Nicolò Amati—which a good expert will feel instinctively—then it must be classified as a work by Amati even if younger hands helped complete it.

The earliest violins attributed to Stradivari show the influence of the "small pattern" model of Nicolò Amati: they are now called *"Amatisé"* Stradivaris. They were not copies, for Stradivari's artistic orginality was already pronounced at an early age. His *Amatisé* violins have much of his early genius: they are bolder, more adventurous, perhaps more masculine than the lovely, somewhat "feminine" small pattern violins made by Nicolò Amati. In tone, however, they were very similar. "The tone of the violins Stradivari made previous to 1684 (the year Nicolò Amati died) cannot be distinguished from that of the average medium-sized Amati," the Hills admit. "There is the same bright soprano, woody quality of perfect purity, the freedom of response which is so helpful to the average player, and the sufficiency of volume for all purposes other than that of the rendering of solos with a large accompanying orchestra in a great hall."

Stradivari was wholly familiar, of course, with both the small and the grand pattern Amati model. He followed the smaller model because there were customers for it. Players were than less interested in sonority and carrying power than in easy response and sweet tone; there were no large orchestras, no large halls. Even professional players in the 1680s were happy with a Nicolò Amati violin or an *Amatisé* Stradivari.

Stradivari's *Amatisé* violins were often covered with a golden yellow varnish similar to Amati's. But Stradivari could not afford imported wood, obtaining his from Lombardy. He often cut maple on the slab, as his teacher had taught him. But, as time went on, his personality became more pronounced; his scroll, often expressive, is cut deeply into the wood; he already placed his signature on his early violins. And he seems to have had his own customers. Obviously Stradivari's name was becoming known among the *cognoscenti*. In 1682, he got an order from Michele Monzi, a banker from Venice, for two violins, a viola, a small and a large cello: all to be presented to King James II of England. The instruments, beautifully ornamented, were sold for one hundred ducats; unfortunately they have since disappeared. Stradivari also received an order from Cardinal Vincent Orsini, archbishop of Benevento, for two violins and a cello. In 1686, the cardinal granted Stradivari an appointment (a copy of the lost document is reproduced in the Hills' book). The cardinal noted "the faithful service and kindly affection" which Stradivari had shown and desired "to rank him among our familiar friends," and exhorted all and everyone "that they show him the same favor, esteem, and due honor." This friendship continued when Cardinal Orsini became Pope Benedict XIII.

Stradivari also made a beautiful quartet of instruments for the court orchestra of King Amadeus II of Sardinia. He made (and personally delivered) a cello for the duke of Modena, later honored by the duke in the presence of the court. According to Fétis, Stradivari at that time made not only violins, violas, and cellos but also viols with six and seven strings, quintons with flat backs, lutes, guitars, and other instruments. The more accurate Hills mention only two violas da gamba, later converted into cellos; a tenor viol (which Vuillaume converted into a viola, substituting his own arched back for Stradivari's flat one); two small viols; two guitars; two *pochettes;* and a harp, one of three attributed to Stradivari.

But Stradivari, still in his *Amatisé* period, could create surprises. In 1679, he made a famous inlaid violin, the "Hellier," named for Sir Edward Hellier of Womborne, Staffordshire, who went to Cremona in 1734, three years before Stradivari's death, and personally bought the violin. (Sir Edward paid the equivalent of about three hundred dollars; it remained in his family until 1875.) The "Hellier" is a beautifully ornamented violin, with fine inlaid work, especially interesting for its large proportions. Its length is 14 1/8 inches, and the bouts are 8 3/8 and 6 13/16 inches wide (lower and upper). The "Hellier" violin expresses a prophetic genius in its symmetry, beautifully cut f-holes, and scroll. Though the "Hellier" is not yet a perfect specimen, being somewhat heavy and incomplete, Stradivari was already ahead of himself.

He continued to make *Amatisé* violins until 1690, but the models were already changing as he experimented. The scrolls vary from one instrument to the next. Some made between 1686 and 1690 remain "unsurpassable...in point of sharpness, accuracy, and beauty of finish" (Hill). In 1690, he made the "Tuscan," a very famous violin that year; and the Medici grand duke Cosimo III commissioned a set of instruments. Only the "Tuscan" violin, the "Medici" viola, and a fine violoncello, also attributed by the Hills to 1690, still exist; yet they already show his genius.

Incidentally, I will not call a Stradivari violin a "Strad": it implies an intimacy that is justified neither by history nor familiarity. An Amati is not called an "Am," nor is a Guarneri a "Guar." The good old Cremonese name of Stradivari has a beautiful musical sound that almost conveys the image of the great violins that Antonio Stradivari created. The least we can do for the genius of violin making is to use his name correctly.

During the fifteenth, sixteenth, and seventeenth centuries, the famous viol makers took pride in their inlaid and ornamented instruments. Gentlemen amateurs were expected to have "a chest of viols." Princes ordered them ornamented—ivory, tortoiseshell, silver, pearls, and precious stones were used. The custom went out of fashion with the emergence of the violin. The early makers justly considered their violins beautiful in themselves, without special decoration. (Only secondary parts—fingerboards, tailpieces, bridges, and pegs—occasionally were ornamented.) But a prominent maker sometimes received a special order from a prominent customer. Such was King Charles IX of France, for whose court Andrea Amati made a set of twenty-four instruments, each bearing the king's coat of arms. Ninety years later, Nicolò Amati made a beautifully decorated violin for the French court of Louis XIV. Once in a while he made a violin with double purfling, with inlaid corners and small stones. Perhaps the great violin makers wanted to prove they could equal what the early viol makers had done.

Stradivari met such challenges in customary style. His ornamented instruments are the finest. Only ten are known to exist—eight violins, a viola, a cello. The earliest inlaid violin was an *Amatisé* model made in 1677, which Stradivari proudly showed to his teacher Nicolò Amati. The last was in 1722, the inlaid "Rode" Stradivari (named after the French virtuoso Jacques Pierre Joseph Rode). Two years later, Stradivari's "intimate friend," Don Desiderio Arisi, had written:

he has made many [instruments] of extraordinary beauty which are richly ornamented with small figures, flowers, fruits, arabesques, and graceful interlaying of fanciful ornaments, all in perfect drawing, which he sometimes paints in black, or inlays with ebony, all of which is executed with the greatest skill, rendering them worthy of the exalted personages to whom they are to be presented.

Among these was King Philip V of Spain, for whom Stradivari made three beautifully ornamented violins in 1709. But the best-known inlaid viola, made in 1696, is the "Greffuhle," named after a former owner, Vicomte de Greffuhle. A glance explains its beauty better than a thousand words. The ornamental purfling, the beautifully painted sides, and the head demonstrate the artistic perfection of Stradivari. He made all designs himself—some drawings still exist—and personally carried out the inlays and ornamentations. Arnaldo Baruzzi in *La Case Nuziale: The Home of Antonio Stradivari, 1667–1680* claims that Stradivari made relatively few instruments after his marriage in 1667 because he earned more money as a skilled carver and inlayer, and made violins only as a sideline.

Around 1690 Stradivari began to experiment with a model now known as the "long" Stradivari. (The French expression *allongé*— "lengthened"—is more accurate.) A "long pattern" violin made in 1690 has a length of 14 5/16 inches, five-sixteenths of an inch longer than the great fourteen-inch violins he made in his best previous years. Many experts believe that he was inspired by Giovanni Paolo Maggini's sonorous, large instruments, made in Brescia; these have a fascinating dark timbre and a powerful tone. The typical *"allongé"* Stradivari was one-sixteenth of an inch longer than the so-called "small pattern" Maggini (14 1/4 inches). Stradivari's sense of symmetry and feeling for harmony is evident in the new pattern. He did not merely lengthen the body of the violin, but he changed the whole outline of the design in artful relation to the new length. He made the bouts longer, less curved; the sound holes are little wider than on his earlier instruments; sometimes the scroll is imperceptibly longer; the elegant purfling conveys a graceful impression. One of the finest *"allongé"* violins is the "Harrison," made in 1693, which belonged to the Henry Hottinger Collection. A somewhat unusual model, it is beautiful with a symmetry of its own.

Stradivari's genius is very apparent when one plays one of the "long pattern" instruments. The tone is quite different from the *Amatisé* instruments. It responds less easily than those he made in the style of Amati, but there is a new, soothing, dark timbre and great carrying power. Stradivari proved to himself that he could do what the Brescians had done, and he did it more beautifully.

Many connoisseurs today love the *allongé* violins, but apparently there weren't enough when he made them. Around 1698 he stopped, and reverted to the ideas of Nicolò Amati and to the "grand pattern" violins that Amati had made in the 1660s. Most were fourteen inches long with a width of 8 $1/4$ inches, harmonious and beautifully finished. No wonder Stradivari, now a mature artist, was deeply impressed by the enormous challenge to improve the almost perfect Amati model—and around 1700 he achieved it. He used beautiful wood and, often, a soft, orange-red varnish. Many experts call the early eighteenth century the beginning of Stradivari's "golden period." Yet, understanding the greatness of Stradivari is to know that the master never stopped looking for wider horizons. To catalogue arbitrarily the changing creations of a genius is to misunderstand them; obviously Stradivari made some of his greatest instruments when he was in full command of his physical powers and deeply understood the intricate psychology, the sound, of the violin. But he made some great instruments when he was relatively young, and he made others toward the end of his life.

For it is not the beauty or the sound of his best instruments that has made Stradivari the greatest violin maker the world has known. The beauty, elegance, and finish of some of Nicolò Amati's violins have never been surpassed, not even by Antonio Stradivari, and many modern artists claim that the sensuous, exciting sound of certain masterpieces made by Guarneri del Gesù is unique. What makes the supremacy of Antonio Stradivari is the evidence of his artistic restlessness, his unceasing striving for perfection, and the enormous range of his creation. A quiet man, he led a rather unspectacular life, while his works went through an almost incredible evolution, from his earliest *Amatisé* violins to the mellow, mature works of his last years. An achievement that some would set beside those of Titian, who created masterpieces until his death at ninety-eight, or Michelangelo, who was an old man when he decorated the dome of St. Peter's. I think, also, of Joseph Haydn, who invented the string quartet in his early twenties and wrote his last masterpieces, full of wisdom and beauty, in his late seventies—or of Verdi, who at seventy-nine created the unfathomable miracle of love and humor, his finest work, *Falstaff.*

After 1700, Stradivari's designs are entirely his own. Now certain about the thickness of the wood, he had learned the secret of creating instruments that had everything—an easy response, carrying power, and velvety smoothness. An artist who plays a *pianissimo* or *morendo* on one of these great violins will be be heard in all corners of any concert hall blessed with good acoustics—Vienna's Musikverein, New York's Carnegie Hall, Boston's Symphony Hall, Philadelphia's Academy of Music, Amsterdam's Concertgebouw—and he will also be clearly heard against the powerful *fortissimo* accompaniment of a modern symphony orchestra. These violins have both beauty of appearance and sound. Yet, incredibly, Stradivari created them when the violin music he knew was still far from exploiting the instrument's possibilities. Sitting in his workroom in a sleepy provincial Italian town, Stradivari, with prophetic genius, created instruments that would fulfill the increased tonal requirements of the next three centuries.

In 1704, Stradivari made one of his most famous violins, the "Betts." The original owner is unknown, rare in the case of an outstanding instrument. The "Betts" is often compared to the finest Amatis but surpasses them in design and finish. The purfling, rather close to the outer edges, has been admired and studied by generations of violin makers. The f-holes are often reproduced in violin books because they seem perfect.

The known history of the "Betts" masterpiece begins in 1820 when Arthur Betts, an English violinist who had studied with Viotti, happened into the violin store of his brother John Edward ("Old John").

On that day in 1820 "a stranger of unprepossessing appearance" came into the store and offered Arthur "the magnificent Stradivari which bears his name for twenty shillings"; the bargain of the century—the violin is certainly worth more than $100,000 today. It is one of the five Stradivari instruments that Mrs. Gertrude Clark Whittall purchased to be kept "in perpetuity" at the Library of Congress in Washington, D.C.

Arthur Betts may not have known immediately that he'd purchased a Stradivari, but he was doubtless aware that it was a beautiful instrument. When his brother died, he and his nephew Charles Vernon took over the store. By then, both knew the value of his Stradivari; when the nephew demanded that their partnership include the instrument, Betts refused, and their business relationship was dissolved. In 1852, after Arthur's death, the "Betts" was sold to John Bone, a retired judge and amateur player; he sold it nine years later to J. B. Vuillaume, and the names of its subsequent owners are known. Eventually, the violin was bought by the Hills, then by R. D. Waddell, a well-known collector in Glasgow, and then by the Wurlitzer firm. Mrs. Whittall bought the "Betts" in 1937.

Before 1709, Stradivari made mostly a fourteen-inch model; later, he occasionally made violins with a length of 14 1/8 inches. He continued to experiment, making violins varying in width and depth of sides. He never stopped working for long, and he loved what he was doing. He had found his greatness and knew he had no competitors. He must have respected the later art of Giuseppe Guarneri del Gesù, but del Gesù's development was not steady and unbroken.

Between 1710 and 1720, starting when he was nearly seventy, Stradivari made some of his greatest violins. Among that decade's more famous are the "Dancla" of 1710, with which Nathan Milstein enchanted audiences for years; the "Parke" of 1711, named for W. T. Parke, an obscure English oboist, though for years it was the solo violin of Fritz Kreisler; the "Boissier" of 1713 on which Pablo Sarasate performed during his last years; the magnificent "Batta" cello of 1714, long the instrument of Gregor Piatigorsky; the "Dolphin" of 1714, made famous by Jascha Heifetz; and the "Alard" of 1715, for which Henry Ford once unsuccessfully offered $150,000.

"It would be incorrect to single out any of these violins as supreme in merit," the Hills write. "We cannot emphasize too strongly that amid all the finest Stradivaris still existing, there is not one which can with justice claim absolute superiority over all others." Not even the "Messiah," made in 1716, which the Hills donated to the Ashmolean Museum at Oxford University, where it is kept as a national treasure.

The "Messiah" is called the "perfect" Stradivari because it was never exposed to the rigors of climate or the use of ordinary men. Stradivari himself considered it something special; he never sold it, though he must have had many offers. Perhaps he liked to have it around to enjoy it and to use as a demonstration model for pupils and other violin makers. His sons Antonio and Paolo later inherited it, with the rest of the estate. Paolo, the textile merchant, sold it in 1775 to Count Cozio di Salabue; Count Cozio sold it to Luigi Tarisio, also a superior collector and dealer; after Tarisio's death the "Messiah" was acquired by Vuillaume, then inherited by his son-in-law, the French violinist Delphin Alard. Later it was sold to the Hills, passed through other hands, reverted to the Hills, and is now forever in Oxford.

In 1716, Stradivari also made the celebrated "Cessole" and "Medici"; the latter somewhat resembles the "Messiah." Charles Reade wrote about its varnish: "When a red Stradivari is made of soft, velvety wood, and the varnish is just half worn off the back in a rough triangular form, that produces a certain beauty of light and shade which, in my opinion, is the *ne plus ultra.*"

In 1724, Stradivari was eighty (if we accept 1644 as the year of his birth). His work showed no serious sign of age—only an expert will note that the sound holes are cut less precisely or that the purfling is less elegant than that of ten or twenty years before. Sometimes the wood isn't as beautiful as in his earlier violins, but in some years not even Stradivari could get the wood he wanted. He needed help and had a number of assistants in his workshop. At least a dozen of those said to have been there later became celebrated makers, such as Guarneri del Gesù, Lorenzo Guadagnini, Carlo Bergonzi, Francesco Gobetti, Alessandro Gagliano, Domenico Montagnana, and Tommaso Balestrieri—not to mention Stradivari's sons, Francesco and Omobono.

Today it seems agreed that of this entire list, only the two sons were certain to have helped their father. Even Carlo Bergonzi, long believed to have been Stradivari's favorite pupil, has now been eliminated. No one still claims that Guarneri del Gesù ever worked with Stradivari. Del Gesù studied with his father, "Joseph filius Andreae."

In his eighties, Stradivari went on working. Even nonexperts can now notice small irregularities in workmanship. The purfling is not perfectly made, nor are the sound holes. The varnish is still beautiful but not applied as carefully as before. But most of these instruments still retain a very beautiful tone; they prove that Stradivari had learned the relationship between the exact measurements of a model and its "voice." Perhaps his hands were trembling, but his instinct was unfailing. While putting together the parts of a new violin and measuring its length, width of bouts, and height of sides, he could "hear" how the finished violin would sound (conjecture, to be sure, but confirmed by the tonal excellence of his very late instruments). Rarely, for example, is the height of the sides the same at top and bottom; the upper height is often a sixteenth of an inch less than the lower height. He also sensed how the composition and application of the varnish would affect the tone. But he was an artist, perhaps also a scientist; he was a magician only in what he created with his mind and hands.

The artist expresses his ideas in materials. When Stradivari didn't get the finest wood, he had to work with the next best. He had long realized that the tone of an instrument was more important than its appearance. In the late 1720s and early 1730s, del Gesù was more careful in his workmanship, perhaps somehow trying to equal Stradivari. Del Gesù's finest-sounding violins were made after the death of Stradivari in 1737. They are also often rather carelessly made. After 1730, Stradivari often made violins that were bolder, more robust in outline, less graceful and finished than his earlier instruments. These late violins have a powerful, incisive tone, closer to the del Gesù sound than to the Amati sound. By that time Stradivari knew the fascinating violins made by Guarneri del Gesù, with their almost "Brescian" sonority. The old master knew that some of del Gesù's violins were sloppily made. But there exists no proof that he was aware of Guarneri's discovery of sonority. Still, one can believe that old Stradivari heard the sound of the future in the violins of del Gesù. And there was no reason why he, Stradivari, a mere octogenarian, shouldn't produce the sound of the future too.

Stradivari's universality remains unique among the greatest makers. None of them had traveled so far, from the sweet beauty of the *Amatisé* violins to the darker sound of the *allongé* instruments, then to the perfect beauty of Stradivari's masterpieces, and the passionate power of his late violins. Even Nicolò Amati's most ardent admirers cannot claim that his beautiful instruments are ideal for the soloist performing, with a large orchestra, the concerti of Brahms, Bruch, or Alban Berg. For such tasks, a fine Guarneri del Gesù is preferable. But the fanatical partisans of del Gesù cannot claim that his instruments are ideal for the purity and fineness of chamber music. For that purpose, a quartet of Amati instruments seems the perfect choice.

Only the violins, violas, and cellos of Antonio Stradivari seem to suit every musical purpose. They are effective in the largest halls, holding their own with no difficulty against a large orchestra; Oistrakh, Milstein, and Menuhin all play the great concertos on Stradivaris. And the sound of the late Budapest String Quartet performing on the Stradivari instruments of the Gertrude Clark Whittall Foundation at the Library of Congress remains unforgettable to all who once heard it. The sound was perfect, regardless of whether classical, romantic, impressionist, or modern chamber works were played.

In the past three centuries, popular taste in sound (as in everything else) has changed. What was once considered sweet and mellow may now be called weak or precious; sound now admired as big and sonorous might have once struck its hearers as coarse, perhaps exaggerated. People may be shocked by the mystical art of El Greco, or the physicality of Rubens and Fragonard, but the universality and power and charm of Leonardo da Vinci, Pieter Brueghel, and Rembrandt seem to survive oscillations of taste and therefore of price. For the past hundred and fifty years, Stradivari prices have been highest on the international violin market; if a late del Gesù, made after Stradivari's death, surpasses the highest price ever paid for a Stradivari, it will not be for aesthetic or tonal reasons but rather a response to the iron law of supply and demand.

Experts, as well as ordinary violin lovers who have the chance to hear several prominent violinists perform on the same Stradivari, are always amazed by the miraculous capacity of this great instrument to adapt to the personality of the player. Great violins don't change their tonal character, but a great Stradivari is extremely flexible, almost merging with the player's style. They form such a happy unity that it isn't always possible to separate the player from the violin sound; in every case, they belong together. The sound has its own beauty, woodiness, brilliance, depth, power, and magic and always incorporates the player's timbre, charm, and personality as well. If there were an "ideal" violin sound, this is it.

Stradivari's first wife, Francesca, died in 1698 and was buried on May 25. A bill for the funeral expenses is one of the few preserved documents signed by Stradivari. Already a man of wealth and standing, he gave his wife "a first-class funeral." The bill lists fees to 150 religious organizations, assorted orphans, beggars, and torchbearers, and sums for bell-ringings at three churches, including the Cremona cathedral.

Sixteen months later Stradivari married Signora Antonia Maria Zambelli, twenty years younger than he and very pretty. It was again a good marriage; he'd had five children with his first wife, and Antonia gave him five more, one daughter and four sons. There were probably few dull moments in the house, with its two sets of children, apprentices, friends, and important customers from all over Europe coming to admire his instruments or place orders. Still, we know so little about his life, not even how he looked. The often-published pictures are always the same and not authentic. Giovanni Battista Polledro, the well-known violinist, provides our only hint: "He was tall and thin in appearance, invariably to be seen in his working costume which he rarely changed, as he was always at work." But Polledro was born forty-four years after Stradivari died and was merely repeating what he had heard.

Signora Antonia died in 1737 at the age of seventy-three and was buried on March 4 in the family grave in the Chapel of the Rosary in the Church of San Domenico. Stradivari survived her until December, and was buried on the nineteenth. The record, made from the register of San Matteo, calls him "a widower, aged about ninety-five years," and this was confirmed by the register of San Domenico. But even if Stradivari was born in 1644, he would have been only ninety-three. Other members of his family were buried subsequently in the family grave. The last was his son Giuseppe Antonio, who died in 1781.

For one hundred and thirty-two years, Stradivari's remains were at rest in the Church of San Domenico. In 1869, lacking money for urgent repairs and restoration, the church was pulled down. Alfonso Mandelli, an eyewitness, was later quoted:

> When the work was in full swing, the masons cared not which part was to be attacked; the pickaxe, incessantly in use, had already rained down its blows upon the Chapel of the Rosary.... I was present on a certain day when several distinguished people were assembled around the tomb of Stradivari...and I recall, just as if I heard them now, the following words being pronounced by one of these gentlemen: "There is such a confusion of bones, without any special mark whatever, that it seems useless indeed to make any further search." On the same occasion, I heard repeated, several times, the name of Stradivari; but I was young and ignorant of the significance of the name, and did not grasp the

> importance of the search which these gentlemen were disposed to
> undertake. During the following days I saw men with baskets clear that
> tomb of all human bones found within it.... I learnt afterwards that the
> men themselves interred the bones outside the city....

Later Mandelli wrote, "The matter of the desecration of this grave
was perhaps too lightly decided on. In fact, the reverence now felt for
everything appertaining to Stradivari had then penetrated but little ever
in Cremona."

That reverence seemed to have penetrated no further by 1948, when I
first came to Cremona. Like other pilgrims, I came hoping to find something that would evoke the city's glorious past, the memory of its great
violin makers. I found nothing at all. The houses where they had lived
had disappeared. No streets were named after them, not even a great
Cremonese violin was left in the city where they all had been created. At
first, no one I talked to knew the great names, or if he did know, was not
pleased to be asked my questions. It was as though the Amatis,
Stradivaris, and Guarneris had been the town's black sheep. I know now
that the community had a sense of guilt for the lack of reverence, which
had lasted for generations. According to a travel folder, Cremona was
noteworthy "chiefly for its gastronomic specialities, such as butter and
cheeses, mustards and sausages, marmalade and *torrone*," candy made of
nuts, fruits, honey, and sugar.

The visit was no loss, though, because I met Mario Stradivari, a sixth-
generation descendant of Antonio. A famous criminal lawyer and an
imposing man, tall and big, he might have been part of a Renaissance
sculpture with his furrowed face, large aquiline nose, and high forehead.
He walked with long, swaying steps, had a booming bass-baritone voice,
and he moved and spoke with grandeur. He told me that he might have
inherited from his great-great-great-great-grandfather "the big nose, the
high-domed forehead, the curved mouth, the long fingers"—then immediately ridiculed the idea. His father, Libero, also a famous lawyer, had
been a follower of Garibaldi and a friend of Puccini. (Libero left his son
a signed photograph of Verdi, but nothing from their famous ancestor!)

Mario Stradivari, a man of wit and irony, told me that in 1937 in
Cremona there had been an exposition of Stradivari violins to com-
memorate the two-hundredth anniversary of Antonio's death. Some

forty violins were shown. Mario hadn't been officially invited, nor had he ever seen a genuine Stradivari. He went to look at the violins. They seemed beautiful, and he wanted to take one into his hands to have a good look at it, but an attendant "came staring at me down his nose, and said the public was not permitted to touch the instruments—would I please leave, or he would have to call the police."

At Mario's house I met Renzo Bacchetta, Cremona's outstanding expert on Stradivari, who informed me that this didn't make him popular with the townspeople. They cared little about Stradivari or violins, only that the price of cheese should stay up. If Stradivari had invented a new kind of cheese, they would have built him a monument. As it was, none had been raised to Antonio Stradivari.

Later that night, the three of us went to Piazza Roma, the modern square in the center of town where Piazza San Domenico had been. On one side was a small park, exactly in the former place of the Church of San Domenico. On the other side was the sumptuous marble façade of a palacelike office building, with the big glass windows of Cremona's most elegant café on the street floor. High above one window was a marble panel reading *"Qui sorgera la casa dove Antonio Stradivari recando a mirabile perfezione il liuto levava alla sua Cremona nome imperituro di artifice somo"*: "Here stood the house where Antonio Stradivari brought the violin to admirable perfection and left to his Cremona an imperishable name as master of his craft."

Bacchetta told me that Stradivari's house had been torn down by the Mussolini government in 1928, because the site was needed for this office building. Mussolini was said to like violins, and Bacchetta had tried to stop the authorities, but failed. He remembered the old building well; it had a tailor's shop and a poolroom with billiard tables on the ground floor, exactly where Antonio Stradivari had had his workshop.

We walked across the square into the small park with play areas for children and gravel paths. At a half-hidden spot near the far side, behind two benches, Mario Stradivari showed me a block of stone three feet high that looked as though left there by mistake. On the lower part, near where the stone touched the ground, I read the name STRADIVARI. Bacchetta, overcome with grief, told me what he called "the saddest story in the history of Cremona"; it tallied with Mandelli's version of the destruction of the old Church of San Domenico. Bacchetta intimated that a

Milanese wrecker had paid the city of Cremona forty-two thousand lire for the right to demolish the church and cart off the materials, which he later sold to his profit. No one had done anything to assure the reburial of the bones of Antonio Stradivari and his family. Said Bacchetta, "Maybe the workers took them to the local cemetery and threw them into a common grave. I hope so, though no such grave is known. Or maybe they just walked to the bank of the Po, only a few minutes away, and threw the bones into the river."

After centuries of neglect, the city at last put up a small monument on the approximate location of Stradivari's grave in the Church of San Domenico. Via Stradivari now leads off Piazza Roma, where once Stradivari's house stood. And most important, where the tombstone and other relics are also exhibited, there is now a Stradivari violin at the Municipal Museum. Made in 1715, and called "Il Cremonese," it was formerly owned by Joseph Joachim, who had at least eight Stradivaris.

In *How Many Strads?* Ernest N. Doring calls the two violin-making sons of Stradivari "perhaps the greatest enigma in the story of the old Italian violin makers." Of the two artists—Francesco, born in 1671, died in 1743, and Omobono, born in 1679, died in 1741—Francesco is now considered the more important.

When the sons took over after his death, their father's workshop surely contained a number of violins that had not been completed; it is also assumed that there were several instruments that the old man had put aside because he was not satisfied with them (he no longer burned such instruments, as he did earlier). Did the sons sell these instruments under their own names? George Hart answers, "Many of the later works of Antonius Stradivaris have been erroneously attributed to his sons," but he does not supply convincing proof. In 1890, the catalogue of Lyon and Healy in Chicago listed Francesco Stradivari's "Le Besque," with an Antonio Stradivari label dated 1734: "The violins of Francesco Stradivari are among the most artistic of any that came out of Cremona. Although not such a genius as his father...nevertheless a great artist in the highest sense...Francesco aimed to produce in his violins a beautiful quality of tone which, with sufficient volume, would combine the best features of the work of Antonius Stradivarius and Carlo Bergonzi...." On the other hand, Arthur W. Dykes wrote in *The Strad* of August 1929: "Francesco Stradivari remains a shadow, as no violin by him is known, so far as I am aware, but the instruments by Omobono, which exist, prove the latter maker to have been an artist of great ability and...one more fully inoculated with the manner of Antonio than any other master in Italy." René Vannes disagrees: "Omobono has produced little. He seems to have done mostly repairs and trading in violins." But Doring's book shows three violins made by Omobono Stradivari, all dated 1740, and all doubtlessly authentic works. One, which belonged to Eric Sorantin, much resembles Antonio Stradivari's late violins: the f-holes, arching, purfling, beautiful wood, and red-brown varnish. It certainly doesn't look like the work of a master who "seems to have done mostly repairs."

To be the son of a genius is not easy. For a long time the experts argued whether the sons alone had made any violins. The Hills wrote in 1902: "Not a single authentic example of Francesco's work has been hitherto identified by us." Yet the Hottinger Collection contains a beautiful, authentic violin by Francesco; the Wurlitzer catalogue calls it "the finest example of Francesco, in a perfect state of preservation." Made in 1742, and called the "Salabue," it was one of the instruments Count Cozio di Salabue purchased in 1775 from Francesco's surviving brother, Paolo. It is a beautiful violin with magnificent tone and easy response—I have played on it—and is the favorite of Mrs. Lee Wurlitzer Roth, who has refused several offers for it.

Francesco died at seventy-two on November 5, 1743, and with that the Stradivari violin dynasty came to an end. Today the violins attributed to Antonio's sons are justly called Stradivaris—they are Stradivari violins in every respect. I wish there were more of them.

Paolo, Antonio Stradivari's youngest son (born in 1708), installed his textile store on the ground floor of the house in Piazza San Domenico, where his father's workshop had been for over fifty years, but by 1746, Paolo moved the store to a better location near the Duomo. Antonio's old pupil, Carlo Bergonzi, occupied Stradivari's house, but he died the following year; the Bergonzi family kept the house until 1758. Other tenants came until the house was finally sold in 1777 by Antonio Stradivari, the son of Paolo and grandson of the great maker.

The exact number of instruments made by Stradivari is another mystery, and there has been wild guessing among the experts for the past two hundred years. It is not known how much time Stradivari needed to create one. Don Desiderio Arisi mentions the visit to Cremona in 1715 by Jean-Baptiste Volumier, then director of the court music of the king of Poland; Volumier came to pick up the twelve violins King Augustus had ordered, and he stayed three months. Some historians deduce that Stradivari made one violin per week during that time. Count Lütgendorff, long considered the leading Stradivari expert in Germany, wrote about "Stradivari's unbelievable productivity": "Even if he completed only one violin each week, that gives us three thousand violins through the sixty-year period of his working life." This statement seems unbelievable.

There are few facts. Count Cozio's correspondence tells us that, at his death, Stradivari possessed ninety-one violins, several violas, two cellos, and a set of inlaid instruments. Cozio does not mention any catalogue kept by Stradivari; a conscientious man might be expected to keep records of his production, but Stradivari was either too busy to bother with paper work or, as his few documents suggest, had trouble writing and making records. Years of thorough research led the Hills to a lifetime total of 1,116 instruments, basing their deductions on all the instruments they had seen or knew about. The available evidence also convinced them that Stradivari's output varied considerably. Relatively few early instruments exist from the years 1660 to 1684 when he worked for, and later with, Nicolò Amati. After Amati's death in 1684, the number of Stradivari instruments with original labels increases, and it keeps up well until about 1725, when he was perhaps eighty-one. During the last twelve years of his life his productivity decreased, but it seems miraculous that three violins of great tonal beauty were made then, and to a considerable extent, by his hand.

Stradivari made mostly violins, and perhaps one cello for every ten or twelve violins; it took about twice as long to make a cello. He also made a relatively small number of violas; they are very valuable. No double bass made by Stradivari is known.

There are no instruments with Stradivari's label from the years 1673, 1674, 1675, 1676, and 1678; either he was working for Nicolò Amati, or, as some Italian historians assume, elsewhere as a carver and inlayer. Even after 1700, his output is sometimes bewilderingly inconsistent. From 1705 we have only five violins, for example, and four from 1706. But these were hard years; in 1706, the Austrians occupied the fortress of

Cremona and turned the castle of Santa Croce into a major Lombardy stronghold. The fortification cost over eleven million francs, much of the money exacted from the Cremonese. All citizens had to billet soldiers in their houses, and Stradivari probably was no exception. It was not a good time for making fine violins.

But 1709, contrarily, remains Stradivari's vintage year: "twenty-one violins and one cello." And, during the great years of 1715, 1716 (the "Messiah"), and 1717, he made thirteen, fifteen, and thirteen violins, respectively, and three cellos. (These instruments were actually seen by the Hills; Stradivari probably made more. Doring's tabulation lists many as "uncertain.") From 1725, only five violins and two cellos remain, but 1727 was another banner year, with sixteen violins and one viola. In 1734, when he was presumably ninety, the Hills attribute five violins to him, Doring seven. Writing in 1902, the Hills had accounted for 540 violins, twelve violas, and fifty cellos, in all 602 instruments; these figures were never claimed to be complete. And if it is frustrating not to know how many instruments Stradivari made, it is worse not even to know how many exist today. "In the case of the violins," the Hills wrote, "we unhesitatingly express our belief that we have only succeeded in recording three-fourths of them, as we have traces, more or less clear, of one hundred more."

Certain instruments, known to have existed, have been traced for centuries without success. In 1690, Stradivari made a set of five instruments for the Tuscan court. They were later borrowed by players and collectors who became so enthusiastic about them that they failed to return them. Where are they now? Of the pair of violins, only one, now the much admired "Tuscan" Stradivari, later turned up in Florence. A quintet of inlaid Stradivari instruments, and various instruments by the Amatis, Jacob Stainer, and Guarneri del Gesù, were purchased by Charles IV, king of Spain. They were last seen in 1790 at the Royal Palace in Madrid; the year before came the French Revolution, then the French occupation of Spain and bad times for fine violins. In this instance, only four instruments remain. Palaces, churches, and monasteries were ransacked and destroyed in many cities and countries. The Napoleonic wars turned the continent of Europe into a battlefield, and countless fine works were undoubtedly plundered and destroyed.

The situation improved in 1815, when the Congress of Vienna

brought relative peace and stability. But there were other disasters and catastrophes. In 1808, when Covent Garden burned, a Stradivari violin owned by W. Ware, the orchestra leader, was lost in the flames. The wars of 1866 and 1871, and World Wars I and II, probably destroyed many fine instruments. It is not yet known what became of the instruments in Russia since the Revolution.

Hardly a week passes when a violin dealer does not have someone step into the store to offer a "genuine" Stradivari. And whenever a newspaper comes out with a story about the discovery of an allegedly old violin in an attic, well-known dealers are deluged with telegrams and long-distance calls from people who think they own a master instrument. Such optimism is understandable, based on circumstances somewhat like the following: an old violin has been cluttering up the attic or a closet for some time. The owners have wanted to give it away, but found no one to take it; when they read of the discovery they open their violin case, finding inside a dusty fiddle bearing the label "Antonius Stradivarius Cremonensis Faciebat Anno...." Now they recall their parents saying that Grandpa brought a violin from the old country in the 1850s. They are convinced that they have a treasure (fifty thousand dollars—that's what it said in the paper).

All dealers are eager to find a genuine old Italian fiddle, but they know that their chances are infinitesimal. Many precious instruments have disappeared in the wars, catastrophes, revolutions, upheavals, fires, and accidents of the past two hundred years. Consequently, the experts are convinced that the history of almost all important instruments is now known, even though their whereabouts cannot always be traced, and that almost all instruments felt to be missing are likely destroyed. The career of most fine violins can be followed back for fifty to a hundred and fifty years. The entire history of some outstanding instruments is known, from the time they left the maker's workshop.

The experts agree that a few masterpieces may still be hidden, but not in the attic of a North American home. Certain violins mentioned in letters, diaries, and old journals have disappeared; they might be in Italy, France, England, or Spain in the possession of wealthy or aristocratic families who are aware of what they own but choose to say nothing about it. A major unknown quantity is the Soviet Union, where the former aristocrats owned many fine instruments. During the Russian

Revolution many that did not disappear were transferred into the vaults of the state. The state lends them to eminent (and "reliable") artists; David Oistrakh, for example, played for years probably the finest Stradivari in the Soviet Union. In the past years, prominent artists have invested hard currency earnings in fine instruments, with permission of the Soviet authorities.

Perhaps a half dozen Stradivari violins and a number of other fine Italian instruments—violins, violas, cellos—remain in the Soviet Union. We don't know exactly how many; some so-called authentic instruments might turn out otherwise, and some genuine ones may still be unidentified. The saddest story is that of Italy, where most of the fine instruments originated, and where very few now are. "If a Cremonese wants to look at our great heritage, he must go to New York, Hollywood, Switzerland, or Germany," Renzo Bacchetta once said. The chief culprit was an Italian, the expert dealer Luigi Tarisio; during the first half of the nineteenth century he took perhaps more than a thousand violins from Italy to Paris and London.

Ever since my article about rare old violins in *The New Yorker* in 1953, I've had letters telling about the "treasures" found among American family heirlooms, asking me where to take them. It seems useless to explain that American households have undergone too many upheavals to make such a discovery probable; I suggest that they take the instrument to the nearest reputable dealer or send him photographs of it. But owners of "old" violins are incorrigible optimists. They will make a long journey to a dealer and try to persuade themselves and him that their forty-year-old violin has been in the family for over two centuries. They accuse the dealer of lying when he tells them the unpleasant truth; they announce they will go to another dealer—who, of course, tells them the same thing. They go home, not quite convinced; some believe that all dealers are crooks. They put the violin back in the attic. In thirty years their children will think they've found a treasure. It's a vicious circle. No one ever throws a fiddle away, no matter how bad it is.

Once in a lifetime—if he is lucky—a dealer may discover a previously unknown masterpiece. At the end of World War II, Rembert Wurlitzer, on his first trip to Spain, found a Stradivari, made in 1720, that was not known to any dealer. He bought the beautifully preserved violin, christened it the "Madrileño," and brought it to New York.

One day in 1911, Emil Herrmann traveled to Posen, at that time in Germany, to deliver an instrument to a customer. He was told that an old postal clerk in the town owned several violins, "among them even a Stradivari." Herrmann was only twenty-three but already a convinced skeptic, as a violin dealer has to be to stay in business. But a sense of duty made him go to the clerk's apartment; his skepticism deepened when the living room looked like a second-rate antique shop. The postal clerk showed him a dozen factory-made violins, and Herrmann was about to leave when the clerk brought a battered old case and opened it. Herrmann often described the scene, the moment every dealer dreams about: "I couldn't have been more surprised. It was a Stradivari; no doubt about it. An *Amatisé* instrument, made in 1684, with a one-piece back and a light-brown varnish. It was in a bad state of repair, with several cracks, but it was definitely genuine. I offered to buy it, along with some of the other violins. The clerk didn't want to sell. I paid him several hundred marks for some bad china and bric-a-brac, in the hope of establishing good will, and said I'd be back. Two weeks later, I returned with four thousand marks in gold—nine hundred and fifty dollars in those days. The clerk still didn't want to sell. We argued all afternoon and well into the evening. Finally, around ten o'clock, I took out the money and put the whole four thousand marks, in twenty-mark gold pieces, on the table—four long rows of fifty coins each. It was a tempting, gleaming sight, and he couldn't resist."

It would be more difficult today. Gold coins are no longer legal tender, while the sight of banknotes, inflated paper money, might not have the same effect.

In 1945, in *How Many Strads?* Ernest N. Doring quotes a letter from Alfred Ebsworth Hill:

> You ask me to help you trace Stradivaris that found their way to the States. This is asking for much for it has amazed me to note how easily your countrymen part with their instruments and how quickly they pass from one end of the States to the other! Consequently, I am no longer well informed as to the whereabouts of these instruments....

Fridolin and Emil Hamma, noted dealers in Stuttgart, agreed. "Among the many transactions which have taken place in recent years, you can no longer keep track. One believes a certain Stradivari to be found in the possession of a German family, only to hear that it has already long been in America!"

The majority of the great instruments has now shifted to the United States. The dollar may no longer be what it was, but America is still the land of the rich. There are more collectors in the U.S. than in any other country, and some now own magnificent quartets of great instruments. The former Hottinger Collection, the most important of its kind, was sold to Rembert Wurlitzer, Inc., whose vaults at 16 West 61st Street today contain more treasures than those of any other dealer. America is where the violin action is. In the golden days of Hollywood, the 1940s, in the orchestras of the major movie studios, more Stradivaris and other great instruments were played than in any other city of comparable size.

The concertmasters and leading string players in the larger American orchestras own some great violins. Rafael Druian, the concertmaster of the New York Philharmonic, owns the "Nightingale" Stradivari, made in 1717. Back in 1960, Isaac Stern played the Beethoven Concerto with the New York Philharmonic under Leonard Bernstein, at Carnegie Hall; during the first movement, the E string on Stern's Guarneri del Gesù broke, but he exchanged his Guarneri for the concertmaster's Stradivari so adroitly that he missed only one measure.

Granted, no one will ever know how many instruments were made by Stradivarius; Lütgendorff's estimate of three thousand is ridiculously high. The estimates of the Hills (a grand total of 1,116) and of William Henley (1,400) seem closer to the truth. Of these, Doring estimated in 1945 that 509 Stradivari instruments had survived. Herbert Goodking, in his latest estimate in *Iconography of Antonio Stradivarius*, lists 630 violins, fifteen violas, and sixty cellos but does not claim that all these are fully authenticated. Dario d'Attili, of Rembert Wurlitzer, Inc., believes that about 550 Stradivari instruments still exist.

The bitter truth is that roughly half of the instruments that Antonio Stradivari made are lost forever.

Timeless Taste

FERNAND POINT
The Finest Butter and Lots of Time

WHEN I WENT TO FRANCE this summer, after an absence of more than a year, I was pleased to find that, for the first time since the end of the war, my Parisian friends had stopped griping about the black market and rationing and were again discussing, passionately and at great length, the heady mysteries of *la grande cuisine*, which, next to women, has always been their favorite topic of conversation in times of content. Once more, with the air of brokers divulging something hot in the market, they were confiding to each other the addresses of good restaurants.

The finest restaurant in France, and perhaps anywhere, it was agreed by my always well-informed friends, is not in Paris. If I wanted to have the epicurean experience of my life, they assured me, I would have to go to Vienne, a town of twenty-three thousand inhabitants in the Department of Isère, seventeen miles south of Lyon, at the confluence of the Rhône and Gère rivers. There I would find the Restaurant de la Pyramide and its proprietor, the great, the formidable, the one and only M. Point.

"Ah, Fernand Point!" said one of my French friends with a deep sigh. "The greatest epicures in France and Navarre sing his praises. His *gratin d'écrevisses* reaches perfection. The yearbook of the Club des Sans-Club awards him the mark of Excellent—its highest. I once had a *volaille en vessie* there that...."

"Point's hors d'oeuvres alone are worth the trip from New York," someone else said. "He calls them hors d'oeuvres but they are a meal in themselves—and what a meal! There is a pâté...."

"Last year at Point's I had the best lunch I've had since Escoffier left the Ritz," a third gourmet friend told me. This friend is a man of seventy-four years and three hundred and twenty pounds, and he has spent most of the former in increasing the latter with good food. "In short, you must go to Point's restaurant."

I objected mildly that I wasn't much interested in the showplaces of *la grande cuisine.* Since the disappearance of the black market, France's restaurants have returned to their prewar standard, which is, by and large, the best in the world. I could see no reason, I said, for patronizing fancy establishments when there is such an astonishing number of small restaurants all over the country where one can get a delicious omelet, a succulent veal stew, a fine cheese, and a bottle of honest *vin du pays* for less than six hundred francs, or something under two dollars.

"Ah, but Point's restaurant is not a showplace," my old friend said. "It is a temple for gastronomes who know that *la grande cuisine* must be well orchestrated, that it must be surrounded by careful details, ranging from the temperature of the dining room to that of the wines, from the thinness of the pastry shells to that of the glasses, from the color of the fruits to that of—"

"All right," I said. "I'll go."

"But it's not a question of whether or not you will *go*," my friend said. "The question is will M. Point let you eat in his place? He has thrown out American millionaires and French ex-ministers when he didn't feel like serving them. Only last week, a friend of mine called M. Point long distance and asked him to reserve a table for the next day. That, of course, was a mistake, because M. Point usually insists on being notified at least three days beforehand. My friend gave his name—a *very* important name in French politics, I assure you. Ha! Mr. Point pretended to be totally unimpressed and kept saying, 'Would you mind repeating the name?' Before long, my friend had lost his celebrated poise and could only mumble that he was being recommended by M. Léon Blum. And what do you think M. Point said to that? He said, 'And who is M. Blum, if I may ask?'"

My friend chuckled. "But I think I can help you out with an introduction. I have a British friend, Mr. Piperno, who happened to be among the Allied troops that liberated Vienne, and I'll have him give you a letter that will open all doors to you. Any friend of Mr. Piperno's is treated royally at Point's. But be sure to call M. Point well in advance to reserve your table. And for heaven's sake, don't think of ordering your meal! You don't order at Point's. *He* tells *you* what to eat."

A few days later, I received a note from my friend enclosing an amiable letter of introduction from a Mr. T. H. Piperno and decided to put in a person-to-person call to M. Point without delay to reserve a table for lunch some day the following week. Finally, after some misunderstandings involving Point's name, my name, and the name of a girl, Denise Something, who had a lovely way of yawning and seemed to be the long-distance operator in Vienne, I got hold of a man with a high, querulous voice who said yes, he was Point, and there were no tables available for the next week—or the next two weeks, for that matter. I quickly said that I was a friend of Mr. Piperno's. M. Point voice abruptly dropped several notes as he said, "Oh!" Then he precipitately told me that I might come any day I like, absolutely, it would be a pleasure, and how about tomorrow? And in whose name should the table be reserved? I began to spell out my name, but M. Point must have got restless, because he said not to bother with the name—there would be a table. He hung up forthwith, without a good-bye.

My friends in Paris had urged me to prepare myself for my monumental lunch by eating only extremely light food, and very little of it, during the preceding twenty-four hours, and I was hungry and cross when my overnight train pulled into Vienne early the following morning. A gentle rain was misting down upon the green trees of the town's miniature boulevards and blurring the outlines of the narrow streets bordered by old houses and small, dark shops. I set out for the nearby Grand Hôtel du Nord, where, again on the advice of my friends, I had engaged a room. "You'd better plan to spend the night," they had said. "No use trying to rush away. You have to relax after a meal at Point's." There were only a few people on the street—pale, stockingless girls who were carrying small lunch boxes, and shabbily dressed men who looked as though they surely had never lunched or dined at Point's.

The Grand Hôtel du Nord was, despite its name, an unassuming establishment that did not indulge in such extravagances as elevators, a bathroom on every floor, and warm water after nine in the morning, but my room was clean and the comforter on my bed was filled with eiderdown. I had a pleasant view of two sides of a square—on one flank the town museum, on the other the Café du Commerce et des Voyageurs, and its clients, all of them, I was sure, were busy in lively discussions of politics, soccer, and the high cost of living. I washed up, read a newspaper I had bought at the station (politics, soccer, and the high cost of living), and finished my interrupted sleep. When I awoke, it was getting on toward twelve o'clock and nearly time for me to present myself at the Restaurant de la Pyramide. As I stepped into the street, I was stopped by a young man wearing a raincoat and a beret and carrying a pipe. He smiled at me like a Fuller Brush man, asked my pardon for his presumption, and informed me that he was Jean Lecutiez, an archeologist sent to Vienne by the Ministry of National Education to dig up the ruins of the houses, temples, aqueducts, baths, and assorted monuments that the Romans left there two thousand years ago.

"I happened to be visiting my friend the desk clerk of your hotel as you came in, and I saw on the registration blotter that you were a writer," M. Lecutiez said. "Right away, I told myself that I would make it my business to take you around." I tried to protest, but he said, "Oh, don't worry—no bother at all. My two colleagues will carry on with the work. There are three of us archeologists here—a very old man, *un homme mûr* [a mature man], and myself." M. Lecutiez prodded me energetically with the stem of his pipe. "You must realize, Monsieur, that Vienne, the old Vienna Allobrogum, was the capital of the Allobroges in the first century B.C. Julius Caesar established a colony here. Later, the Romans went up north and founded Lugdunum, which eventually became Lyon. Naturally, the people in Lyon don't like to hear this, but it's true—"

"I'm sorry," I said. "That's wonderfully interesting, but I have a luncheon engagement at..."

M. Lecutiez ignored this interruption. "Vienne, like Rome, is built around seven hills," he went on as he grasped my arm and relentlessly walked me away. "They are Levau, Mont Salomon, Mont Arnaud, Mont Pipet, Sainte-Blandine, Coupe Jarret, and Mont Saint-Just. I'll take you up on every one of them. Now, this afternoon we're going to start with—"

"It's almost lunchtime," I said. "How about an apéritif? Then I'll really have to run for my appointment."

"Thank you, I never drink," he said. "Would you like to see the pyramid?"

"Ah," I said. "That's exactly where I'm going. I'm lunching at Point's."

"The restaurant, *je m'en fiche,*" said M. Lecutiez. "I mean the real pyramid, which for hundreds of years was commonly, and erroneously, thought to be the grave of Pontius Pilate. There is nothing like it anywhere. Come, it's no distance at all." As we crossed the street, a wild bicyclist almost ran us down, but M. Lecutiez seemed not to notice. "It was the great French architect Delorme who first stated that the pyramid dates from the fourth century and was the domed center of the spina, or longitudinal center wall, of a Roman circus, where chariot races were held. Now we turn here, and *voilà!*"

There before us, an island in the middle of the street, was the pyramid, a monument, perhaps fifty feet high, that looks like a giant metronome. Its square base is pierced by four arches. The thoroughfare it stands in is one of those drab, deserted side streets that one sees in so many small French towns.

"Excavations undertaken in 1854 by Constant Defeu proved Delorme completely right," M. Lecutiez went on, hardly pausing for breath. "We are indeed standing in the middle of what was once a vast Roman circus. It was a big arena, fifteen hundred feet long and…"

On the other side of the street, set in a ten-foot wall, was a gate, and beside it a black marble plate inscribed in red letters: FERNAND POINT, RESTAURATEUR.

"…and the chariots must have come from over there," M. Lecutiez was saying, pointing up the street. They would pass right where we're standing and then—"

"It's been a tremendously instructive talk," I broke in, "and I am most grateful to you, but I must go." M. Lecutiez looked at me with a hurt expression, but I walked firmly across the street toward the gate in the wall. On the left, the wall connected with a decrepit three-story building that looked as if it should have been condemned long before the Renaissance; on the right it joined a house that was considerably newer but seemed rather run-down, and in need of a coat of paint. The rain had stopped and the sun had come out, but even under these favorable conditions the exterior of M. Point's temple for gastronomes presented an unprepossessing appearance. I walked through the gate and found myself suddenly, without any transition, in another world. I was in a garden with clean gravel paths, green lawns, beds of flowers, and a terrace shaded by old maples and chestnuts, and covered with white tables and wicker chairs still wet from the rain. The courtyard walls of the building that I had thought should have been condemned were completely cloaked with ivy, which blended admirably with the beautifully landscaped grounds. To my right was a two-story house—the one that from the front I had thought was run-down. Its garden side was immaculate. The frames of its wide windows were freshly painted, and the whole building looked as clean and spruce as a Dutch sugar house. I walked up three steps, scuffed my shoes on a mat, opened the big door, and entered the hall of what seemed to be a handsome country residence. On the wall were paintings and an old print of the pyramid, bearing the caption "Un Monument Antique, Vulgairement Appelé le Tombeau de Pilate."

A man in a white jacket approached from the rear of the house, greeted me cheerfully and took my raincoat, hanging it in the hall, as is the custom in French homes. I said I wanted to see M. Point and was ushered into a small, pleasantly furnished salon. The walls were hung with paintings and mirrors; a gold pendulum clock stood on a buffet, and a large glass-topped table sat in the middle of the room. On the table were champagne glasses and a half-empty magnum of champagne, and behind it was standing a huge man. He must have been six feet three and weighed three hundred pounds. He had a longish, sad face, a vast double chin, a high forehead, dark hair, and melancholy eyes. I couldn't help thinking that one of M. Lecutiez's sybaritic Roman emperors had come to life. He wore a comfortably large suit, and a big bow tie of black silk ornamented with a flowery design, like those the eccentric citizens of Montparnasse and flamboyant Italian tenors displayed in the old days.

I introduced myself and we shook hands. I gave him Mr. Piperno's letter. M. Point read it casually and shook hands with me again. "Sit down!" he commanded with a magnificent gesture. "For the next few hours, this house will be your home. I'm delighted you came early. Gives us a chance to talk and drink champagne. Quiet, Véronique!" On a chair beside him, a precisely clipped brown poodle was making hostile noises. "Véronique belongs to the family," he said. "We also have a nine-year-old daughter, Marie-Josette. Enfin!" He filled two of the champagne glasses and said, "A votre santé."

We drank. "I like to start off my day with a glass of champagne," M. Point said. "I like to wind up with champagne, too. To be frank, I also like a glass or two in between. It may not be the universal medicine for every disease, as my friends the champagne people in Reims and Epernay so often tell me, but it does you less harm than any other liquid. Pierre—our sommelier—and Mme Point and I go to the champagne district every year to buy. And, of course, to Burgundy, too. Last week, we visited a great friend, the Marquise de la Tourette, the proprietor of one of the great Hermitage vineyards." M. Point filled the glasses again. *"Ah, quelle grande dame!* She won't sell her wines in the commercial market. You have to be her friend, and you must literally force her into selling the stuff. She is over eighty, and every day she walks from her château to the church and back. Permit me to drink the health of the Marquise de la Tourette!"

While we were solemnly drinking the health of the Marquise, a man came in wearing a beret and the light-blue overalls and apron that are the uniform of France's winegrowers and sommeliers. He had a shriveled face that looked as though it had been chiseled out of a piece of seasoned wood.

"Ah, Pierre," said M. Point. "Monsieur, this is Pierre Chauvon, our sommelier and a great connoisseur of that ever new miracle, wine."

The old man scratched his head under his beret with his left hand as he gave me his right. *"Allons, allons, Chef!"* he said, embarrassed but quite pleased. "You know a lot about wines yourself, and Mme Point knows even more. Ah, I assure you, Monsieur," he said to me, "Madame is *épatante.* She is *très, très forte.* When we go the vineyards and taste the wines, the winegrowers always look at her first. She's better than I am, and I certainly know my business." He smiled, revealing a few side teeth and almost none in the front. "Unfortunately, Madame always gets hungry around noon, and once you've eaten, your taste and judgment aren't reliable any more. I don't eat when we're out. Mustn't make a mistake, eh, *Chef!"*

"Everybody calls me *'Chef'* here," M. Point explained to me. "Never *'Patron.'* They just won't forget that I used to be my own chef in the kitchen. Now I merely supervise things there, and my wife takes care of the clients in the dining room. Well, Pierre, why don't we show our friend the cellar? Nothing to be ashamed of, is it?"

M. Point led the way out into the hall, around a few corners, and down a stairway into a big, brightly lighted wine cellar with earthen walls. It was cool, and the dirt floor was as clean as sweeping could make it. All along the walls were shelves on which bottles were stacked horizontally. Tacked to the lower-left-hand corner of each shelf was a small label giving the place of origin and the vintage of the wine. In the center of the room was a table covered with baskets of fresh fruit—enormous pears, Calville apples, lush peaches, and aromatic *fraises de bois*. A roster of the wines in the cellar hung on one wall. It listed two hundred and nineteen names, in four columns. Glancing at random down the second column, I saw Richebourg '42, Romanée-Conti '35, Corton Charlemagne '38, Les Grands Echézeaux '42, Hermitage '98, Romanée-Conti '43, La Tache '43, Hermitage la Cour Blanche '06, Clos de Vougeot '37, Vosne-Romanée '93, Corton Charlemagne '42, La Tache '37, Romanée St. Vivant '40, Pouilly '40, Montrachet '29, Richebourg '29, Chambolle Musigny '21, Hermitage Blanc '40, Marc de Bourgogne '29 and Vire Chapitre '26.

"What a mess!" said M. Point, waving at the chart. "We've always mixed them up—don't know why. Anyway, it's not a bad selection. We have all the great vintage years of Château d'Yquem, back to 1908, and a lot of the fine years of Château Margaux and Château Lafite-Rothschild. You can see we're crowded in here. I had to rent a place down the street for Pierre to keep his champagnes in."

He pointed to a section of the shelves at my right. "How do you like our cognacs?" They were impressive—cobweb-covered bottles of eighty-year-old Otard and *hors-d'âge* Camus, along with batteries of gin, Scotch, apéritifs, and liqueurs. M. Point slapped his stomach. "Before the war, I refused to serve cocktails. Now they bring their own bottles if I don't serve them. My God, after a couple of those concoctions your palate can't distinguish an 1899 Château Mouton-Rothschild from 1949 fountain-pen ink! What's that you have, Pierre?"

The sommelier was examining a small bottle of the sort in which winegrowers send samples to merchants and restaurateurs. "The new Moulin-à-Vent," he said.

"We buy many wines by the barrel—*la pièce*," M. Point said, "and Pierre 'works' the wine, draining it from one barrel into another three times a year. The dregs remain in the old barrel. Pierre knows what he's doing. He wouldn't make a *soutirage*—as the process is called—while a south wind is blowing. The wind must be from the north. Right, Pierre?"

"*Bien sûr, Chef.* I make three *soutirages* a year—in January, March, September. Each barrel of Burgundy contains two hundred and twenty-five litres and each barrel of Beaujolais two hundred and eighteen litres. When the wine is ready, I bottle it myself in my workroom. I've always done it. Had my own *bistro* in Lyon and would go to Burgundy three times a year to buy wines. Those were nice times, before my wife—" He stopped and scratched his chin. "Ah, why warm up those old stories? I'm happy here now. I'm sixty-seven, and I hope to stay here until I die."

"*Allons, allons, Pierre!*" M. Point cried, and his high-pitched voice almost cracked. "What kind of talk is that? Go on, tell me how the wine is."

Pierre uncorked the sample bottle and took a big mouthful of wine. He let it roll over and under his tongue, closed his eyes, and made a gargling sound. Then he spat on the floor. "It'll be all right in three years," he said with authority.

"Good!" M. Point took my arm. "Let's go up to the kitchen and give some thought to your lunch.

The kitchen was large and cheery, with a white-tiled floor and walls. Copper pots hung from hooks on the ceiling, and silver trays were stacked on broad white tables. The ranges and slicing machines were so highly polished that they looked brand-new. M. Point told me that coal was used to cook everything except pastry, which was baked in an electric oven. At the rear of the kitchen were four refrigerators. Through their glass doors I could see hor d'oeuvres and butter in the first, rows of dressed chickens in the second, fillets of beef and veal tenderloins in the third, and potatoes, bunches of white asparagus, and other vegetables in the fourth. The room was a busy place. Cooks and apprentices were washing vegetables, cutting meat, mixing sauces, and doing various other chores, but there was a total absence of haste or nervousness.

A plump and elegant gray-mustached man in a spotless chef's outfit joined us and was introduced to me as M. Paul Mercier, the *chef de cuisine*. "Do you like chicken, Monsieur?" he asked me. He picked one up from a nearby table. "All of ours come from the region of Bresse, the best in France for poultry. Each is tagged with a silver label and serial number. We store them in the refrigerator for four or five days after getting them, but we don't freeze them. They do a lot of freezing in America, don't they?"

"*Malheureux, malheureux!*" M. Point exclaimed, clasping his hands in deep unhappiness. "Of course they do a lot of freezing. It's such a hot country they have to, I am told. But you can't expect to get a good piece of chicken from a freezer. Here we keep everything just above the freezing point." As he talked, his eyes roved over the kitchen, taking note of every bit of activity. "The main thing about cooking is to see to it that only the very best ingredients are used, and used as they should be. When you are interested in *la grande cuisine*, you can't think of money, or you are licked from the start. And you have to go out yourself and get the ingredients. At six o'clock this morning, M. Mercier himself went to Lyon to buy the very freshest strawberries and asparagus he could find in the markets. And butter, naturally. How can anybody expect to cook well without using the finest butter? *Du beurre, du beurre, du beurre,* I keep telling my men—that's the secret of good cooking. And time, lots of time."

I noticed that the bustle in the kitchen had subsided, and that most of the undercooks were listening to M. Point with hushed attention. M. Point solemnly raised his right hand and proclaimed, "*La grande cuisine* doesn't wait for the client. It is the client who must wait for *la grande cuisine.*" He stopped and looked around the kitchen. "*Allons, mes enfants!*" he said, clapping his hands. "Let us go back to work." Ushering me through a doorway, he took me into a small courtyard. "I want to show you our aquarium," he said. The aquarium consisted of two square tanks. In one I saw a couple dozen brook trout swimming around, and in the other a number of crayfish. The water in each tank was kept fresh by a flowing faucet. M. Mercier joined us. "Are we going to serve Monsieur a trout?" he asked. "*Au bleu,* perhaps?"

"I haven't decided yet," M. Point said. He turned to me. "So often our clients ask for what they call 'difficult' things, with long and fancy names. People don't know that the most difficult and also the best dishes are the simple ones. What did you cook for your family on your last day off, Paul?"

"A *choucroute,*" M. Mercier said.

"There you are. Here is a great chef, who can cook a chicken in champagne with truffles the like of which has never before been tasted, and what does he cook for himself at home? A *choucroute*—cabbage, delicious soft ham, Alsatian sausage, and very young potatoes—and what could be better?" He swallowed, and I found myself swallowing, too. My stomach was gnawing. "But it takes experience. What looks easier to make than a *sauce Béarnaise*? Butter, egg yolks, chopped shallots—nothing to it, is there? But years of practice are needed before you can do it right. Forget to watch it for a single instant and it's gone, finished, lost.

Everybody thinks he can fry eggs, and I suppose anybody can, but to fry them so they are soft and mellow throughout, not burned on the bottom and raw on top—*that* is art, my friend. Isn't that right, Paul?"

"Absolutely," said M. Mercier.

"Absolutely. Now, Monsieur, let us return to the salon and think seriously about your lunch."

In the hall, we encountered a slim, middle-aged, efficient-looking woman in a gray tailored suit, who was carrying an order pad under her arm. M. Point introduced her to me as his wife, Marie-Louise. She smiled at me briefly and then whispered in M. Point's ear. "Madame *who?*" he said. "No, no. Tell her we have no table. I don't want her. She smokes before dessert. The last time she was here, she even smoked after the hors d'oeuvres." He escorted me into his salon. The magnum was empty, and he called loudly for another. It was quickly brought in an ice bucket by a frightened young waiter. M. Point watched the youth sternly as he worked out the cork and stopped the flow of foam by pressing a silver spoon over the mouth of the bottle. "A little trick," M. Point said. "Metal will stop the flow. Don't pour yet, Marcel. Always leave the bottle open in the ice bucket for a few minutes." A drop of champagne had spilled on the tabletop, and the waiter, before leaving, carefully wiped it away with this napkin. M. Point nodded in approval. "So many otherwise good restaurants in France don't teach their personnel the importance of attention to detail that makes for flawless service," he said. I saw Mme Point greeting four guests, and a waiter or two scurrying by in the hall. In a minute, a boy in a white apron put his head in the door and said that a M. Godet was calling from Lyon about a reservation, and would M. Point—? For some reason, this seemed to infuriate M. Point. He shooed the boy away, went to the door, and announced down the hall in a loud voice that he was about to have a glass of champagne and that he would be grateful if the world would leave him in peace for a few minutes. Then he shut the door, came back, and sat down.

"Too many people," he said. "Vienne is halfway between Paris and the Riviera, and everybody wants to stop over to break the monotony of the trip. Not many Vienne people come here; most of my clients are from the outside world. It's been that way ever since I opened the restaurant, twenty-six years ago, when I was twenty-six years old." He poured us each a glass of champagne and looked thoughtfully into his. "I was born near here, and I always wanted to cook. My father was a chef. A very good chef. He made me start from the beginning—washing dishes, waiting on tables, peeling potatoes. It's quite important to peel them right, believe me. Then I learned to cook vegetables and make soups and things like that, and after that I went to Paris. Remember Foyot's? Ah, they had a great *saucier!* He taught me a lot. And for a long time I worked at the Hôtel Bristol. I came back home in 1923 and bought this place with my savings. It was just a shack and a few trees then. In time, father and I added the second floor and a new kitchen, the wine cellar, and the terrace. We had the garden landscaped and bought the adjoining lot. Father died a few years ago. All this time I was doing the cuisine myself, always learning, always trying to improve a little, always eating well. You've got to love to eat well if you want to cook well. Whenever I stop at a restaurant while traveling, I go and look at the chef. If he's a thin fellow, I don't eat there. I've learned much about cooking, but I still have far to go."

M. Point leaned back, reached into the drawer of a table behind him, and pulled out a leather-bound book with a gold inscription on its cover: F. POINT, LIVRE D'OR. "I started keeping this on the restaurant's tenth anniversary, in September 1933," he said. He handed it to me. On page one was a short note, *"Quel excellent déjeuner!"* signed by the Aga Khan. "He really knows how to eat well," M. Point said. A couple of pages on, the Fratellinis, France's most famous clowns, had written, "Today we have eaten at Lucullus's," and Colette had written, "The trout was rosy, the wine was sparkling, the pâtisserie went straight to my heart—and I am trying to lose weight! This is definitely the last time I come here—*on ne m'y reprendra pas!"* Farther along there was an unfinished sentence by Léon Blum: *"Si j'en trouve encore la force après un tel déjeuner…,"* a drawing by Jean Cocteau, and an observation by Curnonsky (the *nom de table* of Maurice Edmond Sailland, who in 1925 was elected Prince of Gastronomes by a group of Paris newspapers): "Since cooking is without doubt the greatest art, I salute my dear Fernand Point as one of the greatest artists of our time!"

Nothing was entered from January 1940 until September 2, 1944. On the latter date, someone had written "Premières Troupes Alliées—Merci 1000 Fois!" over an excited, illegible signature. Below was the exclamation *"Vive la France!"* and the signatures of, among others, the Abbé de

Pélissier, F. F. I., Lieutenant Colonel H. C. Lodge, Jr., and Carl F. Gooding, "American Jeep driver." Several pages beyond, I came upon a pasted-in letter, dated December 3, 1946, and typed on the stationery of the War Office (Room 900), Whitehall, London S.W.1. It read, "Mr. Fernand Point: I have the honor to inform you that His Majesty the King has approved the award to you of the King's Medal for Courage in the Cause of Freedom, for your good services in France...."

I asked M. Point about the letter. He shrugged and took the *livre d'or* away from me and threw it back into the drawer. "No time for that," he said. "Time for lunch. If you will go into the dining room, I'll step into the kitchen and see what can be done. I've thought it all out."

At the entrance of the dining room, I was taken in tow by a cheerful headwaiter, who led me to a table. Mme Point came up with the order pad still under her arm. She gave me a long, speculative glance—the kind of glance that wives so often give their husbands' drinking companions—and then she smiled and said that she hoped I would have a nice lunch. She went off, and I looked around the dining room. I had the feeling of being in a comfortable home in the country. The room wasn't so small as to give one a sense of being cooped up with a lot of other people (there were perhaps fifteen or twenty other clients) and not so large as to give a feeling of mass production. There were pretty white curtains on all the windows, and on every table was a vase of fresh flowers. In the center of the room stood a long buffet covered with stacks of big, ivory-colored plates, piles of silver and rows of glasses, and against one wall was a grandfather's clock. When I opened my white napkin of rough linen, it turned out to be almost the size of a small bedspread, and exhaled the fragrances of fresh air and of the grass on which it had been dried in the sun.

A waiter placed one of the ivory-colored plates in front of me, and another waiter served me the first hors d'oeuvre, an excellent *pâté de campagne en croûte*. French cooks are generally expert at baking an extremely light, buttery dough called *croûte,* but never before have I eaten *croûte* that almost dissolved in my mouth. When I had finished, the first waiter replaced my plate, fork, and knife with clean ones, and a third waiter served me a slice of *foie gras naturel truffé* embedded in a ring of *crème de foie gras.* The ritual of changing plates and silver was repeated after each hors d'oeuvre—hot sausage baked in a light pastry shell, accompanied by delicious *sauce piquante;* a pâté of pheasant; crackling hot cheese croissants; fresh asparagus (which M. Mercier must have bought in Lyon that morning), set off by a truly perfect hollandaise sauce. A bottle of wine—an elegant, airy Montrachet—was brought in an ice bucket; the waiter filled my glass half full and gave it a gentle swirl to spread the bouquet. It was a great show and a fine wine. The last hors d'oeuvre was followed in person by M. Point, who informed me that I had now completed the "overture." "The overture merely indicates the themes that will turn up later," he said. "A good meal must be as harmonious as a symphony and as well constructed as a good play. As it progresses, it should gain in intensity, with the wines getting older and more full-bodied." Having delivered himself of this pronouncement, he returned to the kitchen.

Whenever I think back to that lunch, I feel contentedly well fed; the memory of it alone seems almost enough to sustain life. The next course was *truite au porto,* which, the headwaiter told me, had been prepared by M. Point himself: brook trout boiled in water to which vinegar, pepper, salt, and bay leaf had been added, and then skinned, split in half, and filled with a ragout of truffles, mushrooms, and vegetables. With it came a sauce of butter cream and port wine. It was a masterpiece; I was by then entirely willing to take the word of my friends in Paris that Fernand Point is today France's greatest chef. The trout was followed by a breast of guinea hen with morels, in an egg sauce; a splendid Pont-l'Evêque; strawberry ice cream, made of *fraises de bois* that had been picked the day before; and an array of pâtisserie. M. Point had chosen as a wine for the guinea hen a rich, full-bodied Château Lafite-Rothchild '24. And at the end of the meal, with my coffee, there was a Grand Fine Champagne Cognac '04, the taste of which I still remember vividly.

Later, M. Point sat down at my table. The smell of good coffee and good cigars, and the sound of soft, relaxed conversation drifted through the room. M. Point acknowledged my praises with the casual air of a seasoned virtuoso who had expected nothing else. "We always strive for near-perfection," he said. The inevitable bottle of champagne in its ice bucket was whisked up to the table by the headwaiter, and two glasses were filled. "Of course, I know that there is no such thing as perfection. But I always try to make every meal"—he closed his eyes, searching for the right words—"*une petite merveille.* Now, you won't believe it, but I gave a lot of thought to your lunch. I said to myself, 'Maybe he should have a *sole aux nouilles* instead of the *truite au porto.*' I decided against it. It might have been too much, and I don't want my clients to eat too much. Only in bad restaurants is one urged to order a lot. *Enfin,* you are satisfied."

I said he could probably make a fortune if he opened a restaurant in Paris. He nodded glumly. "My friends have been telling me that for years. But why should I leave? I belong here. My men like to work for me. We have thirteen men here in the dining room, and eight cooks and two *pâtissiers,* under Paul Mercier, in the kitchen. Many of them have been with me for over ten years, and some have been here a lot longer than that. They don't quit, as they do in Paris. Look at Vincent, here. He's been with me for twenty years—or is it twenty-one, Vincent?"

The headwaiter filled the glasses again and gave the champagne bottle a twirl as he replaced it in its bucket. "Twenty-one, *Chef,*" he said.

"You can't get rid of them," said M. Point. "I could throw Vincent out the door, and he would come right back in through the window. No, *mon cher ami.* Point stays at the Pyramide." He lifted his glass. "Let us drink to the Pyramide!"

"To the Pyramide!" I said.

We drank a considerable number of toasts after—to France; to the United States; to Escoffier; to Dom Pérignon, who put the bubbles in champagne; and to the memorable day when M. Point prepared his first *truite au porto*—and it was with a feeling of light-headedness and supreme contentment that, late in the afternoon, I paid the bill (which came to no more than the price of a good meal in a good restaurant in New York), bid farewell to M. Point, and went out into the garden. It had rained again, but now the sun was shining. The earth had a strong smell of mushrooms and flowers. I headed back to my hotel. At the corner of Cours Président Wilson, I ran smack into M. Lecutiez. He was talking to an unworldly looking patriarch, who I presumed was the oldest of the three archeologists, but M. Lecutiez introduced him to me as *l'homme mûr,* the mature man. He said goodbye to his colleague and seized my arm with great enthusiasm. "I've been waiting for you!" he said, waving his pipe happily. "We've got lots of things to do. We still have time to climb at least three of Vienne's seven hills."

I said that he must excuse me, because I was hardly able to make the Grand Hôtel du Nord, having just had lunch at M. Point's.

"M. Point has a very interesting place," M. Lecutiez said.

"Interesting?" I said. "They say it's the best restaurant in this country. It's the most remarkable—"

"Oh, I don't mean that," M. Lecutiez broke in. "I don't give a damn about the restaurant. I care only for antiquities, you know, and M. Point has plenty of them buried under his place. When they landscaped his garden ten years ago, they came across a couple of first-class Roman sculptures. I wish we could take over M. Point's place and start digging in earnest. I'll bet there are any number of marvelous relics under his wine cellar."

AFTERNOON AT
CHÂTEAU D'YQUEM

MONSIEUR K. LIVED IN A FINE OLD HOUSE across from an old park. There was the smell of marble and wood and the fragrance of wine that seems to hover over the old houses of Bordeaux, whose owners have wisely invested their wealth in fine wines.

Monsieur K. was sitting in the salon as I came in. His armchair was covered with blue velvet, and his head rested on a needlepoint lace, like a gem in the jeweler's case. He was a fragile, white-haired man with a finely shaped head, delicate features, and the hands of an artist. His art was the wine of Bordeaux. In this city, where fake experts don't last long, Monsieur K. has been respected for decades as one of the great artists of wine. I'd known him for years. He told me how pleased he was to see me again.

"Sit down, sit down," he said, pointing vaguely into space with no chair in it to sit on. "I've been trying to decide about the wines that we are going to have with our lunch."

In the adjoining dining room the table was set up in bourgeois style. Long sticks of white bread, hors-d'oeuvres, and olives were already prepared. Several decanters and wine bottles were standing on the buffet.

"Sometimes my wife can't make up her mind what to cook, and naturally I can't make up my mine before she's made up hers. People make much fuss about great vintages and fine *crus* but they pay too little attention to the relationship of food and wines. They commit the heresy of serving older, full-bodied wines before younger, elegant ones. They serve the liqueurish wines of Sauternes, Barsac, Monbazillac, Anjou, and Vouvray at the beginning of the meal. Afterward, of course, all other wines appear dull and as mild as milk. People waste fine wines by serving them with salad, the enemy of wine. The only liquid that goes with salad is a glass of mineral water."

Monsieur K. shook his head in resignation. *Rien à faire,* he said, the world was going to the dogs. People would enjoy wines much more if they would follow the simple rules—rules that have been set by the palate, not by wine growers or professional gourmets. With fish, oysters, other seafood, and hors-d'oeuvres, serve Chablis, Pouilly-Fuissé, Puligny-Montrachet, Chassagne-Montrachet, Sancerre-Sauvignon, Vouvray *sec,* Graves *sec,* Tavel, Hermitage *blanc,* Montrachet, Alsace. With white meat and fowl, serve red Bordeaux from the Médoc or Graves region; Beaujolais and light red Burgundies; Chinon, Arbois, Bourgeuil. With red meat, game, *foie gras* and cheese, serve Pomerol, Saint-Émilion, Néac; Beaune, Pommard, Volnay, Corton, Nuits-Saint-Georges, Clos Vougeot, Musigny, Romanée, Chambertin, Moulin-à-Vent, Morgon, Juliénas; Hermitage *rouge,* Côte Rôtie, Châteauneuf-du-Pape.

"People serve white wines ice cold when they ought to be moderately chilled," said Monsieur K. "Cold wine never offers its full taste. Even here in Bordeaux some people don't know that red wines need time and warmth to release their flavors. They bring their bottles up from the cellars ten minutes before the meal. Sometimes they place them near the stove. *Ah, mais ça se casse!* The sediments fall down, the wine breaks. A few weeks ago a dinner was given here for some ships' captains. I was asked to select the wines. The following day no one called to commend me on my choice—which was unusual. So I investigated. The stewards had put the bottles into a bathtub filled with warm water to bring them up to room temperature. *Right here in Bordeaux!*"

Monsieur K. put the tips of his fingers together and gave the ceiling a contemplative stare. "People treat wine as if it were a soulless liquid. But wine is a living organism. Its cells act like the cells of a human being. Wine lives even when it seems to be dead in the bottle. Believe me, I've stopped going out to restaurants. I just can't stand the sight of a *type* called *sommelier* who wears around his neck a chain that ought to be tied to his leg. He's a criminal, a murderer! He swings a fine old bottle as though it were a softball. He's never heard of the sediments, a sign of maturity and age, which develop over years of careful storing and must not be disturbed. He doesn't know that the cork must be drawn slowly and steadily, without haste and jerking. He forgets to clean the inside lip of the bottle with a white cloth and to sniff at the cork. Perhaps he knows that wine bottles are stored horizontally, and Cognacs and Armagnacs are not, because they would burn the cork. But does he know what a wine cellar should be like—clean, dark, well-aired, but without drafts, and in a place that has no street trepidations? Ah, it is all very, very sad."

He got up, and returned with a file containing charts and statistics.

"My little treasure chest. Charts for every year since 1847, giving the exact number of rainy days, the summary of medium temperatures for each month of the year, and the hours of sunshine. There seems to be a sort of recurrent parallelism between certain vintages, every thirty or fifty years. Either they cross one another or they meet in pairs. The cycles would be almost perfect if the war years hadn't created disturbances that were not to be expected. Take, for instance, 1895 and 1945. Both vintages have the same characteristics. The red wines were full-bodied and 'roasted,' as we call it, having been produced from overripe grapes. The wines were sweet, oily, round and full of sap. The white wines were sweet, flavory, *savoureux*. Similar analogies exist between 1896 and 1946. Both years produced wines that were harmonious, elegant, deep-colored."

Mme K. came in, a white-haired women of great dignity, dressed in black. She said lunch was ready. Her husband didn't look up from his charts.

"The wines of 1868 and 1869 are similar to those of 1898 and 1899, exactly thirty years later, and again to those of 1928 and 1929. Always an outstanding year followed by a great one. The years of 1869, 1899, and 1929 have produced wines that are almost strikingly similar: round and oily, soft, yet with lots of life, near-perfect wines. Note too that the 1898 and 1928 are still growing in quality, while the 1899 and 1929 are either at their height or declining. *Ça c'est vraiment curieux!* The charts don't lie, my friend. With the help of those charts my father would be able to forecast the quality of the future harvest as early as June. He made a fortune that way. He made only one mistake, 1858, when he didn't know that mildew can ruin a harvest. Almost broke him."

Monsieur K. gazed fondly at a framed portrait on the wall. It showed a sumptuously bearded gentleman radiating the confidence that comes from having remade one's fortune after being broke. Mme K. took advantage of the momentary lull in her husband's monologue to point at the table, with the desperate urgency of the hostess who knows that the roast in the oven is getting drier every moment. As we walked into the dining room, Monsieur K. was reminiscing about his father.

"He used to say: 'No man is born a connoisseur, but with patience and talent you may become one.' But it takes years, many years. When I was four years old, my father let me taste some wine and asked me how I liked it. There never was a meal in our house when wine wasn't discussed at great length. You can't help learning that way."

Lunch was good and the wines were superb. There was a Margaux 1900 that Monsieur K. had decanted a few hours earlier, holding the neck of the bottle against a candle to see when the sediments started to come and it was time to stop pouring. The Margaux was served with a Roquefort that was not too strong in flavor.

Monsieur K. gazed thoughtfully at the robe of the wine, holding his glass against the light. "This Margaux gives me great satisfaction. Back in 1901, when I was a young man, my father and a friend of his went out to the vineyards of Margaux to buy some of the young wines. I was permitted to go along. They tasted this wine, then only a few months old. Must have been quite hard on the tongue. My father's friend said: '*Il est bon mais trop gentil.*' My father shook his head. 'This wine will be great in fifty years,' he said. How right he was! Papa was a genius."

The wines of Margaux have always been my favorites for their delicacy, aroma, and beautiful color, and this Margaux seemed to continue to combine all their virtues. It was round and flavorful, soft and elegant, truly a great wine.

"I gave a little dinner a few months ago for twelve friends," Monsieur K. said. "All of them are lovers of fine wine. I served a Château Guiraud 1875, without showing them the label. They were to guess the origin and the year. All came pretty close. Some voted for the Pontet-Canet 1875 and some thought it was a Léoville-Las Cases 1871. Everybody agreed that the 1875 was *une exquise jeune fille.* Still, these days some people make much too much fuss about vintages. After all, there have been only four unforgettable vintages in the past hundred years: 1847, 1875, 1900, and 1929."

Mme K., who, in the tradition of long-suffering French wives, had not spoken up while her husband was holding forth, asked me to take another piece of the *tarte aux fraises.* Her husband poured the wine, a liqueurish Château d'Yquem 1899.

"No matter what some people may say about Bordeaux wines, they can't say anything about Yquem," he said, with some asperity. "Yquem is perfection. I chose this wine forty-five years ago. It was the month before we got married."

"That was the Armagnac," said Mme K.

"Oh, yes. I'm sorry, *ma chère*. It was the Armagnac. We will have it later. It is pure perfume—all the sharpness and fire have gone." He gently placed his hand on the arm of his wife. "Forty-five years isn't so long in Bordeaux. At a banquet at Château d'Yquem, a few months ago, they had twenty couples, each of them older than eighty years...." He looked at me and said, "Why don't we drive out to Yquem? The afternoon is pleasant."

An hour later we arrived at the gravel-covered courtyard of Château d'Yquem, a large, medieval stone structure with walls a yard thick and a round watchtower overlooking the gentle slopes of the Sauternes district. A heavyset elderly man with a blue beret and heavy bedroom slippers welcomed us. He seemed to be a friend of Monsieur K., who introduced M. Henriot, the *régisseur*. It must be true, as they say in Bordeaux, that people take on the color of the wine that they "work" and drink. M. Landèche's face had the reddish color of the grapes of Château Lafite-Rothschild. And M. Henriot's hue reflected the golden glow of the wines of Château d'Yquem.

We walked past the administration buildings inside the courtyard. A white-haired patriarch, also in bedroom slippers, came out and vigorously shook hands with Monsieur K. He was the château's bookkeeper and had been employed here fifty-nine years.

"I came in 1893," he said, and rubbed his hands. He seemed none the worse for wear. "It was a golden age. A bottle of Château Yquem cost fifty sous."

"Fifty *gold* sous," Monsieur K. explained.

"Yes," said the bookkeeper. "How easy it was to keep books! Today one needs so much space to write down all the large figures. Did the gentlemen taste our new wine, Léopold?"

"I was just going to take them there," said M. Henriot. "Why don't you come along?"

We walked over a graveled path. In front of a small house a parchment-faced, toothless woman was knitting.

"She was ninety-three last Easter," said the bookkeeper. "Last year, at the dance that Monsieur le Marquis gives at the end of the harvest, she was dancing with me and the other young men. She has her glass of Yquem every night after dinner."

"Maybe a couple of glasses," said M. Henriot. The young men smiled and Monsieur K. clicked his tongue appreciatively.

Presently we were in the cellar. I saw rows of barrels of wine forming straight lines, like soldiers at a parade. M. Henriot, moving about silently in his heavy slippers, brought us samples. The one-year-old wine was still somewhat dry and rough-cornered, but the two-year-old was sweet and luscious, and already had the peculiar flavor of Yquem. I took a swallow, and then I drank up my glass.

M. Henriot chuckled. "*Doucement, doucement,*" he said. "This wine is made of overripe grapes. *La pourriture noble,* we call it. It contains more alcohol than any of the red wines in the Médoc. Ah, our wonderful, wonderful Sauternes!"

His face was brightened up by the supreme bliss that I had noticed earlier on Monsieur K.'s face when he tasted his wines. "Isn't it a ray of sunshine, caught in the glass—a bowl of liquid gold?"

We moved to another barrel, and then to the one behind, sampling more wines. A mood of contentment seemed to settle down over the cellar, and us. The old bookkeeper talked of the Cardinal de Sourdis, an archbishop of Bordeaux in the seventeenth century, who had greeted a bottle of Sauternes with the words: *"Je te salue, o roi des vins,"* and Monsieur K. sat on a barrel, dangling his thin legs, quoting Baudelaire,

> *J'allumerai les yeux de ta femme ravie,*
> *A ton fils je rendrai sa force et ses couleurs....*

From the chateau's chapel came the sound of the Angelus bell. Through the open door of the cellar I saw the sun go down behind the softly rounded slopes of Sauternes with their rows of Semillon and Sauvignon vines. The sky took on the golden glow of the liquid in my glass, and the air had a mellow fragrance. M. Henriot shuffled around in his slippers, refilling our glasses with the liquid gold of Yquem.

A Lyric Life

A VERY LATE CONFESSION

MOST REMINISCENCES of the Prohibition era were written by people of authority—historians and experts—or by men then desperately trying to get a drink. Some, as you can gather from Waverley Root's amusing account, showed ingenuity and perseverance, even bravery. My own contribution to the literature of that heroic epoch is in the minor key, I'm afraid, and you might stop reading right here. I wasn't trying to get a drink; I was trying to sell it. I didn't care for the stuff then. (I do now.) It's rather late to confess, but better late than never.

In the wonderful year 1928 I was twenty-one, a student at the Sorbonne in Paris. I also studied law at Prague University, which took some Continental commuting. To support myself I played the fiddle in obscure joints around the Place Pigalle, where I lived on the top floor of a small hotel, with a sign reading *eau chaude* that fooled many people. There was no hot water. On our floor the rooms were rented by the month; those on the lower floors were let by the hour. Physically and psychologically, it was a salubrious experience, highly recommended, as they say in the guidebooks.

One day in July, I was given a chance to see America for the first time when I was offered the position of second violinist in the mini-orchestra of *La Bourdonnais,* a mini-steamer owned and operated by the venerable Compagnie Generale Transatlantique. There was nothing venerable about *La Bourdonnais,* whose name was mercifully unknown to most American travelers of the period. They would sail on the French Line's elegant ships, the wonderful (earlier) *France,* with her four funnels and at least forty old tapestries, the fashionable *Paris,* or the unforgotten *Ile de France.* Remember midnight sailings, champagne corks popping, streamers, confetti? Very nice, but not for *La Bourdonnais,* of which the French Line executives must have been somewhat ashamed. They wouldn't let us sail from Le Havre. *La Bourdonnais* slipped out surreptitiously from Bordeaux at dawn's early light (when decent citizens are asleep in Bordeaux and elsewhere). We went straight south and southwest, making stops in Santander and Vigo in Spain, continued northwest to Halifax, Nova Scotia, and south again to New York City—

eleven days of zigzagging, too long for most Americans who were in a hurry even then. Our long-suffering passengers were Spaniards and Canadians, who, I soon noticed, were not an ideal mixture. The two groups were openly antagonistic and had to be seated on different sides of the dining room.

I noticed other things too. *La Bourdonnais* seemed only slightly larger than the *bateaux-mouches* on the Seine, on which no one would ever want to go to Halifax. On my first trip we lost the upper part of the only funnel we had. The lifeboats were not tested, so far as I remember. It was common knowledge aboard that the ship was mystically held together by rusty nails and the nightly prayers of the elderly *femme de chambre*. It was rumored that *La Boudonnais* was listed as a liability, not an asset, on the books of the French Line. Then why did I sail on such a decrepit boat? Because I wanted to see New York, which, I thought, was America. That's a perfectly good reason, and I am not ashamed of it to this day.

We sailed from the Quai des Chartrons in Bordeaux, where, I learned much later, *les aristocrates du bouchon,* the great wine merchants and well-known shippers, kept their offices and hundreds of thousands of bottles of vintage claret in large cellars. I couldn't have cared less. I'd never heard of claret, and I didn't know what a vintage was. I was only familiar with the *pinard* they served at my *prix fixe* restaurant near the Place Pigalle, along with the *raie au beurre noir* (skate with brown butter), *boudin blanc* (white sausage), and other good things. Today some people in the trade would call my *pinard* a *grand ordinaire*. And sometimes I go to three-star restaurants where they wouldn't serve such vulgar but wonderful things as *raie au beurre noir,* where all the wines are vintage, and where the sommelier might be shocked if asked for a *pinard*. But I fondly remember my little *prix fixe* at seven and a half very old francs, including plenty of bread and half a bottle. So much for all that snobbish talk about vintages.

My colleagues on this memorable trip were Maurice, a short, rotund, red-faced Alsatian cello player, and Dimitri, a tall, handsome, melancholy White Russian pianist from Vladivostok. I don't remember the name of the first violinist, a Frenchman. He never played with us, and I became *the* violinist. The nonplaying fiddler was active in the bathroom of our small musicians' quarters down on C-deck, where he skillfully diluted the contents of bottles of gin, rum, Cognac, and whiskey that

Maurice had purchased on the musicians' account from the second-class barman at the fifty-percent-reduced crew rate. Since we would be paid only after the return trip, the barman had to finance the operation. It seemed unusual to me, but Maurice said they always "did things that way." On the second day I asked the nonpaying French violinist what he was doing with all the bottles.

"Stretching the stuff. I can make three bottles of whiskey out of two. Even the king of England wouldn't notice."

"But why?" I asked. He gave me a long, hard stare. I still remember his look, though I cannot think of his name.

"Listen," he said. "Why did you take this job?"

"I wanted to see New York."

He almost dropped a precious bottle of scotch. Fortunately, he caught himself, and the bottle, just in time.

"*Tu es fou* (you're nuts)," he said, shaking his head. Afterward he ignored me. I went to see Maurice, the cellist, whom I liked. He was the oldest of us. He said he worked on ships because he had a wife in America and *une petite amie* in Paris, eighteenth *arrondissement,* and he liked to keep them both happy. I asked him why the French violinist was working with all those bottles in our bathroom.

Maurice looked at me pensively. It was a nice soft look; he was a sweet fellow.

"*Ecoute, mon petit,*" he said. "You are still young but you will learn by experience. Just enjoy yourself and don't worry. And please leave our colleague in the bathroom alone. He isn't much of a violinist, but he's a pretty good chemist, see?"

Looking back now, I admit I must have been a little stupid, but this was 1928, my age of naïveté. There were too many mysteries. Take the second-class barman who sometimes offered me a glass of brut champagne that he charged to a tipsy Canadian passenger. Able and handsome, the barman, too, was an expert in diluting drinks. The lonely Canadian women admired him while they sat on the high stools, sipping their cocktails. Once I asked him why he didn't work on the *Paris* or the *Ile de France,* where he would make more money on tips, with all those American millionaires aboard. He stopped wiping his glass, winked at me, and said, "Are you kidding, *mon petit?*" After that I asked no more questions.

In those incredible days we musicians had no uniforms, no union cards, no steady working hours, and certainly no discipline. We played for the apéritif hour before lunch and dinner, and later there was an evening *concert classique,* followed by *le dancing,* when Maurice put the cello aside and performed miracles on the drums. It was a lovely era, with lovely songs. Remember "Always," "Tea for Two," "Ain't She Sweet," and all the others?

We would mingle freely, sometimes too freely, with the first-class lady passengers and had our meals in a corner of the first-class dining room, before the general service, in the company of noisy babies and their suffering mothers. Each of us was entitled to two bottles of wine with each meal, labeled *Rouge Supérieur* and *Blanc Supérieur.* This was before the French wine laws known as Appellations d'Origine were passed, and I have no idea what was in the bottles. Maurice, our expert, said maybe wine from the south of France that arrived in Burgundy or Bordeaux in large tank trucks that looked like they transported gasoline. Occasionally (Maurice said) they mixed up the trucks and that was why the red wine sometimes had a slight aftertaste of not yet fully matured Mobil oil. Maurice forbade us to drink the white "superior" wine, which, he said, was almost as bad as water, and water "makes frogs grow in your stomach." After each meal we took all the bottles down to our staterooms and stored them under the beds. Occasionally we invaded the dining room after the main service and removed all the wine bottles that the Canadian passengers had left on their tables. Most of them disliked wine and drank water. The Spanish passengers unfortunately drank most of their wine, even the whites.

I don't want to convey the impression that we didn't work. We played Massenet's "Manon" and Tchaikovsky's "Nutcracker," arranged for trio, and I played solo pieces of what the Viennese call "Salonmusik." I had some success with Albéniz's "Pavane Espagnole," Kreisler's "Caprice Viennois," and especially Gounod's "Ave Maria," which made some Spanish women cry. Maurice's great hit was Saint-Saens's "Le Cygne" (The Swan), which made even some hard-boiled Canadians cry. Maurice said he had "studied" the piece with Pablo Casals. Maybe. Unfortunately he (Maurice, not Casals) was unable to play a legato after his fifth glass of wine, and he rarely had less than eight at dinner. Dimitri said it was "the situation" that drove Maurice to drink. "He always has to say good-bye, either to his dear wife in America or to his dear *amie* in Paris. That's enough to make a man an alcoholic." Dimitri had neither a wife nor *une amie,* but he drank milk with vodka when he was depressed, and homesick for Vladivostok, he was often depressed.

On the afternoon prior to our arrival in New York, my three colleagues were getting quite busy. Dimitri swiped the mouthwash glasses from all unoccupied staterooms in the vicinity. Maurice, completely sober for a change, stored several bottles of sweetish *goût american* champagne in his second cello. It had a detachable back and contained his laundry and a collection of interesting photos, such as those offered to tourists by unshaved North African *types* around Pigalle. The chemist-violinist arranged his bottles in the bathroom, which looked like the barroom in a Marx Brothers farce. Maurice told Dimitri to get enough ice cubes, whereupon our pianist broke into tears. He said ice cubes reminded him of Vladivostok.

I was too excited to go to bed that night. Long before the pilot boarded the ship outside New York harbor, I saw a reddish glow in the dark sky way ahead. Maurice, who was with me on the bridge, said it was the reflection of the lights of Broadway. He hadn't touched his wine at dinner. He said he never drank while in New York.

"There's too much to do what with all the business we're going to have. And my wife approves of Prohibition. In fact, she's quite strict about it."

We passed the Statue of Liberty and slowly sailed past Lower Manhattan: the Battery, Wall Street. It was very beautiful. The sun had just come up and was reflected in the windows of the tall buildings. A fine haze was hugging the tops of the skyscrapers. Maurice gave a low whistle and said it was going to be a very hot day, "good for business." I hardly listened. One arrives in New York for the first time only once in life. Nowadays I often watch my fellow passengers when we arrive by plane at Kennedy Airport. I'm afraid it's not the same thing. They miss most of the excitement. I was luckier that hot morning in July 1928.

We passed the *Ile de France,* lying at the large French Line Pier 57 at the foot of West Fifteenth Street. The foghorn of *La Bourdonnais* greeted the *Ile,* but she didn't answer. She was inaudibly ashamed of her shabby relations. The second-class barman spat over the railing and said something terrible. There were other fine ships at various piers. We passed them all and continued north until we could go no farther. We stopped at the last pier, number 99, at the foot of West Fifty-ninth Street. The neighborhood was not very chic, with a row of tall chimneys belonging to the municipal garbage disposal plant. Pier 99 is still there, falling to pieces, but whenever I ride past it on the West Side Highway (which was not there in 1928) I have a warm feeling in my heart.

We docked quietly. A few Spanish-looking people stood down on the pier, gloomily awaiting the arrival of the dear relatives they would have to put up with now. The Canadians had disembarked in Halifax. A few American mongrel dogs barked. Two customs men down there waved at Maurice, and he waved back.

"They are our friends," he said. The second-class barman glared at the customs men. I said to Maurice the neighborhood was depressing.

"Don't be silly," he said. "It's the perfect setting. We are concealed here. Only one customs man on duty at the gangway. Do you know how many there are at the *Ile de France*? Sometimes ten and more. Impossible to do any business there. Let's go down. Our friends will drop in."

The two customs men dropped in and were greeted with enthusiasm by my three colleagues. I was introduced. Even Dimitri stopped being melancholy. The chemist offered our friends two mouthwash glasses filled with scotch whiskey, straight. I noticed with amazement that he'd opened a new, undiluted bottle. Obviously the customs men were *very* good friends.

There was not time for questions, though. Maurice gave me my debarkation card and a piece of paper with a score of names and phone numbers.

"Now this is where you come in," he said. "*Écoute bien, mon petit.* You walk eastward, all the way to Columbus Circle. You'll find a drugstore there. They've got pay phones in it. You put one of these coins in." He gave me a handful of nickels. It's hard to believe now. Nickels!

"You dial and ask for the first name on the list. You'll get the secretary first. These are all important men and have secretaries. You tell the secretary you want to talk to Mr. So-and-So. If she asks you anything, you tell her, 'I'm from *La Bourdonnais*.'"

"But will Mr. So-and-So talk to me?" I asked. "He doesn't know me. Also, I cannot speak English."

"*T'en fais pas* (don't worry)," said Maurice. "Those *types* are waiting for your call. They'll be delighted to hear your voice, even if you talk Czech. All you say is, '*La Bourdonnais* is here, good-bye.'"

By that time I should have guessed the facts of life, but I still didn't realize that I had just become a bootlegger's apprentice. I walked up to Columbus Circle and found the drugstore with the telephone booths inside. It was terribly hot. I dialed the first number on my list and got the secretary and then the important man himself. I said, "*La Bourdonnais* is here." He understood right away, for he emitted a yell and said something *I* didn't understand, but he sounded happy. My English vocabulary was extremely limited: a few dozen words, not all of them very elegant ones. But Maurice had been right. I had no problems. By the time I reached the last name on the list, I was soaking wet. New York is perhaps a wonderful place, but not in a phone booth in a Columbus Circle drugstore in July. I had a few nickels left and got myself a chocolate soda, asking for chocolate ice cream instead of vanilla.

"That's called 'all black,' sonny," the man said. I still remember the taste of my first American chocolate soda. I thought it had been worth it to come all the way to America for that soda.

I looked around Columbus Circle and ventured along Central Park South, all the way to Fifth Avenue, and then I walked down to Times Square and up to Broadway. The heat got worse, but it didn't bother me. It was exciting. In Columbus Circle I thought of having another chocolate soda, but one must not overdo a good thing, and I walked back to the ship. At the gangway Dimitri was welcoming two straw-hatted, prosperous-looking Americans. Dimitri told our friend, the customs man on duty, that the gentlemen were friends of the musicians.

The customs man nodded understandingly. "Music makes friends all over the world," he said. One of the two men laughed so hard that he dropped his straw hat.

"They look like millionaires," I said to Dimitri as we followed them on the way to our staterooms.

"They are," he said.

There were already a dozen friends of music downstairs, sitting on chairs and beds and cello cases and even on the floor. Some were fat and others were tall, some had hair and some hadn't, but each had a mouthwash glass filled with (diluted) liquor in his hand. All seemed happy and very thirsty. No wonder, on such a hot day. Almost all had taken off their jackets. In the bathroom our chemist was busy washing the glasses and filling them again, but he found time to make a check on a list with names every time he brought the friends of music another drink. I was now quite sure that he was no violinist. No fiddler ever kept a list like that. I asked Maurice why the second-class barman hadn't been asked to help out. He said the second-class barman had had some "trouble" and must not get "involved," and, anyway, didn't I know that the ship's bars were closed while *La Bourdonnais* was in the territorial waters of the United States of America?

More friends of music dropped in, and some brought along their friends, who didn't even know we were musicians. Maurice had said I would learn the facts of life, and I learned them that afternoon—very fast. Unpleasant ones, too. Some friends seemed in such a hurry to get down as much liquor as possible that they drank too fast. They had to catch "the five-sixteen for Chappaqua." That sounded like another code word to me. One friend was a powerful-looking, bald character; Maurice said he was the president of a large corporation as rich as half of Czechoslovakia. The president fell down flat on his stomach. Dimitri and I dragged him to a nearby stateroom, and Dimitri threw two glasses of water in the president's face, which seemed a strange way of treating a president. At last the president opened his eyes and said what he needed was something to make him *really* awake.

"Black coffee?" I asked hopefully.

"Nope, gin," he said. He turned over on the floor and was asleep again. We called for help. A few friends gave us a hand in carrying the president into another stateroom where they stored old mattresses, and we put him on top of them. He was sound asleep; he wouldn't make Chappaqua, or whatever it was called, that night.

By late afternoon there were at least three dozen presidents, board chairmen, and ordinary millionaires in our staterooms and in the corridors. I was sure I hadn't called all of them, but Maurice said it was always like that. The friends would bring along their customers and business associates, and, he said, "One hand's washing the other." Most of them behaved well, but there were a sad few who were, as Maurice said, "*pauvres types* who had never learned to drink."

The evening remains hazy in my memory. I know that Maurice asked the customers—he'd stopped calling them "friends"—to rinse their mouths with milk before going ashore. Then he would sniff each man's breath. If he detected a trace of liquor the customer was given a coffee bean and asked to chew. Don't ask me where the coffee beans came from. Apparently, my colleagues were great organizers who had thought of everything. Some customers hugged me before leaving and said they hoped I would come and have lunch with them *any*time, and they would be glad to do *any*thing for me. Here I was in America less than twenty-four hours and already I had a lot of friends in very important circles who would do *any*thing for me. America was certainly a wonderful country. Europe had never been like that.

One millionaire was stretched out flat on the floor and sat up only to drink some more. I indicated in my poor English that maybe he had had enough, but he pointed at his stomach and said, "Son, what you've got in here, no one can take away from you," and then he began to cry, very quietly. Maurice said "Prohibition!" and spat contemptuously.

Our two customs men had left and there was a tough-looking man at the gangway, but he wasn't really tough. He had dinner with us and a couple of the presidents in our corner of the dining room. The presidents gave enormous tips to our steward, and everybody was happy. One of the presidents asked for more whiskey and refused the wine. Wine, he said, was only for sissies. Whiskey was for men, and, he said, "It's the only thing that goes with everything. Oops!"

We had a late visitor, the first violinist from the *Ile de France*. They were sailing for Le Havre at midnight. He looked at the happy customers all over the place, and he saw that Maurice and Dimitri had their pockets stuffed with American money. He was disgusted.

"I wish I were here," he said. "That damn *Ile de France!* Impossible to do something there with all those customs men watching each other. *C'est la barbe.* Would you care to take my place on the *Ile?*" he asked me.

"No, he wouldn't," Maurice answered for me. "He loves *La Bourdonnais*. He hates those luxury liners. Am I right, *mon petit?*"

I nodded emphatically. I had learned a great many facts of life on my first day in America. It had been an instructive day.

La Bourdonnais sailed from New York three days later. Our departure was anonymous and quiet, no good-bye parties and very few passengers, mostly elderly Spanish Americans. Maurice said they'd made some money in America, and now they were going home to Spain to die.

"There are good places in Spain to die," he said. Most passengers would come aboard in Halifax.

When we reached the open sea, we threw the empty bottles out of the portholes. Maurice gathered all the money, counted it, and divided it by five. The second-class barman was getting his share, too; he had certainly earned it. Each of us got over three thousand francs, which was more than three times our round-trip salary as members of the ship's orchestra. On several successive trips we made even more. Toward the end of the year I went back to Prague to continue my studies at the university. Everybody said it must be a great life to be a ship's musician, to see the world, and to get paid for it.

I said, sure, it was all right, but I didn't tell them of my nonmusical activities in the territorial waters of the United States of America. My fellow law students might not have understood.

MY FATHER'S CUFF LINKS

I HAD MY FATHER'S CUFF LINKS with me when I went to America, and I often wore them, even on occasions when more elegant ones were called for. Instinctively I preferred those with my mother's portrait, the ones my father had ordered and had liked so much. I owned gold cuff links, but I rarely used them. Once, a woman in Hollywood—it would be Hollywood—asked me why I didn't wear "the gold things." I told her the story of how my father had gone to a gifted silversmith in Vienna with a photograph of my mother and had the cuff links made to order. She listened and nodded, as though she were apologizing. "Of course," she said. "Of course."

Not long ago I noticed, here in Vienna, that the subtle mechanism that holds the cuffs together didn't function properly anymore. The tiny lever, shaped like a miniature boat and fixed by a thin metal thread to the stem of the links, seemed precariously low, on the verge of breaking off. Once I did lose the left cuff link—fortunately at home where I later found it on the rug. Had this happened outside in the street, it would truly have been lost. Someone might have found it, but would he take an old silver cuff link—worthless, so to speak—to the nearest police station?

I wrapped the cuff links in soft tissue paper. I would take them to the small, old jeweler's shop in Vienna's Operngasse. From the entrance, one can see the southwest corner of the State Opera. The small shop is only a few years younger than the opera; it has been there since 1891. It cannot compete with the fashionable modern jeweler not far away, who usually exhibits only one large diamond in his window. An impressive stone, lying in a small box lined with blue velvet, illuminated at night by two powerful lights from above. No alarm mechanism is visible, but it's quite obvious that a modern one was installed. Vienna, like so many other big cities, is no longer a safe place.

The smaller shop exhibits certain old things that cannot compete with the commercial value of the large diamond. They have had great sentimental value to their owners, though. The store window facing the street is filled with an odd profusion of medallions, old bracelets, brooches, gems, and chains made of semiprecious stones. There are small and large watches, among them a Schaffhausen pocket watch exactly like the one my father had worn on a chain and which later "disappeared." The store specializes in old pieces. The owner buys them from elderly people who need the money, or from younger people who do not care about silly heirlooms—people who think they need the money so they can spend it quickly. Lately there has been much demand for old things, and the owner of the store ordered some pieces reproduced. But she is a decent woman and tells you the truth: some things are not really old; they only look old.

Inside there are vitrines filled with an assortment of old glasses, china, ivory, jade. The finest piece—it is not for sale—is the ancient regulation clock, over two hundred years old, whose round pendulum ticks off the seconds with imperturbable calm. The clock is run by a bronze weight hanging from a chain. Once a year it is wound with a special key, and the bronze weight is lifted up. The clock is said to be as accurate as its modern electronic rivals.

I had discovered the lovely old store a while ago when it was necessary to have my old alarm clock repaired. That is another heirloom dear to me: as long as I can remember, it stood on my mother's bedside table. It was made around the turn of the century—at the same time as the cuff links—in the Swiss Jura, and survived despite many improbable dislocations. The clock is housed in a rectangular glass case held together by a brass frame, proudly displaying its inner secrets. On top, visible under the glass, is the small wheel that watchmakers call the balance, swinging back and forth. When you press a small button on top, the chimes will tell you the time, very pleasant at night when you lie in bed and don't want to turn on the light. The dial has Roman numerals— once fashionable, later outdated, and nowadays again fashionable.

The clockwork's sound is pleasant and melodious, unlike modern alarms that are often shrill and make an awful racket. The old alarm clock will wake you, but gently. The chimes ring every quarter of an hour, and they are sweet and soft and don't disturb your sleep. On the contrary, one would miss them in their absence.

Whether my mother bought the clock or my father gave it to her, I cannot say. But after my father had gone and we were "suddenly" poor, and my brother and I slept in my mother's bedroom because she had to rent the children's room, the alarm clock was always on her bedside table. On school days, when I had to get up in the morning, she would set the alarm for seven-fifteen. It always worked and woke me, and I slipped effortlessly from morning slumber into consciousness. The clock was on my mother's bedside table when I left my hometown and went to Prague and, in the summer of 1938, to America.

For a while, I missed the sweet sound of those chimes. But when one is young one doesn't miss possessions for very long; more important things came up, and the sound of the chimes was forgotten. We were immigrants in New York, concerned with the many important problems of survival, and later we went to southern California because people said it was less expensive to live there. It was cheaper, yet it also was a very strange life, and I don't like to think of it. But I remember the day when we were notified that a large wooden box had arrived from Ostrava. It was late in 1940. My mother had packed some things that she wanted us to have, "before it is too late." Perhaps she already sensed she wouldn't be able to keep them. Fine old linen, tablecloths and napkins, embroidered with her initials, some of the old silver she had loved so much, and a few pieces of Meissen china. And the dear old alarm clock, in its original black leather case, with the key in a special compartment. You pressed the top of the case at a certain spot, the top opened, and the clock could be taken out.

I pressed the top and took out the clock and the key. I had no hope it would be running after that long journey. Much of the Meissen was broken. My mother had been unable to get expert packers; how she managed at all to get the wooden box out of German-occupied Czechoslovakia I cannot say. She must have fought a stubborn battle with some minor Nazi bureaucrats and must have had to have filled out innumerable documents. Perhaps she had had the secret help of some Czechs who hated the Nazis. She never wrote about it, she didn't dare. Somehow the box had reached a German port—I believe it was Hamburg—and started its long, slow voyage across the Atlantic, through the Panama Canal, along the west coast of the United States, until it arrived at the port of Los Angeles.

I remember well how I slowly wound the clock, with no hope, and suddenly the small wheel started running back and forth. The clock was all right! The chimes too were working, the familiar sound. We placed the clock on the mantel above the fireplace. The fireplace didn't work but the clock did, its chimes marking each quarter hour. When we had company, people were delighted with it. It was no longer an alarm clock but a minor work of art in the living room.

Later the clock accompanied us as we drove from the west coast to Connecticut, and as we took the boat back to Europe. We didn't dare ship it, as it had become too precious; we carried it in our luggage. Here in Vienna, I again keep it in the living room. Not above the fireplace, because in Vienna there are no fireplaces, but on the top of a baroque chest, next to a wooden Madonna. The Madonna and the old alarm clock seem to like one another.

Eventually time caught up with the clock, as it does with us. Clocks have much in common with human hearts. Someday both stop running. The alarm didn't stop suddenly. I suppose it was too well brought up to quit overnight. But it had to be wound more frequently, and it badly needed cleaning. I had never taken it to a watchmaker, afraid he might repair it so thoroughly that it would never run again. But now there was no alternative. I took it to the small jeweler's store. I had seen two similar pieces in the shopwindow. Perhaps they had a skilled watchmaker to whom we might entrust our old clock. I wouldn't take it to one of those modern stores selling quartz crystal watches that look like small computers and tiny computers looking like wristwatches. Nothing looks like itself any more; appearances are intentionally deceiving. I believe that an alarm clock should look like one. At the old store they might understand the clock. They might have patience with it.

I had never been inside. When I opened the door I expected a bell would ring—it was that kind of door. But it didn't. Two old, fragile ladies sat behind the counter. They reminded me of the sweet sisters of *Arsenic and Old Lace,* though of course they wouldn't have murdered anyone. When I came in they seemed worried rather than pleased. I understood. They had heard all those stories of jewelers being held up. A man coming in alone was suspicious.

The smaller one—later I found out she had been the owner since the death of her husband, who had been an expert watchmaker—had asked her cousin to stay with her. She admitted there was little they could do if a determined would-be burglar came in. They couldn't afford a modern alarm system.

Apparently I convinced them that I wanted to take nothing. On the contrary, I wanted to leave something there. The ladies relaxed. They admired the old alarm clock, so much more beautiful than the new ones now made in Germany and elsewhere. Some had rich, gold-plated frames; the old ladies, though, liked the bronze frame better. Did I know that such a genuine old clock was now worth at least seventeen thousand schillings (more than fifteen hundred dollars)? No, that wasn't the point, certainly not, the cousins said. But these clocks went back to the generation of our grandparents, and someday they would all be gone. Both ladies sighed. I liked the way they looked at my clock, as though it were an old person.

I had been right. They still had an old artisan—one "should really call him an artist," said the smaller one—who understood those clocks. He was probably the only real expert in the city. They spoke of him with respect, almost with awe. They didn't mention his name; he was to remain a nebulous figure. Right now he was busy and could not be bothered. But eventually he would get around to my alarm clock, would take it apart—"very, very carefully, do not worry"—and clean it. The job would take a long time and—here they coughed apologetically—it would be expensive. Such repairs were no longer made commercially, routinely. The artist was getting two hundred and fifty schillings an hour, almost fifteen dollars, and he worked only a few hours a day because his eyes were getting bad.

In fact, said the owner, it might almost be less expensive to buy a new imitation, with a one-year guarantee and a sturdy, noisy alarm that would wake up even the soundest sleeper.

"Of course, you wouldn't want a new clock," said the cousin. She pronounced the word "new" with distaste.

Of course not, I said. I understood also about the expense, as long as it was treated gently by a man who understood it. The two ladies were delighted. Just then a hard-boiled woman came in and, without bothering to wait her turn, said she had a little extra money, "over ten thousand schillings," and wanted to buy something that had value and would look nice on her. She turned and looked at herself in the mirror, but I don't think she liked what she saw there. Well, she said to the two old ladies, how about showing me some things?

The small women seemed flustered and looked at me. I said it was all right and left my name and telephone number, and asked them to call me when the clock was ready. They looked at me gratefully and I walked out. Turning left, I stood in front of the State Opera. At least some things didn't seem to change—or did they? Now it wouldn't occur to me to climb up to the fourth gallery, though the acoustics there are still the best. How many times had I run up the stairs, arriving with my heart beating fast, to get a good place in the first row of standees? Later my heart might beat again when somebody sang especially well, and we members of the claque started the well-deserved applause.

Nowadays I sit downstairs in the stalls. Very comfortable, and I am surrounded by substantial-looking people who can afford the prices. But their hearts don't seem to beat faster when somebody sings exceptionally well, and the claque in the rear and upstairs is noisy and shouts and protracts the applause—something we would never have done—until the people around me start to get annoyed and hiss "*Sh.*" In such moments I look up. I almost wish one could turn the clock back, but one cannot.

The ladies called to tell me the old alarm clock had been repaired. When I went there they told me the clock was almost as good as new. The soft chimes still tell the quarter hour. The alarm doesn't function properly, but I said I no longer needed the alarm. No more school, no more early trains and planes.

A little later, when I lost and luckily recovered the left cuff link, I naturally took them there. They might have an old silversmith who would be able to fix the mechanism. The old ladies nodded understandingly. When I told them the little angel was really my mother, they both had tears in their eyes.

"Your mother when she was very young?" the smaller woman asked.

"Yes. I wasn't even born yet."

"And you still have them," said the cousin, nodding, stating a simple fact. "And you are afraid to lose them."

They looked at the mechanism, which was still working but seemed fragile. The owner said yes, they had a silversmith. Even older than the watchmaker, and he didn't work much any more, only if a special job appealed to him.

"He might do it," she said. "Or he might not. It's hard to say. Goodness, he may even be the man who originally made these cuff links. It's fine Viennese workmanship."

I said that would be too much of a coincidence, and besides, I no longer believed in coincidences.

She said, "He's a decent man. When he thinks the repair will be too expensive he suggests that the customer buy something new instead. But I suppose in your case —"

"Yes. I'm not going to buy a new pair of cuff links."

Two weeks later they called and asked me to come by. When I stepped in, the owner of the store went to the small safe in the rear and opened it. She took out the cuff links as though they were jewels of great value.

She said the old silversmith couldn't remember having made those cuff links, but he'd had a couple of friends when he was young who had specialized in that sort of work. They had died long ago.

I looked at the cuff links. They didn't seem to have been touched.

"He explained to us he would be afraid to repair them," said the owner. "He would have to use a soldering lamp and might hurt the silver profile. The dark color might go. And the lovely profile might disappear entirely. You would have a sturdy clasp but no longer the cuff links you like so much."

She looked at me. "I am sure you wouldn't want that to happen."

I shook my head.

"Take them with you," she said. "Wear them at home where you are sure to find them if you lose one or both links. Actually, the mechanism is still working well though it looks brittle. But don't take any chances, don't wear them outside. You wouldn't want to lose your beautiful cuff links, would you?"

No, I don't want to lose them. I put them in my pocket, and I thanked the two old ladies and left.

I still have my father's cuff links.

NO OBSTETRICIAN IN OUR QUARTET

LONG BEFORE I BECAME A WRITER, I wanted to be a famous violin virtuoso or a conductor. Music was my youthful passion. Years ago, Herbert von Karajan, then in charge of the Vienna State Opera, told me how much he'd liked an essay I'd written about the opera house. He looked into space, wistfully, and said if there was anything he would rather do than conducting, it would be to write. I said that I'd often wished I could conduct Verdi's *Otello* or Wagner's *Parsifal* as he did, and on that slightly sad note of mutual admiration we parted. Conducting attracts me because it is a mysterious art. George Szell, perhaps the greatest interpreter of classical music today, once told me that "there are matters in conducting that cannot and should not be explained." He said if he wore a mask and stepped for the first time in front of an orchestra that he had never conducted, the players would at once recognize that he knew his business. Some call it the conductors' "magic." Perhaps it is the unanalyzable phenomenon of personality.

My early dreams of glory shouldn't convey the impression that I was an unusual boy. I went through the normal phases of wanting to be a soccer player or a mountain climber—the elation of reaching the stillness of an Alpine summit is not unlike the elation one feels in blessed moments of performing beautiful music. Among my boyhood heroes were Giacomo Casanova, not for his alleged sexual successes but because he once jumped from a second-floor bedroom window into a Venetian lagoon when the irate husband showed up; and Bronislaw Huberman, the Polish-Jewish violinist, because he was the only great master of the violin who performed in my hometown. Today some bloodless esoterics might claim that Huberman "overplayed"; he was an emotional artist who "lived" music. I've since learned that all great artists "live" music, even though they have accepted the necessity of near-perfect performing.

As a youthful violinist, I looked upon pianists as playing a "mechanical" instrument with no soul. The violin literally contains a "soul." The French call it *l'âme*—the slender cylindrical rod made of pine that is forced into the violin's body between back and belly, underneath the right foot of the bridge. This sound post transmits the soft belly's vibration to the hard, maple back. A violin without a sound post would have a hollow tone that wouldn't carry far. I thought it fascinating that a little piece of wood, about one quarter of an inch thick, determined the tone and timbre of the instrument, its brilliance and power. Were it shifted less than a millimeter, the violin's character would be completely changed. Of the many secrets of the mysterious violin, the "soul" is perhaps the most enigmatic. I know as little about my violin as I do about the people closest to me.

My father and mother liked music in a casual way; neither played an instrument. At home we had an early gramophone with a gleaming brass horn, exactly like the one shown on RCA Victor records, with the little dog listening to his master's voice. Marie, our elderly cook, disliked the gramophone because she had to polish the horn once a week. I spent thrilling hours sitting on the floor in front of the brass horn, like the little dog. I remember the voice of Caruso. I didn't know who he was, but his voice did something to me. Though these were bad acoustical recordings, Caruso's voice projected through all musical and mechanical shortcomings. He sounded glorious even when he seemed to take liberties in "Una furtiva lacrima." I was fascinated by his *legato* and *mezza voce,* and forgot to change needles when I played and ultimately ruined his records.

Our record collection reflected my mother's catholic tastes. She particularly liked the recordings of people she knew personally. Caruso was the exception; he was everybody's exception. Thus, she collected the records of Leo Slezak, from the nearby capital of Brno, who, so to speak, belonged to the family; and of Selma Kurz from nearby Bielitz, the celebrated coloratura diva of the Vienna Opera and Zerbinetta in the world premiere of Richard Strauss's *Ariadne auf Naxos.* My mother called her Selma, reminding me that the diva had "almost" married Uncle Bernhard, who later married my mother's sister, Aunt Mella. It wasn't clear to me who had turned down whom. Selma seemed to have recovered from the shock, for she later married Professor Halban, a famous obstetrician in Vienna. I looked up "obstetrician" in my German encyclopedia, but the explanation was too technical, or I was too young to understand it. My mother also loved Johann Strauss's "Frühlingsstimmen Walzer," performed by the great Alfred Grünfeld, whom she'd once met in Aunt Bertha's salon in Vienna, which, I gather, was different from our salon at home. Again, the encyclopedia was no help.

The record I liked best was *Der Traum des Reservisten* (The Reservist's Dream), a medley of sound effects, trumpet solos, and melodies describing a day in the life of an Austrian army reservist during the autumn maneuvers. My father bought it in the gay epoch prior to 1914, when playing soldier had been fun. The record was mercifully forgotten after 1918, when it was no longer fun, but recently was reissued by a Viennese firm and is again popular with many people who forgot much and learned nothing since 1918.

A year after my father's death—I was eight—I had my first violin lesson. My mother said my father would have liked it; he wanted me to learn something he had missed. I became everybody's ordeal at home; a practicing fiddler is worse than a dripping faucet. My mother bravely encouraged me to practice "another five minutes." Marie, the cook, escaped into the Old Church, where it was quiet and peaceful. Fraulein Gertrud, our governess, quickly dressed up my younger brother, and they went for a walk.

My musical mentor was Uncle Bruno, my mother's youngest brother. He'd wanted to become a musician, but life turned him into a paper salesman. A first-rate musician and fourth-rate salesman, Uncle Bruno became my mother's partner when they opened their stationery store in the early 1920s, on the advice of Uncle Heinrich in Olmütz, who had a successful stationery store there. It was a bewildering experience for my poor mother. Once she'd been the wife of a rich man, with servants at home, a dressmaker in Vienna, traveling with my father to Biarritz and Monte Carlo when few people could afford to go there. Now she had to sell pencils, erasers, and office supplies. She never complained; she didn't want to depend on her relatives' charity. She let Fräulein Gertrud go, rented out half our apartment, economized radically, and somehow managed to send my brother and me to good schools.

The stationery store was no success. Uncle Bruno was not interested in onionskin, and Uncle Hugo, who later joined them, had just gone through his third bankruptcy. (My mother had twelve brothers and sisters, and my father had ten; there was an abundance of aunts and uncles.) Like many bankrupts, Uncle Hugo was a perennial optimist, and began to "reorganize" the store, changing the price system, and ruining the store a couple of years later. My mother cried and made me promise that I would never go into business with relatives. She also told me never to lend money to relatives and friends. "Either give it to them outright and forget about it, or refuse," she said. Sound advice, though my father, a banker, might not have agreed.

Uncle Bruno should have become a musician; he would have had fun and made more money than he did selling paper. He played the violin, the viola, and the cello (well), the piano (fairly well), the clarinet and the French horn (poorly) and was popular among the local amateur musicians and much in demand. His bachelor apartment, across the street from ours, had little furniture but enough instruments to furnish a small chamber orchestra, piles of music, and a dozen chairs and music stands. He and his friends were making music almost every night. Uncle Bruno selected the three-quarter size violin on which I produced my early, ugly efforts. Later, he gave me a cheap viola with a fake Stradivari label inside, and a half-broken cello that we fixed up together. Even Marie didn't mind my practicing the cello; she said it had a nice, human sound.

My first violin teacher was Herr Böhm, but Uncle Bruno soon fired him and hired Herr Ascher, who said that everything that Herr Bohm had taught me was wrong: my posture, my fingering, my bowing. After he was fired, my third teacher, whose name I don't remember, condemned the methods of my first two teachers and taught me his own, which were declared void and useless by my fourth teacher. I wonder how many young musicians have been ruined by the conflicting methods of their teachers. Fortunately, Uncle Bruno taught me that the beauty of good music transcends the incompetence of bad teachers. He also taught me the essentials: taste, style, self-discipline. Uncle Bruno, a dilettante, loved music more than many professional musicians.

He introduced me into the wonderful world of chamber music when I was eleven. The second violinist of his steady string quartet was a women's doctor (I still couldn't pronounce the word "obstetrician") who was sometimes suddenly called away in the middle of a quartet because of an emergency. I wouldn't have an obstetrician in my own quartet now, no matter how well he plays.

One evening, around nine o'clock, Uncle Bruno came to our apartment, breathless from running up the stairs.

"Take your violin and come along," he said. "The gentlemen are waiting."

Today I understand the catastrophe befalling three men who looked forward all day long to an evening of string quartet playing, one of the most civilized and enjoyable pursuits of Western culture, and then the fourth man doesn't show up, or worse, is called away in the third movement of a beautiful Beethoven. In modern society, no man is said to be irreplacable. The president is assassinated, but the government continues to function. Management goes on, though the chairman of the board has a heart attack or runs away with his secretary. But a string quartet is sunk without one of its regular members.

Twenty-five years later, when I went to Hollywood, where I was lonely for string quartet music and knew no players, I bought a couple of quartet study recordings with the first-violin part left out. While the record was playing, I was supposed to perform the first violin part from the attached music with my audible but invisible fellow players. It didn't work out. Quartet playing is a subtle give-and-take among four people brought together by their common love of music. I had to follow the recording, but my three anonymous fellow players wouldn't follow me. In a moment of elation, when I sang out a melody and made an imperceptible *rubato,* I was brutally called back to reality by my fellow players, who performed with the merciless beat of a metronome. I gave up; better no music at all than anti-music.

Eventually, I found chamber music players in the hills and canyons of Hollywood. They are the same everywhere, no matter where they come from or what language they speak; lovable lunatics conversing in the universal language of Haydn, Mozart, Beethoven, Schubert. That four people who may not know each other by their first names are able to establish a psychological rapport, as they sit down to make heavenly music, is one of the few miracles left in this era of cold rationalism.

After half a century, the memory of my first chamber music evening is still very strong. Normally a soft-spoken, kindhearted man, Uncle Bruno became a tyrant and madman when he sat down to play a string quartet. I can see him still putting the Breitkopf and Härtel parts on the stands: Opus 18 No. 4, one of the early Beethoven quartets.

It was a terrifying experience. Uncle Bruno cursed like a top sergeant, stamped the floor, used his fiddle bow as a conductor's baton and riding whip. He didn't mind my playing a few false notes; he knew this was my first effort at sight-reading. He was also lenient with the viola player, a prominent lawyer who couldn't keep up with the *alla breve* passages of the final movement. But he got furious when the cellist showed a lack of zeal in the *Minuetto* and threatened to throw him out the window. I'd just learned in school about the Prague defenestrations and the trouble they'd caused, and I got frightened. So did the cellist, a powerful industrialist feared by a legion of underlings.

In the *Scherzo* the two violins play a ticklish *spiccato* passage together, while the viola and cello rest. I adjusted to Uncle Bruno's light bowing and didn't lose a single semiquaver. At the end of the movement, I was commended by the lawyer and the industrialist. Uncle Bruno stared at me hard through his thick eyeglasses, and then he smiled and lightly touched my right shoulder with the tip of his bow. It was a great moment in my youthful life. At the age of eleven, I had been knighted, chamber musically.

I've played in small ensembles ever since, except when wars, travel, sickness, and assorted disasters created an unavoidable interval. There is almost nothing that would now keep me from an evening of chamber music. It's more than a hobby; it is a love affair that never ends. In this kind of music, I've at last achieved the switch from passive listener to active participant. I agree with Henry Peacham, the seventeenth-century British essayist, who wrote of chamber music, "I dare affirm, there is no science in the world, that so affecteth the free and generous spirit, with a more delightful and inoffensive recreation, or better disposeth the mind to what is commendable and vertuous."

The playing of chamber music—"the music of friends," as it is called—engenders an atmosphere of warmth unknown to most virtuosos or prima donnas. For them, music is a competitive business, a race that goes to the fastest and loudest. Not so with chamber music. It is based on the proposition that all players are equal. It is a garden of musical fellowship from which the law of the jungle has been banished, and in which egotism cannot thrive.

But if chamber music is noncompetitive, it is far from being lukewarm. Nothing could be more wrongheaded than the view that chamber music players are austere, bloodless esoterics, as anyone can attest who has watched a string quartet in action, soaring to the heights of happiness when a movement comes off, and plummeting to the depths of despair when (as happens more often) it doesn't. Like Uncle Bruno, I freely tolerate imperfection on the part of my fellow players; but the slightest lack of enthusiasm, no, never.

Chamber music was written for the enjoyment of amateurs, rather than for the display purposes of professionals. Some composers had a high opinion of good amateur players. Beethoven wrote some very difficult quartets to be played in the houses of his aristocratic patrons. They had to hire professionals to play these quartets as they should be played. But even the cold-blooded professionals were conquered by this music and became "friends."

String quartet music is the pure essence of beautiful music. Composers of far more ambitious works have turned to it from time to time as a means of distilling the sort of divine beauty that big orchestral compositions, with their brasses, woodwinds, and percussion instruments, cannot duplicate. From the player's point of view, chamber music is uniquely rewarding and wonderfully satisfying. Personally, I went through a long evolution until I reached the present, final stage, where I play this music for the sake of music, not trying to prove something to myself or others. We play in congenial surroundings, and we are alone; no one's ego is injured if something goes wrong, as it does, inevitably. Technical mistakes are forgiven, but not mistakes against the musicality. In certain blessed moments, when all goes well, I sense the exaltation that I imagine mountain climbers experience on silent peaks above the clouds, or perhaps skiers on a downhill ride through powder snow and March sun.

In earlier years, when I hadn't quite got to that stage, we often performed for relatives and friends. We might have played as many as five or six quartets, into the early morning hours, eating and drinking and playing yet another quartet, until the irate neighbors called the police. I hereby apologize to them, though where they are now, they can no longer collect the lost hours of sleep. In those days I would sit down to play with people I'd just met and might never meet again. I wouldn't do it anymore; it's the wrong way of making "the music of friends." In Hollywood, I played with professional musicians who were highly respected members of studio orchestras and made more money than the members of celebrated symphony orchestras in Europe. They were superb technicians, but chamber musically, many of them had "gone Hollywood," talking more about their expensive instruments than about the music. Many owned Stradivaris and other rare old Italian instruments, and they listened more to the gorgeous sounds of their precious fiddles than to their fellow players. In chamber music, one must play and listen at the same time.

Sometimes a world-famous soloist joined us for the evening. He played his part with bravura, as though it were a concerto accompanied by three other instruments. We admired the great virtuoso, but we weren't truly playing chamber music, which is an expression of musical democracy, an exercise in compromise, a display of human fellowship. The virtuoso played a solo performance, the antithesis of chamber music.

A happy amateur string quartet is a greater miracle even than a happy marriage, since twice as many people are involved, and each member has to get along with his three fellow players. A string quartet is a blend of different temperaments. If the four players are not on the same wavelength, musically or psychologically, the spell is broken. I remember a very able player who irritated us because he always pushed a little bit, driven by impatience, unable to discipline himself. There was the woman player who talked too much between the movements when we three were still "in the music." There was the second fiddler who would collapse in the fast movements. There was another woman player, a very good musician, who brought along her husband; he read the newspaper, turning the pages during the *pianissimo* passages, smoked a cigar, and afterward told us what we'd done wrong. One violinist always came with his wife, though she hated chamber music and fell asleep during the slow movements. And there were others who had to be dropped for one reason or another.

Now, at long last, the four of us lead a happy chamber musical life in Vienna, where I spend several months of the year. My fellow players and I are all of the same age. Our backgrounds are different, but we have all grown up in the musical landscape of Viennese classicism. We always return to the great masterpieces of Haydn, Mozart, and Beethoven that form the gold reserve of string quartet music. We are on the same level technically; no one outshines the others, and no one stays behind. We argue vehemently, but we always reach agreement, since we have the same musical tastes. We respect traditions and classical style and try to read the composer's intentions. Musical annotation is, at best, hopeful expectation. A Brahms *adagio* is different from a Beethoven *adagio* or from a Dvořák *adagio*. We listen to one another—while playing *and* afterwards. Everybody is asked to criticize.

We played together for years before we knew each others' first names. We called each other Herr So-and-So, in the polite Viennese manner. I knew the telephone numbers of my fellow players but not their wives or professions. At supper, after the music, we would talk about missed rests or the exaggerated tempo of a famous professional quartet that had performed the final movement "for effect," twice as fast as the composer prescribed it. The violist collects string quartet recordings and tells us how the various celebrated quartets played the Beethoven we've just finished. The cellist is an amateur musicologist. The second violinist knows Haydn's and Mozart's letters and always has some interesting quotes.

Chamber music comes naturally to the Viennese. The modern string quartet originated in Vienna, in 1755, when Joseph Haydn, then twenty-three, was invited to spend some time at the country house of Karl von Fürnberg in nearby Weinzierl, where he composed his Opus 1 No. 1, now generally regarded as the world's first string quartet. He wrote eighty-four quartets altogether, in which he brought this noble art from birth to maturity. Mozart wrote twenty-five and Beethoven, seventeen. When Beethoven died in 1827, the classical period of chamber music died with him.

Not surprisingly, quartet playing has always been a way of life in Vienna. Prior to the Hitler invasion (or "liberation," as some Austrians then called it), there were perhaps two hundred steady amateur quartets in this city. A great many chamber music players who belonged to the Catholic and Jewish intelligentsia perished in the war or in the concentration camps. When I came to Vienna after the war, it was almost impossible to find an amateur quartet. Only in the past few years has chamber music made a slow comeback in the city where it originated. string quartet playing emigrated, with many other things, to England and America.

After playing with them every two weeks or so for the past ten years, I've learned a little about my fellows. The second fiddler is a retired executive of the Vienna Streetcar Company, much envied because he has a pass entitling him to free rides on all municipal cars and buses. His first name is Felix, as in *"Tu, felix Austria, nube,"* and he is a man of felicitous disposition, a cheerful philosopher who takes long, solitary walks in the Wienerwald. The viola player is a retired civil servant, and at one time played with the Vienna Symphoniker, an excellent orchestra permanently frustrated by the overwhelming presence of the more famous Vienna Philharmoniker. The cellist is a dentist, handling the sturdy pegs of his instrument with the physical force he applies to the recalcitrant molars of his patients. He spends long vacations skiing in the mountains. When he isn't skiing, the viola player takes a cure against rheumatism, and when they are both in Vienna, I may be in America. Sometimes it is as hard to get the four of us together as if we were Messrs. Heifetz, Oistrakh, Primrose, and Piatagorsky.

All this makes our music evenings important private events. Every hour counts. Every time may be the last. We don't make small talk. There are no listeners in the music room, though occasionally somebody may be in the next. All lights are turned off except the lamps with the soft silk shades between our four stands. This is chamber music playing as it should be—no distractions, no pretense, only the music and us. Years ago we played four quartets, but now we usually play only two, though with great dedication and deep intensity. In chamber music, as in lovemaking, depth of feeling eventually replaces physical exuberance. One of the two pieces is often a late Beethoven. Ernst Heimeran, a noted German publisher and chamber musician, called their interpretation "a veritable devotional act of music." To be able to play these quartets, perhaps the greatest music ever written, and play them so the music emerges, behind and between the notes, is the supreme aim of all amateurs. My fellow players are uninterested in my income or the sale of my books, but they watch me carefully while I play the difficult first-violin runs in the opening movement of Beethoven's late, and very great, Opus 132.

Several years ago we noticed that we made no artistic progress just playing through one quartet after another. Now we often use the first hour for study. It's hard work, but it pays rich dividends. We begin to hear the hidden details, while the structure of the work itself becomes clearer. After practicing the more difficult passages of a quartet, the whole piece sounds quite different afterwards. When we are exhausted, which happens often nowadays, we end on a cheerful note with the music of Haydn or Mozart, God's antidote to our age of anxiety. They leave us with a sense of exhilaration. On Saint Anne's Day in 1799, an Italian musician walked into Saint Michael's Church in Vienna to listen to one of Haydn's masses. "I perspired during the *Credo* and was terribly sick, but then my headache went away, and I felt cured mentally and physically," he wrote.

Haydn's and Mozart's therapeutic powers remain as strong as ever. I often feel low and demoralized at the beginning of the evening. My work didn't go well, or it's the dreaded *Föhn*—the wind from the southwest that lowers the blood pressure and has a depressing effect on people. In Vienna, the *Föhn* is used as an excuse for everything, from driving through a red light to beating one's wife.

The viola player, who has had a couple of heart attacks, announces that he won't be able to do more than the Beethoven tonight. Even the second violinist and the cellist, who represent the outdoor life and health cult, are under the weather, and I've certainly had it. At that point I prescribe "a little Mozart." (An imprecise manner of speaking; there is nothing little about Mozart.) After the first bars we feel rejuvenated, and our headaches go away by the end of the opening movement. I leave the explanation to the medical experts, but for me there is no doubt that "the music of friends" is healthy, a remedy for body and spirit. By the time we sit down for supper, we are tired but happy.

The Bund Deutscher Mädel

THE CHILDREN OF LIDICE

ON A VISIT I MADE to my native Czechoslovakia shortly before the recent Communist coup, I drove fifteen miles northwest of Prague one day to the little green valley, in the softly rolling hills of central Bohemia, where the village of Lidice once stood. On June 10, 1942, when SS troops and Gestapo men arrived with orders to "erase" it, Lidice was a typical ancient Czech village, with low, cream-colored houses clustered around a six-hundred-year-old church that had a baroque cupola. Nobody in Lidice had much money and nobody was very poor. Automobiles, radios, moving pictures, and newspapers were practically nonexistent. There was a school, a firehouse, a sports club, and a reading circle. The men worked in the coal mines and foundries of the nearby town of Kladno, and the women tended the fields and gardens on the slopes behind their houses. On Sundays, they gossiped in front of the church after the service; the children played under the trees along the brook that ran through the village; and the men dropped in at the inn for a glass of beer. Exactly five hundred men, women, and children made up the population of Lidice.

As I gazed down on the site of Lidice from a hilltop overlooking the green valley, it was not difficult to imagine the village as it once was. It was harder to visualize the details of what had happened to it, even though I had just been over all the available historical data, now assembled in Prague. The SS and the Gestapo men drove into the village in trucks and staff cars at half past two o'clock on the morning of that June day six years ago. It has been indisputably established by German documents and statements since then, that the people of Lidice were guilty of nothing. In the opinion of Adolf Hitler, however, the population of Czechoslovakia, then occupied by the Germans, needed "a terrifying demonstration of the strength of the Third Reich." The choice of Lidice as the scene of this demonstration was apparently arbitrary. The SS troops formed a cordon around the village under orders to let nobody out. Hauptsturmführer Harold Wiesmann, chief of the Kladno Gestapo, who was in charge of the expedition, stood in the village square and read to his lieutenants a *Führerbefehl* (leader's command) that, he said, he had just received. The *Führerbefehl* charged that the inhabitants of Lidice had given aid to the assassins of SS Obergruppenführer Reinhard Heydrich, who had been attacked and mortally wounded outside Prague a week before. It also charged that the people of Lidice had been storing arms and ammunition, reading forbidden printed matter, and illegally listening to foreign radio broadcasts. "Because the inhabitants of this village broke the law so recklessly," it concluded, "the Führer himself has ordered that the village be razed to the ground and its name erased. Men over sixteen years of age will be shot, the women deported to concentration camps, and the children taken away where they will have suitable upbringing."

Weismann then sent for František Hejma, the mayor of Lidice, and ordered him to hand over all the cash in the municipal treasury and all public documents. Squads of SS men, each accompanied by a Czech-speaking member of the Gestapo, went from house to house, woke up the inhabitants, and ordered them to go to the square. There the men and boys over sixteen were separated from the women and younger children. "The women were all hysterical," one of the SS men afterward wrote to his wife. "Throwing their arms around their husbands and sons, crying like mad. Children weeping, dogs barking, and chickens and pigs all over the place—what a mess!"

The women and children were put into buses and driven away. A hundred and ninety-two men and boys, the youngest sixteen, the oldest eighty-four, were taken to some stone-walled stables on the outskirts of the village. The Germans carefully checked the names of these men and boys with the police registration files, apparently to make sure that no one was missing. Then they piled mattresses taken from the houses against the back walls of the stables, so that no bullets would rebound, and shot all their captives, ten at a time. The bodies were thrown into a mass grave dug behind the stables. A *Schnellkommando* (emergency squad) summoned from Prague drove away the cattle, gathered up the pigs and poultry, and loaded the agricultural machinery on trucks, along with all the bicycles, sewing machines, and baby carriages in the village. Wiesmann picked out one baby carriage as a present for his wife; she was seen the following day on the streets of Kladno pushing their child around it it. Finally, SS men and soldiers placed cans filled with gasoline in the cream-colored houses, in the school, the firehouse, and the church and ignited them. Whatever withstood this holocaust was dynamited, and the fragments plowed into the earth. A camera crew took motion pictures of all this, and the films were duly filed away under *Kulturfilme* in the office of the Czech Reichsprotektor where they were discovered after the war.

From my hilltop, I could see that, topographically, the erasure of Lidice had been complete. The Germans planted wheat on the site and over the mass grave. The dynamite blasts even changed the course of the brook that ran through the village. I had been told in Prague that the only visible traces of Lidice are in Kladno, and I decided to go there. It was to Kladno that the women and children of Lidice had been driven in buses, while the men and boys were being shot. On the next morning they were assembled in the high school, their names listed, and the children were taken away from their mothers. There were, altogether, two hundred and three women and a hundred and five children. Townspeople two and three blocks away, through the closed windows of their houses, heard the desperate cries of those women and children; the citizens of Kladno had been instructed to keep their windows shut and stay off the streets that morning. The women were sent to concentration camps in Germany, and the children were scattered over Europe. Of the two hundred and three women, fifty died of torture and mistreatment; a hundred and forty-one returned to Czechoslovakia and have been domiciled by the government in a little colony of renovated houses in Kladno, a drab town of coal mines and coal dust, factory chimneys, tenements, and freight yards. As I drove through it, its dreariness was relieved solely by the noise of the children playing in the streets, but when I came to the colony in which the women of Lidice live, there was not even the sound of children playing. Only sixteen of the hundred and five children of Lidice came to Czechoslovakia. The rest are still unaccounted for.

A sign on one of the houses said *Národni Výbor Lidice* (National Council of Lidice). I walked up a wooden stairway to an office on the second floor, where I met Josef Novák, the secretary of the council. Novák, a friendly, soft-spoken man with a Slavic face, is a sort of liaison between the Czechoslovakian government and the survivors of Lidice. I asked him if I might talk to some of the children. "Only a few of them, the older ones, remember what happened to them," he said. "The younger ones, who were a year or so old when they were taken away from their mothers, don't remember anything much, or else they can't seem to talk about their experiences. Of those who were really old enough to understand what went on, only nine have come back." He telephoned the principal of the local school and arranged for three of the older children, a boy and his sister and another girl, to be sent over.

Two women dressed in black entered the office, and Novák gave them a friendly greeting and handed each one a document. "Sign here," he said. He took a sheaf of paper money from a desk drawer and counted out some bills. The women thanked him as they picked up the money. One of them said, "Nothing new?" as if she were stating a fact instead of asking a question. "No news, I'm afraid," said Novák. They nodded and went out. These were two of the widows whose children are missing, and they had come to collect their allotment. "Every surviving woman gets a monthly pension of two thousand crowns from the government," Novák said. "In addition, the Association for the Restoration of Lidice, a private organization supervised by the government, pays a thousand crowns to every woman under thirty-five years of age and fifteen hundred crowns to women over thirty-five. The children get from six hundred and twenty to nine hundred crowns from the government, according to their age, and five hundred crowns from the society. A thousand crowns is about twenty dollars, so even though their houses are rent-free, it's not much, with the cost of living going up all the time. But the women say they would gladly give up their pensions if only they could be back in Lidice. Not a day goes by without some of the women walking out to the place, which is about six miles from here. They sit down on the ground and cry for hours."

The coalition government had promised to build another village near the old one and to make a national shrine of the original site, but it had indicated that this probably would not be done until next year. (No word has yet come out of Czechoslovakia as to what the Communist plans for Lidice, or for its women and children, may be.) "I keep telling the women there is a serious shortage of building materials and not enough manpower," Novák said, "and that many other important buildings, with higher priorities, must be put up—hospitals, railroad stations, and schools—but they say, 'What about priorities for Lidice? Has the government forgotten our sacrifice and suffering?'" He sighed and shifted in his swivel chair behind his rolltop desk. "Fortunately," he went on, "children are able to forget most unpleasant things and remember only the pleasant ones. It's an entirely different story with the women of Lidice. The government settled them here in Kladno after the war, because it was felt that being away from the place of the tragedy would make it easier for them to forget." He gave an unhappy shrug. "It didn't work out that way. The women hate to live here. They want to go back to Lidice as soon as possible. To those who lost husbands and children, the tragedy is still as sharp and painful as if it had happened only yesterday. In their homes, the pictures of their husbands, brothers, and sons are draped with black cloth, and most of them are still wearing black dresses. When they get together, they talk of scarcely anything else. But maybe it will be better for them when Lidice is rebuilt."

There was a timid knock on the door, and the children Novák had sent for came in. They were Václav Hanf, now fourteen, his sister, Maruška Hanfová, now seventeen; and her girlfriend Marie Doležalová, now fifteen. They were in a group of ninety children shipped to Poland by the Germans. These three were moved from one place to another in Poland, Germany, and Austria until the war ended. Then Allied agencies brought them back to Czechoslovakia. Václav took off his cap and nodded gravely when he was introduced to me. He is a slim, earnest blond-haired boy with remarkably fine features and sad blue eyes, and I noticed at once that he looked much older than fourteen. He limped across the floor to sit down next to Novák. The two girls made themselves comfortable on a leather couch, and began whispering and giggling. Václav just sat still, very serious and grown up.

"Václav is the only boy in the group who has returned," said Novák, giving him an encouraging smile. "All the other children of that group who have come back are girls. Every year, on the anniversary of the destruction of Lidice, there is a mourning ceremony at the site of the village, with many officials and hundreds of thousands of people attending, and Václav acts as Lidice's unofficial ambassador. He has spoken in front of the president and members of the government and Parliament, and for the newsreels." Václav acknowledged this with a casual nod. The girls laughed, and Maruška said, "And he's very glad that he could come here now and doesn't have to sit in school." Maruška is a healthy, happy-looking girl with a shrewd peasant face, red cheeks, and white teeth. She was wearing a pleated skirt and a dark blouse, and her sturdy legs were bare. The other girl, Marie, slender, pretty, and vivacious, kept bouncing up and down on the couch.

For all their noisiness, Václav hardly ever glanced at the girls as he told me his story. He and his two sisters, Maruška and Anna, were, he said, together on the train to Poland. There were three third-class carriages for the children, and one car each for the escort of SS men and women of the N.S.V., a welfare organization. The journey lasted three days and two nights. The children had no light at night, and in the tiny, dirty washrooms there was no water. Quite a few of the children were toddlers and needed attention, but the Germans didn't bother, and the older girls looked after the little ones as well as they could. I gathered that Maruška, who was then twelve, and one of the oldest and most energetic of the lot, took unofficial charge. Every evening, an N.S.V. woman brought the daily food ration—a few pieces of stale, dry, and sandy bread and some dark, lukewarm water that smelled faintly of barley. All the children were extremely hungry, and the first night there was a scramble among the older ones for the bread, but Maruška told them that they must not forget the babies. She and three other girls managed to distribute the bread and soup evenly. The bread was too hard for the babies to eat, so the older children chewed it first to soften it up for them. After dark, the babies cried because they were cold and the older children cried in terror and homesickness, but by midnight most of them were asleep.

On the third evening, the train arrived at a big railroad station, and the children were told to get out. Václav saw a sign that said "Litzmannstadt," and learned later that this was the new German name for the Polish city of Lodz. The children were loaded into buses and taken to a building that Václav discovered was the *Rasse and Siedlungsamt* (Race and Settlement Office). "We were put into two big rooms," he said. "Along the wall were two tiers of beds, like a sleeping car I have seen in an American motion picture. I was on one bed with Maruška and Anna. When I stood up on it, I could look out of a little window, and I saw a barbed-wire fence around the place and a tower with two German sentries in it. An old woman brought us hot soup and dried potatoes. She was Polish, but she understood a little Czech, and when I asked her whether our mother or father would follow us here from Lidice, she gave me a funny look." Václav pressed his lips together tightly for a moment. "She knew. Today I realize that she knew everything, but wasn't permitted to tell us. That's why she brought us paper and an envelope and said we should write a letter to an uncle or an aunt. I asked her why not to Mother or Father, and she said, 'No, no, better write to somebody in Prague. Don't you have anybody there?' My sisters and I said yes, we had Aunt Wolfová in Prague, so we wrote her and asked her please to send us warm clothes and some food. Aunt Wolfová didn't get our letter for several months. When she did, she mailed us three packages, but we never got any of them."

Early one morning, a few days later, a group of men came to see the children. The men wore white coats over SS uniforms and addressed one another as *Herr Kollege* and *Herr Doktor*. One man told the children to line up against the wall and be quiet, and then he walked slowly down the row. He was Dr. Walter Robert Dongus, head of the Lodz Race and Settlement Office, whose job it was to pick out those children who had what the Nazis called the "characteristics of Northern race" and were *eindeutschungsfähig* (literally, Germanizable). "Most of the kids were ordered by him to go and stand against the opposite wall of the room," Václav said. "When he saw one with dark hair, he wouldn't even look twice but would send him to the other group. He looked into my eyes and at my hair, and he took a pencil and held it in front of my face and moved it around as if he were measuring my forehead and my nose and the space between my eyes. He looked at my sisters the same way and turned around to his men and said something in German. Then he told my sisters to go to a corner of the room, where there were three or four other girls. Maruška asked whether I was coming with them, but he shook his head and said I must join the group against the other wall. Maruška and Anna began to cry and said they wouldn't go without me. Dongus said, '*Nichts*, we already have enough,' but when they kept on crying, he shrugged and looked at me again, and then he said something to the other men, and then he let me go over to my sisters."

Václav was sitting especially erect now and his hands were playing nervously with his cap. "If Maruška and Anna hadn't cried so much, I wouldn't be here today," he said solemnly. "Perhaps I wouldn't be alive." He glanced around and smiled at Maruška, who crossed her legs and looked proud. When we all smiled, too, she blushed. I asked what had happened to the large group of children. "They were taken away that night," Václav said. "We have never heard of them again."

"What happened to them?" I asked Novák.

"Nobody knows," he said. "They are just missing. There are many who fear they may have been sent to Chelmno, in Poland, where—well, let Václav tell you his story first. We don't want to keep the children out of school all day long."

"Why not?" said Marie.

Everybody laughed, even Václav, but as he cleared his throat before going on with his story, his face grew serious again. "I saw the ones in the large group being driven away in trucks that night," he said. "We had been awakened by some German women when it was still dark and told to get dressed. There were seven of us—my two sisters and I, and Marie, and three other girls. I asked one of the German women where they were sending us, and she hit me in the mouth and said I mustn't talk Czech. We were taken to the *Rasse und Siedlungsamt* camp in the town. We stayed there only a few days before we were put on a train again."

The seven children were sent to the Polish town of Puschkau, near Posen, where they were enrolled in a *Heimschule* (home school), one of several such establishments set up in Eastern Europe by the Reichskommisar für die Festigung Deutschen Volkstums (Commissar for the Consolidation of the German Nation) to mold foreign children into Germans, once it had been established that they were Germanizable. ("All children," read the Reichskommissar's directive on the subject, "will undergo racial and psychological tests of their ability to become Germans.") Václav remembers vaguely a lot of incomprehensible examinations. The children were then given a few lessons in German and told never to speak anything else. Their clothes were washed regularly, they were assigned clean rooms, and they got enough to eat. "The food was cooked by Polish women," Václav said. "I used to go to the kitchen and talk to them."

The two girls burst out laughing again. "All he remembers is the food," Marie said. "He was always hanging around the kitchen, always telling us that he would like to eat a piece of sausage. Tell about Höpfner. Tell how she let you stand barefooted in the corridor all night long." Václav didn't say anything, so Novák explained to me, "Václav was a good Czech. He didn't want to talk German, so the woman in charge of the *Heimschule,* Meta Höpfner, cut down on his food. At night, she would make him stand barefooted for hours in the cold corridor. That was the first winter—1942–43—wasn't it, Václav?" Václav nodded. "Yes," he said. "And it was very cold."

A pale, tired-looking middle-aged woman, dressed in black, came into the office. Novák introduced me to her, and she glanced at me with the swift, instinctive suspicion of Europeans who have gone through hell and find it hard now to maintain their faith in people. She was a woman from Lidice, Mrs. Růžena Petráková, an aunt of Marie, with whom Marie now lives. Her own two children are among the missing. In the afternoons, she helps Novák with his clerical work. She sat down beside Marie and gave her a stern glance. "Sit quiet," she said. "Don't bounce up and down so."

"Did you wonder what had happened to your father and mother?" Novák asked Václav.

"Of course I did," Václav said. "Once I went to the Höpfner woman and asked her when my parents would join us. She looked at me as if she would beat me, and then she shrugged her shoulders. She said we mustn't be impatient, that our parents would come soon."

"They told us a similar story in the Ravensbrück camp," Mrs. Petráková said. "Whenever we women from Lidice grew hysterical, the Germans promised that the children would join us any day. Lying was part of their system to avoid trouble. We in Ravensbrück never knew about the gas chambers at the other camps until we were liberated by the Red Army and they showed us those places. The Germans had everything beautifully organized so that they could kill millions without any complications."

Václav has only hazy recollections of the months and years he spent in "school." It is difficult for him to put together the pieces, because there was one after another, and they were all so much alike. The children were taught the German language, German history, and German songs. If they uttered a word of Czech, they were beaten. There were afternoons when they had to recite the glorious deeds of Adolf Hitler, and there were cold winter mornings when, before daybreak, they had to stand in the snow in the schoolyard, take off their shirts, and do exercises. The exercises and the schooling and the beatings became a dreary routine.

It was in the summer of 1943 that Václav was taken out of the

Puschkau *Heimschule* and began his journeys from school to school. He counted on his fingers and said he thought there had been seven altogether. His sisters, he added, had already been sent away from the *Heimschule*. A German woman had come for Anna, and a few months later another had come for Maruška. Václav was told that his name was now Hans Joachim Strauss and that later on he would be sent somewhere or other to live with a family named Strauss. He had been spending more time with his classmates, most of them Polish boys, than with his sisters; he was nine, and his playmates had become more important to him. He still wondered what had happened to his father and mother, but the other boys at the *Heimschule* said that he shouldn't worry, that everything would be all right, and he began to think about them less often. By now he knew the "Horst Wessel Lied" so well that he could sing it when drunken SS men woke him up at two in the morning, which they often did. They came into the dormitories whenever they felt like it, and every boy had to stand at attention on his bed and sing the song. Some Polish boys who had trouble remembering the words were made to stand barefooted in the snow in their nightshirts. Three of them died of pneumonia. Václav came to hate the "Horst Wessel Lied" and the German language. Later, in a school at Oberweissburg, in Austria, he was locked in a dark room for a week and given only bread and water because he didn't want to repeat the wonderful things he was taught in class about the Führer.

He thinks that it was late in 1944 when a train on which he and a group of Polish boys were being moved to another school was attacked by English planes. Václav could see the markings on their wings. "The train stopped, and then there was gunfire from all sides and the SS men ran for cover," he said. "One of them stumbled over me, and he got up and kicked me in the knee, and then I was hit in the arm by a bullet." Václav rolled up his sleeve and proudly showed us a long scar. "Didn't it hurt?" asked Marie. "The arm hurt less than the knee where the SS man kicked me," Václav said. His arm is all right, but the knee still gives him trouble, especially when he walks fast or runs, and it is a handicap when he tries to play soccer.

"Why don't you tell about what happened in Mariaschnell?" Maruška said. Václav seemed to shrink down in his chair. Then he shrugged and said, "In the Mariaschnell camp, in Austria, there were many Polish,

Hungarian, Norwegian, and Ukrainian boys. One morning, the Germans called us out to the courtyard for an assembly. Three SS men brought in a Hungarian boy who had come to the camp only three days before. His hands were tied behind his back. They made him kneel down, and one of the SS men said to us that if we didn't behave, the same thing would happen to us." Václav paused before he said matter-of-factly, without raising his voice, "Then they cut off his head with a sword."

Marie, I noticed, stopped bouncing up and down for a moment and watched my face to see what effect Václav's words had on me. Novák, after a moment's silence, asked Václav whether the other boys ever found out what crime the Hungarian boy had committed. Václav was astonished. "What crime?" he asked shrilly. "You didn't have to commit a crime to be beheaded! Well," he went on more calmly, after another pause, "that was shortly before the Anglo-Americans liberated us. They gave us chocolate and so much bologna sausage!" He smiled and swallowed. Everybody laughed again, and Marie said, "Didn't I tell you that Václav thinks only of food? Once, in the Puschkau *Heimschule,* I asked him what he would like for Christmas if he could have anything, and he said, 'A bologna as long as a telegraph pole.'"

"Marie, behave yourself," said her aunt. "One hears no one but you here."

The Anglo-Americans, as Václav called them, put him into a UNRRA camp in Austria and told him that his name was no longer Hans Joachim Strauss, and that he didn't have to speak any more German, which pleased him almost as much as the bologna. He soon made friends with an American mess sergeant from Cleveland, who felt the same way about Germany, and seemed to have an inexhaustible supply of bologna. The main thing that troubled Václav at that time was that he didn't know what language to speak. He had forgotten most of his Czech, German was hardly advisable, and he knew very little English. He and the other boys in the camp—Hungarian, Polish, French, Russian, and Norwegian—developed a language of their own. No one else understood it, and that gave the boys the pleasant feeling of being members of a secret society.

Then, one day, a woman from Prague came to the camp and talked to all the children, one after another. When Václav told her that he was from Lidice, she began to cry. He learned later that she was searching for her nephew, one of the missing children of Lidice, but he didn't ask her any questions then; he had learned that one usually got beaten when one asked questions, and he hadn't yet shaken off the feeling that he was a prisoner of the Germans. He was given some new clothes, and a few days later, the woman took him with her to Prague, where he arrived the day before Christmas. His Aunt Wolfová met him at the station and took him to her apartment. When the door opened, Václav saw a big, lighted Christmas tree inside. Standing beside it were his two sisters, whom he hadn't seen in more than two years.

"Poor Václav!" Maruška said to me. "He stood there as if he'd lost his mind. He didn't even come toward us or say anything. He was afraid of us all. He just stared around, and then he mumbled something, but we couldn't understand him. We had to talk to him in German. It was terrible. There were so many people in the room and everybody was crying and Václav just standing there like a little donkey. Somebody said that Anna and I should talk to him alone, and so we took him to our bedroom." There they told him that their father had been shot in Lidice on that terrible morning three years before, that their mother had died the next year in a concentration camp, and that Lidice existed no more. "We went back to the living room, where the tree was," she said. "Václav hardly looked at his gifts. Later we all sang 'Silent Night, Holy Night' in Czech—all but Václav, who didn't know the words any more. I asked him whether he could sing something else, and he said, 'I can sing the "Horst Wessel Lied," but I won't.' The next morning, we drove out to Lidice. He didn't remember the way. He didn't even know how to get there."

Václav shrugged, and he looked like a tired old man. "How could I remember?" he asked. "Even the road was gone. They had changed everything. When we passed by the Buštěhrad Cemetery, I heard some geese cry, and then I remembered the geese we'd always had in back of our house, and then the brook that ran through our village." He gave his sister a scathing look. "Maybe I didn't remember the road," he said, "but at least I didn't wear a uniform, the way you did."

Maruška blushed again, and then, apparently feeling that an explanation was due, began to talk. Meta Höpfner, the woman in charge of the Puschkau *Heimschule,* had sold her, she said, to an elderly German couple named Richter. I asked her whether she actually meant *sold,* and she nodded. "The Höpfner woman got fifty marks for me from the Richters.

They took me to Dessau. Richter was a locomotive engineer on the German State Railroad, and they had a small one-family house—very clean, but it always smelled of warmed-up cabbage."

"What of it?" Václav said. "I like cabbage. Especially when it's been warmed up."

"Quiet, Václav, said Mrs. Petráková.

"The Richter woman liked to listen to the radio," said Maruška. "When Hitler's name was mentioned, there would be tears in her eyes, and she said to me once, 'What a wonderful man is our beloved Führer!'" Maruška sat up straight to imitate the stiff posture of the German *Hausfrau*, and her voice took on a Prussian harshness. Everybody laughed again. The Richters told her that her German name was Marga Richter, and to make it official they had her rechristened; she was given a new white dress one morning and they went to a church, where the priest said a prayer and sprinkled white wine on her face and also on her white dress. "I tried to wash out the stains, but they stayed in," Maruška said. "It ruined the dress. Later the Richters hired a tutor for me and I had German lessons every afternoon, and they sent me to a millinery shop, where I learned to make hats. When I was fifteen, they entered me in the *Bund*."

"The *Bund?*" I asked.

"*Bund Deutscher Mädel*," said Maruška. Václav made a sour face, and Marie, bouncing up and down on the couch, cried, "Show us the picture! Show us the funny picture in your uniform!"

Maruška took a dog-eared photograph out of her school portfolio. It showed her, unsmiling, wearing a dark skirt and a light blouse with a swastika armband. She said that she was a great disciplinarian and soon rose to the grade of *Mädchenführerein*, or Girls' Leader.

"She even beat other girls because they didn't sing the 'Horst Wessel Lied' loud enough," said Václav contemptuously.

Maruška tried to laugh it off, but her cheeks were red again. "I know it sounds terrible now, but I liked *The Bund Deutscher Mädel*," she said. "It was fun."

"Fun!" said Mrs. Petráková.

"We didn't talk about politics," said Maruška defensively. "We had games and sang, and almost every night there was a victory celebration. Frau Richter told me that Václav was still at the *Heimschule*, and I had letters from Anna, and I hoped that Father and Mother were all right and that I would see them someday. My sister Anna came home first of the three of us. She was with a German family in Kottbus, in February 1945. When the Russians came in, they ordered that all foreign children be sent back to their homelands. Anna went to Dresden, where she met a Czech railroad man, who brought her to the Czech border station of Podmokly, and the first person she saw there was our Uncle Václav Tyč."

Maruška came home a little later. The Richters had told her to go to Berlin and from there to make her way back to Czechoslovakia. In Berlin, she went to the American military headquarters and talked to an American officer. She told him she was from Lidice. He incredulously started to question her, suddenly got very excited, and made a lot of telephone calls. Two days later a Czech army officer came for her. "I didn't know then how silly I must have looked," she said. "A Lidice child wearing the insignia of a *Mädchenführerin* in the B.D.M.!"

"Well, Maruška, you were not the only one," said Mrs. Petráková, giving Marie a significant glance. "Ask this little frog here how she behaved when I found her," she said to me.

Marie giggled and swung her legs. She had gone from the Puschkau *Heimschule* to the house of Herr and Frau Alfred Schiller, in Posen. Herr Schiller was a picture dealer. "We lived on the Hindenburgstrasse," said Marie, and laughed. Her aunt asked her what was so funny about that. "I can't help it," Marie answered. "Today, those German words just sound funny to me." Maruška nodded approvingly, and Václav raised his eyebrows. "They were always funny to me," he said.

"She learned German very well," said Mrs. Petráková. "She didn't even want to listen to me when I came for her and spoke Czech."

Marie said that in the beginning she was not happy in the Schillers' house. They gave her a tiny room behind the kitchen, and she had to do the housework. She was permitted to eat at the table with the Schillers, but she had to listen to frequent arguments about her. Frau Schiller didn't like having another mouth to feed. "It's difficult enough to get food for the two of us," she would say to her husband. "You and your party friends! Why do they pick *you* to take this girl?" Herr Schiller would angrily shout, "They have ordered us to make a German woman out of her and we are going to do it!" and then hammer his fist on the table.

Frau Schiller told Marie that she must never let anybody know where

she was from. "If I ever hear the word 'Lidice' in my house, I will beat
you half-dead," she said. Marie was now called Ingeborg Schiller. That
was all right with her. At night, lying in her bed, she would murmur,
"Marie Doležalová, Ingeborg Schiller," and she came to the conclusion
that Ingeborg Schiller sounded nicer.

"Sounded nicer!" Mrs. Petráková cried. "Did you ever you think of
your father and mother?"

"Yes, I thought of them. I even had a picture of father in my pocket,
but when the Schiller woman found it, she tore it up and burned the
pieces."

"Didn't you wonder what had become of your parents?"

"Yes, I did."

"Marie was too young to worry," Novák said to Mrs. Petráková sooth-
ingly. "Children are always optimists, thank God, or there wouldn't be
any children left."

As time went on Marie got used to her environment and began to call
Herr and Frau Schiller *Vati* and *Mutti*. Frau Schiller became more friendly. The Schillers entertained a good deal, mostly Nazis, and the girl sat at
the table with them and listened to their talk. She had instructions never
to say anything unless she was asked a question. This happened rarely.
The guests were always drinking beer and making long speeches.

I asked Marie whether the guests knew her history. "They knew," she
said. "Sometimes one of the *Parteifunktionäre* would ask me how I liked
it in the Reich, and when I said liked it fine, they would nod at each
other triumphantly and say, 'She will become a good German yet!' The
girls in my school didn't know. They thought I was a *Volksdeutshe* from
the Sudeten, because I spoke with an accent."

By 1944, the SS stopped coming to the Schillers' house, and some of
the *Parteifunktionare* took off their insignia and brown shirts and began
to go around in civilian clothes. *Vati* Schiller looked worried and *Mutti*
kept telling Marie that "the terrible Russians" were getting nearer—"and
you know what they do to little girls like you." Marie never found out
what the Russians did to little girls. When the Russians approached
Posen, the Schillers fled to Hamburg, taking Marie along, and thence to
Berlin, where they were when the war ended. The German population
was ordered by the Allied authorities to report immediately the presence
of any foreign children who had been adopted, and Herr Schiller, always

happily obedient to authorities, took Marie to the *Magistrat.* There she was given a passport with a German, French, Russian, and English text, which stated that she had been "certified by the Municipal Board of the City of Berlin as a victim of Fascism." A few weeks later, Mrs. Petráková, who had been notified by UNRRA of Marie's whereabouts, came to Berlin and picked her up at the small, run-down apartment the Schillers then occupied.

Mrs. Petráková is still angry when she talks about her trip to Germany. "Here I come all the way to Berlin to get my niece, happy that at least one of the children in our family had been saved, and what do I find? A German girl! You should have seen her hair. She wore it long, like those *Hitlermädchen,* and she wouldn't talk Czech to me. Said she didn't understand. Mind you, she wouldn't even come with me. She hung on to that Schiller woman and cried, '*Mutti, Mutti,* I don't want to leave you!'" Mrs. Petráková got up from the couch and paced back and forth. "*Pro Krista!*" she exclaimed. "It made me so mad, I could have beaten her blue. I said, 'This woman isn't your mother, Marie. Your mother is lying in a Prague hospital, dying of tuberculosis that she got in a German concentration camp. Your father was shot by the Germans at Lidice. My two children—your cousins—and almost all your friends from Lidice are missing, and you aren't ashamed to call that woman *Mutti?*' One more year and that girl would have been a real Nazi!"

For the first time, Marie looked meek. Václav nodded and chewed a pencil. "She didn't want to listen to me," Mrs. Petráková went on. "When it was time to leave, she started to whisper with that Schiller woman. Later she confessed to me that she had promised she would come back to Berlin as soon as she could. And you should have seen her on the train! She ignored me and was rude and arrogant. I said to myself, 'That's a nice situation. Her poor mother in the hospital and all the Lidice women, the members of the government, and the newspaper people waiting to welcome this girl—one of the few that have been found. She will be called officially an Orphan of the State, and they will photograph her and write her up, and here I am bringing home practically a *Hitlermädchen!*' I decided to stop for a few days in the biggest town near the German-Czech border—Moravská-Ostrava, in eastern Moravia—and get her acclimatized. I bought her some decent clothes and took her to a hairdresser to have that silly, long German-style hair cut off. Somehow it got around that Marie was a Lidice child. A crowd began to collect in front of the hairdresser's, and people came in and brought her candy and flowers. They looked at her as if she were a saint, and an old man wanted to kiss her hands, and there she sat, shouting—in German—that she didn't want to have her hair cut, *nein, nein, nein!* You should have seen the stunned faces of the people. I was so ashamed, I wanted to hide. The old man who had wanted to kiss Marie's hand got mad and said they should send her back to Germany, where she belonged, but a woman took his arm and said, 'Don't you understand, Jan? This child isn't guilty. It's the Germans who are guilty. Not only did they take our children away from us but they even tried to change them inside so they would never be ours, even if we ever found them.' Well, we finally managed to get her into that hairdresser's chair, and he cut her hair while the tears ran down her cheeks."

Marie was able, after all, to understand and speak Czech again in short order, and in a few days she wrote her mother a note in Czech. She was a very different girl when she arrived in Prague to see her mother in the hospital. The Czechoslovakian government, mindful of the world-wide propaganda value of this human interest story, had alerted a number of newsreel photographers so that they could make a pictorial record of the first reunion of a child of Lidice and a mother of Lidice. When Marie was admitted to the sickroom, her mother was lying in bed, crying silently, unable to talk. Seemingly, she still couldn't believe that this girl, kneeling in front of her, had at last been given back to her. The photographers and cameramen went to work, and the pictures they took were shown all over the world. Marie's mother died a few weeks later. "I don't know what I would do if I didn't have that little frog," said Mrs. Petráková tenderly, kissing Marie's hair. "Thank God, she hardly remembers those years any more, and she speaks Czech as if she had never left the country."

There was a knock on the door, and a boy of Václav's age came in, carrying a soccer ball. He bowed to Novák and asked if Václav could please come with him, because their team was having soccer practice on the field behind the school and needed him. Novák smiled. "Each class has its own team, and they are having a tournament," he explained. "Václav's team is already in the semifinals. Maybe they will win the championship. Run along, Václav, if you wish." Václav shook hands with me. "You can bet we'll win," he said. He didn't show a sign of a limp as he and his teammate ran out of the door. Marie and Maruška went along to watch the boys practice.

I sat and talked to Novák and Mrs. Petráková for a while longer. I asked Novák again if he could tell me anything about the children of Lidice who had been separated from the Germanizable ones at the Race and Settlement Office. "At Chelmno, in Poland," he said, "there was a crematorium built especially for children. We know that more than six hundred thousand Jewish, Polish, Norwegian, French, and Czech children were killed by gas at Chelmno and burned in the crematorium. We don't know whether the missing children of Lidice were sent there or not. But there are some indications that they were."

"But there's no proof," said Mrs. Petráková.

"That's right, there's no proof," Novák said.

"I haven't given up hope," Mrs. Petráková said. "You wouldn't give up hope, either, if you had two children who were missing. None of us have given up hope. There were a hundred and five children, and sixteen have been found already. There will be others."

ACKNOWLEDGMENTS

The essays collected in *Trifles Make Perfection* originally appeared in the following books and periodicals;

HENRI SOULÉ: *The New Yorker* (March 25, 1953).

WARBURG: Joseph Wechsberg, *The Merchant Bankers* (Boston: Little, Brown & Co., 1966).

ALBERT SCHWEITZER: *The New Yorker* (November 20, 1954).

THE BOIS DE BOULOGNE: *Gourmet Magazine* (May 1976).

VIENNA: AN INTRODUCTION: Joseph Wechsberg, *Vienna, My Vienna* (New York: Macmillan, 1968).

PERFECT SERVICE: *Gourmet Magazine* (February 1973).

A QUESTION OF REVERBERATION: *The New Yorker* (November 5, 1955).

THE BUDAPEST STRING QUARTET: *The New Yorker* (November 14, 1959).

STRADIVARI: Joseph Wechsberg, *The Glory of the Violin* (New York: Viking, 1973).

FERNAND POINT: *The New Yorker* (September 3, 1949).

AFTERNOON AT CHÂTEAU D'YQUEM: Joseph Wechsberg, *Blue Trout and Black Truffles* (New York: Knopf, 1953).

A VERY LATE CONFESSION: *Gourmet Magazine* (August 1974).

MY FATHER'S CUFF LINKS: Joseph Wechsberg, *The Vienna I Knew* (New York: Doubleday, 1979).

NO OBSTETRICIAN IN OUR QUARTET: Joseph Wechsberg, *The First Time Around* (Boston: Little, Brown & Co., 1970).

THE CHILDREN OF LIDICE: *The New Yorker* (May 1, 1948).

About the Author

JOSEPH WECHSBERG was born in Ostrava, Czechoslovakia, in 1907 and died in Vienna in 1983. After a very brief but false start as a lawyer in Prague, he began his life as a traveler, amateur musician, and writer by playing violin in a modest tourist ship orchestra, eventually emigrating to America in 1938 and joining the U. S. Army as a translator in the Second World War. "Going Home," a wistful description of a return to his battle-ravaged birthplace in a newly Communist country, was, in 1946, his first publication in *The New Yorker*. It marked the beginning of a rich literary output on music and musicianship, science and art, food and wine, biography, European history, and travel—all personalized with a unique, humanist's mixture of praise, pleasure, and sadness that revealed the author as clearly as it did his subjects.

About the Editor

DAVID MOROWITZ was born in Chicago and educated at the University of Illinois and its medical school. At the age of twenty-five, he discovered the writing of Joseph Wechsberg, finding it then, as he still does thirty-four years later, a rich, life-enhancing treasure. The author of a text on gastrointestinal radiology and a part-time photographer and writer, he practices medicine in Washington, D.C. He is married with two children, and lives in Bethesda, Maryland.

Trifles Make Perfection

was set in Minion, a contemporary digital type family created by Adobe designer Robert Slimbach. Minion is inspired by
classic old-style typefaces of the late Renaissance named after
one of the type sizes used in the early days of typefounding.
Minion means "a beloved servant," reflecting the type's
useful and unobtrusive qualities.